NIGERIAN FOREIGN POLICY

Also by Timothy M. Shaw

Cooperation and Conflict in Southern Africa (*co-editor*)
Conflict and Change in Southern Africa (*co-editor*)
Canada, Scandinavia and Southern Africa (*co-editor*)
Zambia's Foreign Policy (*co-author*)
The Politics of Africa (*co-editor*)
Alternative Futures for Africa (*editor*)

Also by Olajide Aluko

Ghana and Nigeria, 1957–1970
Foreign Policies of African States (*editor*)
Essays in Nigerian Foreign Policy

Also by Timothy M. Shaw and Olajide Aluko

The Political Economy of African Foreign Policy (*co-editors*)
Africa Projected (*co-editors – forthcoming*)

NIGERIAN FOREIGN POLICY

Alternative Perceptions and Projections

Edited by

Timothy M. Shaw
and
Olajide Aluko

St. Martin's Press   New York

All rights reserved. For information, write:
St. Martin's Press, Inc., 175 Fifth Avenue, New York, NY 10010
Printed in Hong Kong
First published in the United States of America in 1983

ISBN 0–312–57269–7

Library of Congress Cataloging in Publication Data

Main entry under title:

Nigerian foreign policy.

Bibliography: p.
Includes index.
1. Nigeria—Foreign relations—1960–   —Addresses,
essays, lectures.   I. Shaw, Timothy M.   II. Aluko,
Olajide.
DT515.8.N524   1983   327.669   82–25049
ISBN 0–312–57269–7

Contents

v

Preface

The preparation and publication of this volume not only reflect Nigeria's growing national role in the global political system; they also reflect the importance of the Nigerian statesmanship and scholarship in the global intellectual system. As befits their developing and dynamic country, Nigerian academics are very active in the global university; some of their work is reflected in this project.

The professional association between the editors on which this book is based started in Chicago in 1974 and continued at Ife in 1979-80. Together they organised a pair of panels at the African Studies Association conference in Philadelphia in 1980 at which several draft chapters were presented. And this and other joint editorial tasks have been facilitated by continuing linkages between the University of Ife in Nigeria and Dalhousie University in Canada.

We are grateful for typing undertaken in Nigeria and Canada by Leslie Adamson, Doris Boyle, Tunde Akibu, Segun Oyedepo, Elaine Otto and Marie Riley and we appreciate the collaboration between Macmillan-Britain and Macmillan-Nigeria which made this collection possible. We also acknowledge the earlier appearance of Chapters 10 and 11 in Essays in Nigerian Foreign Policy and Journal of Modern African Studies respectively.

Halifax and Ife
December 1982

Timothy M. Shaw
Olajide Aluko

Notes on the Contributors

OLAJIDE ALUKO is Professor of International Relations at the University of Ife, the first full professor in this subject in black Africa. Dr Aluko holds a doctorate from the London School of Economics and is author of numerous articles in African Affairs, Millenium and Quarterly Journal of Administration as well as of two books: Ghana and Nigeria, 1957–1970 and Essays in Nigerian Foreign Policy. He is also editor of Foreign Policies of African States and co-editor (with Timothy M. Shaw) of The Political Economy of African Foreign Policy.

DANIEL C. BACH is a Research Fellow from the Centre National de la Recherche Scientifique (CNRS) at the Centre d'Etude d'Afrique Noire in Bordeaux University, France. He was previously a Lecturer in International Relations at the University of Ife and holds a D.Phil. from Oxford University. Dr Bach specialises in France's Africa policy, Nigeria's foreign policy and francophone Africa. His essays have appeared in the Canadian Journal of African Studies, L'Année Africaine 1980 and J.-F. Médard and Y.-A. Fauré (eds), Etat et Bourgeoisie en Côte d'Ivoire; he is an editor of Politique Africaine.

THOMAS J. BIERSTEKER is Assistant Professor of Political Science at Yale University. Dr Biersteker is author of articles in International Organization, Paul Lubeck (ed.), The African Bourgeoisie and I. William Zartman (ed.), The Political Economy of Nigeria. He is currently working on industrial investment in Nigeria, a development of earlier research which appeared as Distortion or Development? Contending Perspectives on the Multinational Corporation.

MARK W. DELANCEY is Associate Professor of Government and International Studies at the University of South Carolina and has recently been a Visiting Professor of Political Science at the University of Nigeria, Nsukka and of History at the University of Yaounde in Cameroon. Dr

DeLancey is a review editor of African Book Publishing Record and is author of numerous articles on African international relations in Genève-Afrique, Africana Journal, African Studies Review, Journal of Developing Areas and Rural Africa. He is editor of Aspects of International Relations in Africa and African International Relations and author of African International Relations: an Annotated Bibliography and Teaching the International Relations of Africa.

OROBOLA FASEHUN is Lecturer in International Relations at the University of Ife in Nigeria. Dr Fasehun has written essays on African international relations in Afrika Spectrum, Journal of Modern African Studies and Nigerian Journal of International Studies. His doctorate is from Rutgers University.

SOLA OJO is Lecturer in International Relations at the University of Ife. Dr Ojo holds a Ph.D. from the London School of Economics and has published articles in Africa Quarterly, Nigerian Journal of Political Science, International Studies and Quarterly Journal of Administration. He is co-editor (with Olajide Aluko, Amadu Sesay and Timothy M. Shaw) of Southern Africa in the 1980s and (with Timothy M. Shaw) of Africa and the International Political System.

TIMOTHY M. SHAW is Professor of Political Science at Dalhousie University in Nova Scotia and was recently Visiting Senior Lecturer in International Relations at the University of Ife. Dr Shaw's essays on Nigeria have appeared in Africa Contemporary Record, Journal of Modern African Studies, ODI Review and I. William Zartman (ed.), The Political Economy of Nigeria. He is editor of Alternative Futures for Africa and holds a doctorate from Princeton University.

SONNI TYODEN holds a Ph.D. in Political Science from the University of Lancaster in England and is a Lecturer in Political Science at the University of Jos in Nigeria. Dr Tyoden is working on foreign policy and political economy in peripheral states. His book on The Political Economy of Nigeria's External Relations is forthcoming.

STEPHEN WRIGHT is Lecturer in Political Science at the University of Sokoto in Nigeria. His essays have appeared in Millenium, Round Table and West Africa and he is co-editor of ECOWAS and Regionalism in West Africa. Dr Wright holds a doctoral degree from the London School of Economics.

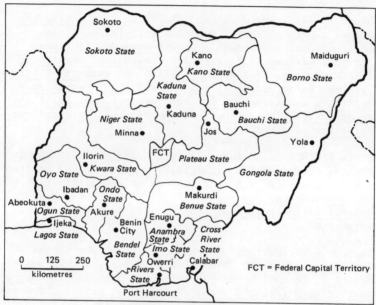

The States of Nigeria, 1982

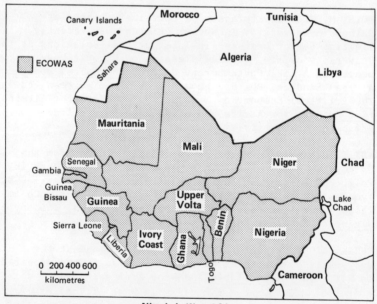

Nigeria in West Africa

1 Introduction: Nigeria as Africa's Major Power

TIMOTHY M. SHAW

Nigeria is in some important respects Africa's most powerful nation.

Andrew Young [1]

Our economy is still oriented outwards and locked into dependency on the West ... Our ruling class appears to be largely confined to the role of ensuring the existence of the political conditions of accumulation. Many are quite happy riding piggy-back to affluence on Western capital ... We have performed poorly in our quest for development ... economic failure poses problems of legitimacy for those in power.

Claude Ake [2]

Nigeria is going to rule the entire world of man as from 1989 ... The future of Nigeria is very bright more than any country on earth. The country has a very important role to play in reshaping the future of man.

G. O. Okunzua [3]

... we do not think that Nigeria the neo-colony of the sixties is the same as the neo-colony of the seventies.

Sonni G. Tyoden [4]

Recognition of Nigeria's relative influence and affluence is now commonplace in Africa, Europe and elsewhere. Yet scepticism remains about the stability of Nigeria's state and status. The country clearly has potential for expanding its capabilities and choices, but whether it can either realise or utilise these is still problematic. This book is intended to contribute to the growing debate about the bases and effects of Nigerian power. The debate is of

1

relevance not only to students of Nigeria in particular or
of Africa in general but also to students of Third World
foreign policies as a whole, especially those of Newly
Industrialising Countries (NICs). For Nigeria is one of
very few African states aspiring successfully for a place
in the 'semi-periphery'. Its position between 'core' and
'periphery' in the global system remains somewhat tenuous
although the nature of its political economy and development
strategy points towards such a role or status, particularly
in the medium-term future.

  Nigeria has always been *primus inter pares* in black Africa,
but with the advent of changes in the global political
economy in the 1970s as well as with the ending of its own
civil war, Nigeria became ever more indisputably Africa's
leading state [5]. Its claim to being the natural leader of
the continent is reinforced by the emerging character of
its political economy. For, as in Brazil, the archetypal
semi-peripheral country, so the central feature of Nigeria's
political economy is 'a complex alliance between élite local
capital, international capital, and state capital ... "the
triple alliance" ' [6]. This book seeks to put Nigeria's
foreign policy, development strategy and political economy
into perspective by offering a description and projection,
explanation and evaluation of this continuing evolution of
Africa's major power.

GROWING EMPIRICAL AND ANALYTICAL IMPORTANCE IN AFRICAN
INTERNATIONAL RELATIONS

Since independence, Nigeria has always been Africa's largest
country: the size of its territory and population and the
diversity of its peoples and resources distinguish it from
most of the continent's other fifty states. But under the
initial Balewa government, Nigeria was both conservative
and cautious: Africa's 'sleeping giant'. If the first civilian administration failed to mobilise Nigeria's potential
in international affairs the first military regimes were
preoccupied with civil strife and then civil war: Gowon had
little time for foreign policy when it affected the outcome
of the national conflict.

  But if the 1960s were characterised by passivity the
1970s were characterised by activity in Nigeria's African
and global diplomacy. The new tempo of Nigeria's external
affairs under the successive post-civil war Gowon and
Mohammed/Obasanjo regimes [7] was the result of an historic
conjuncture at the beginning of the new decade: (1) the
ending of domestic hostilities and internal crises, and

(2) the beginning of international energy and economic crises. Both of these events enhanced Nigeria's external position and together constituted the backdrop to Nigeria's exertion of its capabilities and its transition into the second civilian republic. As Tyoden indicates in his opening quotation: the 'neo-colony' of the 1970s is quite different from that of the 1960s.

Despite the continuity of Nigeria's economic orientation — an essentially dependent [8] and capitalist system — its activism in foreign affairs coincided with a shift in focus from world to African affairs: alignment in economics did not seem to exclude nonalignment in politics [9]. However, over the last twenty years the structure of Nigeria's political economy has not been static as it has begun to achieve recognition as a part of the semi-periphery. As Evans notes in his comparison of Nigeria and Brazil, despite considerable differences between these two countries at the semi-periphery: 'That the Nigerian case appears suitable to formulations of the triple alliance at all is impressive. In fact, the prospects for Nigeria moving successfully in the direction of the triple alliance seem good' [10].

This ineluctable progress towards semi-peripheral capitalism — towards a more industrialised economy dominated by an ever-changing balance of fractional forces among national, transnational and bureaucratic bourgeoisies or capital — underlies Nigeria's evolving foreign and development policy. Nigeria's new Afrocentric activism — which came to shape its attitudes towards other non-African interests and issues — was revealed most dramatically in its surprising recognition of the MPLA regime in Angola and most consistently in its continuing concern for regional cooperation and integration in West Africa [11]. These twin strands in its African policy — liberation in Southern Africa and integration in West Africa — are likely to continue into the future providing (1) its leadership is not changed suddenly and (2) its national income does not go into a precipitous decline. Both of these conditions are likely to be met, at least in the short-to-medium term, given the character of Nigeria's political economy. As Oye Ogunbadejo concludes his own review of the soldier's legacy:

Clearly, the record of the military in the field of the country's foreign relations is, in varying degrees, much better than that of the Balewa regime. But then, this could be explained to some extent by way of Lagos' increased capability for influence. Its oil wealth, particularly in the years after the civil war, provided

Nigeria with the economic base, and thus the confidence, to give more substance to its foreign policy of non-alignment [12].

However, if there is general agreement amongst analysts about the nature of Nigeria's new Afrocentricity and activism in the 1970s, there is less agreement about the definition and direction of its international nonalignment — external, intergovernmental 'alliances' — and its national political economy — transnational 'triple alliance'. And its regional position and role are affected by these global and national situations; that is, by the constellations of international and intranational actors.

As for most states, Nigeria's global and regional relations are interrelated. This is particularly so for a NIC at the semi-periphery of the global system; by definition it is something of an intermediary between centre and periphery, between global and regional systems [13]. In the case of Nigeria, the federal government has at times played the role of mediator or *animateur* at both continental and 'subregional' levels; that is, in Africa in general and in West Africa in particular. In Africa as a whole, Nigeria has been most active in conflict resolution within the OAU system and in political liberation within Southern Africa; while in West Africa, Nigeria has been most advocative in advancing regional integration through the Economic Community of West African States (ECOWAS) and in proposing responses to political changes and crises (e.g., coups in Ghana and Liberia and conflict in Chad).

But such activity or advocacy cannot be separated from continuing issues at the global as well as national levels. Conflict resolution and political liberation in the African continent, and regional integration and political cooperation in West Africa, bring Nigeria up against a variety of extra-African interests and institutions: super and great powers and a range of international and transnational organisations are also involved in such issues. East-West conflicts and intra-Western tensions as well as corporate and religious concerns are all reflected in such ostensibly 'African' issues. The interrelatedness of global and regional factors can be seen in Nigeria's several African roles: in continental, Southern African and West African issues.

First, at the continental level, Nigeria's policy of supporting PanAfrican unity and diplomacy has led it into active involvement in a range of OAU questions. Its encouragement of an African Common Market was symbolised by the April 1980 economic summit and declaration in Lagos [14].

And its concern over Chad generated numerous meetings and proposals, including the dispatch of an ill-fated Nigerian 'expeditionary force' to Ndajema, which pitted Nigeria against Gaddafi's Libya. In general, Nigeria's role as a status quo mediator has not disturbed major external powers, although its advocacy of continental economic union and a peace-keeping force may bring it up against foreign national and corporate interests — but, if the logic of the 'triple alliance' is recognised, then there may be compatible as well as incompatible interests among different national and transnational bourgeois fractions [15].

Second, at the level of Southern Africa, Nigeria's support for anti-racist African nationalism has put it more directly in opposition to various Western countries and corporations [16], although, once again, shared commercial interests moderate antagonisms between centre and semi-periphery [17]. Therefore Nigeria's support of the liberation movements has overall been quite muted and it has emerged as a 'helpful fixer' between the Western 'contact group' and the Front Line States. In general it supports political rather than economic change, although its recognition of the MPLA regime in Angola was, probably mistakenly, taken to be a move towards a more radical stance. Its assistance in the Lancaster House negotiation and agreement over independence for Zimbabwe, however, revealed the essential continuity in Nigeria's Southern African policy, although the insensitivities of the combined Reagan and Thatcher administrations may further strain Nigeria's tolerance of Western perfidy. As Andrew Young, a leading 'activist' in improving US-Nigerian relations under President Carter and General Obasanjo [18], suggests:

Nigeria will endeavour to foster its interest in economic development and stable trade relationships with the West while simultaneously continuing to use its leverage with Western nations and corporations in the interest of its political goals on the African continent — especially with regard to South Africa [19].

The final level at which Nigeria may simultaneously cooperate with as well as confront the advanced capitalist states is in its own immediate region.

Third, then, at the West African level, Nigeria's advocacy of regional integration is based on a pair of interrelated concerns: (1) regional cooperation for development, and (2) regional cooperation to reduce extra-regional penetration (and clearly these two factors of development and vulnerability are interrelated). Nigeria's interest in its own

economic, especially industrial, fortune since 1970 has
coincided with its interest in reducing foreign, especially
European, involvement in the national and regional economies. As Olatunde Ojo indicates in his insightful analysis
of the domestic and bureaucratic policies of Nigerian
diplomacy in West Africa:

> Domestically, one of the factors in Nigeria's active role
> in the formation of ECOWAS was and is the country's desire
> to become the industrial heart of West Africa with all the
> political power that this may bring, not only within
> Africa but also in the world at large. A concomitant of
> this is the desire to undermine or erode French economic
> and political influence which has sometimes been inimical
> to Nigeria's interests in the sub-region. The need to
> utilise Nigerian petroleum revenue, while it lasts, and
> to provide alternatives to oil dependence later came to
> reinforce commitment to ECOWAS. As it became clear that
> this task of reducing dependence could not be solved in
> isolation, the commitment to the success of ECOWAS
> became irrevocable [20].

So much for the logic of the semi-periphery.

But the potential of ECOWAS notwithstanding, Nigeria's
national economy still faces major difficulties in its transition from an oil-extraction and commodity-production base
towards semi-industrialisation. This process of 'dependent
industrialisation' — dependent development in Evans' ter-
minology — is traumatic for any social system. It is especially so in the Nigerian case because of the character of
its inherited social and physical infrastructures: traditional values and communications failures complicate the
process of change. Moreover, oil income although massive is
not completely predictable or reliable over time.

As a part of the global semi-periphery, albeit the newest
and most problematic part, Nigeria's political economy is
still rather dependent in a classical manner and its 'triple
alliance' rather inchoate and unselfconscious. For, as Evans
indicates:

> In an African context the structure of the Nigerian econ-
> omy may appear relatively advanced; in a Latin American
> context it would appear anachronistic. From the role of
> the state to the position of the multinationals, the
> structure of the Nigerian élite is in many ways more sug-
> gestive of the period of classic dependence than of the
> current period of dependent development in Brazil and
> Mexico [21].

Nevertheless Nigeria's place at the semi-periphery seems to be assured for the foreseeable future as external interests come to recognise its potential for dependent development. To cite Evans again:

> Except for the oil industry, which is a classic enclave, (Nigeria) is primarily an agricultural country. The manufacturing investment it contains is a fraction of that which international capital has chosen to locate in Brazil and Mexico. Yet, the international business community is beginning to discuss Nigeria the way they discussed Brazil at the beginning of the seventies — as a potential member of the 'semi-periphery' [22].

The rapidity with which Nigeria achieves, and is seen to achieve, the status of a semi-industrialised state at the semi-periphery depends to a considerable extent on how it reinvests its oil income and, therefore, on the demand for and price of oil.

Nigeria's new dependence on oil revenue [23] is revealed by fluctuations in GDP over the last decade. National income grew dramatically in the 1970s, after the war and before the slump of 1978-79. Revenue was again buoyant as oil prices continued to rise from mid-1979 to mid-1981 but the new dip of sales and prices in mid-1981 led to a rapid decline in both production — down from almost 2 billion barrels a day to 1.0 or 0.5 billion — and price — down from over $40.00 to $36.50 a barrel [24]. Given Nigeria's major commitments to its continental, Southern African and West African policies, let alone its ambitious development plans for industrial expansion and welfare satisfaction, the state cannot easily adjust to a more frugal life-style. In 1978 Nigeria reverted to the Eurodollar market to maintain its rate of expenditure and growth [25]. The continued volatility of the oil market, despite the medium-term upward price trend, may force it to do so again.

Nigeria's need to borrow foreign capital on occasion may be seen as characteristic of its continuing dependence on foreign investment, technology and skills, as well as on foreign supplies and markets. However because of the size and status of the country, few analysts consider Nigeria to be dependent in a classic, chronic manner. Rather, they focus on its foreign and development policies: on the 'output' rather than the 'input', on diplomatic gestures rather than on political economy [26]. Nigeria's essential extra-continental structural dependence — which, to be sure, is not static but continually changing — is overlooked when scholars concentrate on its largely intra-continental

activist diplomacy. Andrew Young, for example, nicely links
these two features of Nigeria in the 1980s without being
critical about the limits that the former imposes on the
latter:

> In general, Nigeria's democratic institutions (patterned
> on those of the United States) and its relatively capita-
> listic economy gear the country toward cooperation with
> the United States ... Massive infrastructural projects
> to develop power, highways, railroads, and a new federal
> capital ... are ... underway. To achieve these goals,
> Nigeria is looking to the West, and particularly the
> United States, for economic partnership.
>
> Meanwhile, Nigeria is playing an increasingly influential
> role in the political and economic policies of other
> African countries. As a consequence of oil wealth and OPEC
> membership, Lagos exercises considerable leadership in the
> Organisation of African Unity and dominates the Economic
> Community of West African States. Nigeria's resources and
> zealous commitment on Zimbabwe made it a virtual partner
> with the Front Line States at various stages in the
> negotiations for a settlement. Its diplomatic corps has
> been central to efforts by West African countries to
> resolve the conflict in Chad [27].

More critical analysts, however, would see a close relationship with the US and/or the EEC as imposing constraints on
the effectiveness of Nigeria's diplomacy in Africa. The
'triple alliance' of multinational, state and local capital
may evolve — and certainly Nigeria's national bourgeoisie
is increasingly influential within this transnational nexus
— yet as a form of fundamental 'conditioning' its impact
remains; not just because of the salience of 'external'
actors but also because of their close identity of interest
with 'internal' bourgeois fractions, both 'national' and
'bureaucratic'.

DEBATES OVER NATIONAL POLITICS, POLITICAL ECONOMY
AND FOREIGN POLICY

Alternative views about Nigerian politics, economics and
foreign policy — about the bases, effects and limits of
Nigeria's political economy in the world system — can be
categorised into three distinct types: the 'idealist' versus
the 'realist' (disagreement over contemporary and future
forms) and the 'realist' versus the 'radical' (disagreement

over historical, current and projected structures). The
majority of analysts of Nigerian internal and international
politics — as befits its place of power at the semi-
periphery — are realists; only a minority are either
idealists or radicals [28].

Characteristic of the dominant 'realist' position, as well
as reflective of differences within this paradigm, is the
work of Bolaji Akinyemi and Olajide Aluko. Both of these
leading scholars — it is not coincidental that they are
Director General of the Nigerian Institute of International
Affairs and Professor of International Relations at the
University of Ife, respectively — take it to be axiomatic
that Nigeria is powerful and influential [29]. They may be
in disagreement about some of the causes of this power and
influence — political direction, bureaucratic style or
economic resources — but they exhibit few doubts about the
overall character of Nigeria's external stature and status.
In this shared assumption they reflect the perspective of
most Nigerian scholars and statesmen, as well as that of
most students of Nigeria: Nigeria is seen as a Newly
'Influential' Country (an alternative definition of a NIC)
at the semi-periphery, as Africa's great power and as a
successful example of 'development' [30]. If any scepticism
about Nigeria's standing is expressed by realists it is
usually about (1) how long oil (and gas) reserves will
last, (2) how long civilian government will last, and (3)
how long contemporary confusion and chaos in the infra-
structure will last. In general, though, such difficulties
are taken to be surmountable given Nigeria's financial and
entrepreneurial resources. In short, the mood is very optimistic and rather heady.

By contrast, the two minority positions are considerably
less optimistic and popular. The 'idealist' view is less
developed and debated than the radical one and is not identified with the work of any single scholar. Rather, there
are elements of idealist views in some of the writings of
several Nigerian scholars such as Oye Ogunbadejo and Aluko
[31] — what should be the bases and directions of Nigerian
foreign policy? In his second chapter in this book, for
instance, Aluko laments the deficiencies in Nigeria's economic, strategic and political structures and argues for
greater attention being given to the national interest
rather than to regional and/or continental affairs: for a
careful balancing of means with ends rather than a reckless
pursuit of grandeur [32]. In general the realist and the
idealist perspectives on Nigerian foreign policy are not
very far apart. Rather, the latter consists of redefinitions
of or revisions to the former; that is, if Nigeria is to be

influential in the future then it must reform its political
economy and federal bureaucracy to make its goals more
readily realisable. In some ways, the idealist position is
preemptive of the radical one: it anticipates future (positive) relations as a way of responding to current (negative)
criticisms.

By contrast, the other minority position — that of the
'radicals' — is much less optimistic or idealistic. Instead
it sees Nigeria as a Newly 'Industrialising' Country (the
more orthodox and cautious conceptualisation of a NIC) confronting all sorts of contradictions and constraints: the
future is less clear than in either of the other perspectives. Rather, both indigenous and foreign analysts in this
genre see Nigeria as an essentially dependent state, albeit
one at the semi-periphery rather than at the periphery: its
place in the world system and its emergent class society —
in Evans' terms the triple alliance — will constrain both
its present and future influence, as suggested in Claude
Ake's opening quotation.

So instead of an assured future, its growth and influence
are seen to be rather unstable and unsustainable: the
favourable conjuncture of forces that generated the oil boom
may not be repeatable. However as a state at the 'semi-
periphery' [33], Nigeria did experience rapid, if uneven,
growth in the 1970s. Nevertheless the projection of the oil-
based boom into the future remains problematic because of
both internal contradictions and external changes, particularly domestic tensions and international demand.

Such radical analysis clearly remains the minority school
of opinion, yet one that is growing in its forcefulness —
as reflected in the balance of contributions to this book
— as Nigeria's rapid growth generates further uneven
development. Moreover, its persuasiveness is reflected in
the fact that the major debate now is between realists and
radicals [34]; the idealist perspective is usually mobilised
only in defence of the realist position rather than in its
own right. One positive and immediate result of this growing
debate is that both realists and radicals have had to reconsider their assumptions and evidence, especially the political and economic bases of foreign policy. Enhanced sophisti-
cation and nuance are revealed in the contributions to this
volume: the debate has been joined.

MODES OF PRODUCTION, ANALYSIS AND RESOLUTION

Nigeria's place in the world system is in part or in the
main (depending on mode of analysis) a function of its mode

of production: the character of its political economy or
substructure. Its external linkages have evolved as (1) its
mode of production has changed, and (2) associated class
relations have developed. Together the mode and relations of
production can be seen to have played a primary part in
determining Nigeria's foreign policy directions and dynamics, a part that is best recognised in radical rather than
in realist or idealist analysis.

At present Nigeria's dominant mode of production — capitalist extractive and commodity production — is in flux,
(1) as the former grows at the expense of the latter, (2) as
both are joined by a burgeoning manufacturing sector, and
(3) as pre-capitalist feudal and peasant modes yield to
capitalism. The juxtaposition or coexistence of extractive,
commodity and 'industrial' modes, given their differential
linkages within external interests, has resulted in uneven
development, in terms of both economic production and social
relations [35].

The dominance of the established merchant class (which
grew to exploit pre-capitalist production and exportation)
is being challenged (1) by a 'bureaucratic bourgeoisie' in
governmental and parastatal institutions, (2) by a 'managerial bourgeoisie' in corporate branch-plants, and (3) by
a 'comprador bourgeoisie' of agents and contractors (a
refinement or reformulation in the Nigerian context of
Evans' 'triple alliance', found in the Brazilian case). The
'bureaucratic' fraction tends to be more nationalistic than
the others, which are more 'transnational' in focus and
tenor. However elements within the 'managerial' bourgeoisie
may become more national over time, possibly leading them to
establish a coalition with the remnants of the merchant
class which may, in turn, become more of a landed aristocracy as land becomes scarce. In any event, class formation
and relations in Nigeria are both growing and complex — as
well as changing — with multiple fractions inside the local
bourgeoisie and divisions within the ranks of labour and the
peasantry. This process in the Nigerian example serves to
support the assertion of Immanuel Wallerstein that competition among semi-peripheral states may 'push the indigenous
bourgeoisie and professional strata of a particular country
to a more politically "radical" stance' [36].

In the Nigerian case, the bureaucratic bourgeoisie seemed
to be ascendant during the Mohammed/Obasanjo period, particularly elements within the military and industry. This was
the period of indigenisation decrees, which particularly
affected the petroleum and manufacturing sectors, and of
'radical' African policy, both of which jeopardised or retarded the interests of the managerial and comprador

bourgeoisies [37]. The return of civilian rule and the simul-
taneous revival of some 'Northern' interests (both within
Nigeria and within the world system) signifies a retreat
towards more 'normal' fractional conflict resolution: the
easing or removal of some indigenisation and importation
rules limits the activities of the bureaucrats and facilitates the tastes of the managers and compradors.

However popular awareness of embourgeoisement is growing
under party government, in part because politicians are
better known and more visible than soldiers, so criticism of
and opposition to any retreat from economic nationalism may
also grow. Moreover, concern about Nigeria's regional role
— seen at times as regional 'hegemony' or 'imperialism' —
is also increasing in West Africa: another potential check
on national politics. And both of these forms of national
and regional resistance are themselves occurring in a world
system characterised by recession rather than by growth.
Transnational linkages between Nigeria and the industrialised states may change in any event in the 1980s as neo-
mercantilist pressures in the latter reduce the global reach
of multinational corporations [38]. In which case, Nigeria
may yet need to revive the indigenisation programme of the
1970s as a form of self-protection in a world of trade wars.

Meanwhile the intermediary position of states like Nigeria
has implications for other countries in the West African
region and is, in turn, affected by shifts in the global
system. On the one hand, Nigeria's role as a semi-peripheral
state may serve to reinforce rather than relieve its neighbours' position at the periphery: hence their ambivalence
about too close an association with Nigeria in ECOWAS. On
the other hand, as already suggested, Nigeria's own status
may shift as the global growth of the early 1970s gives way
to global recession in the early 1980s, especially if it can
confront successfully those countries and corporations at
the global centre: 'In moments of world economic downturn,
semi-peripheral countries can usually expand control of
their home market at the expense of core producers, and expand their access to neighbouring peripheral markets, again
at the expense of core producers' [39]. At the same time,
the semi-periphery may be under increased pressure to maintain purchases from the centre to help the latter through
its economic problems. This is especially so in the case of
the bilateral economic relationships between Britain and
Nigeria and between the US and Nigeria, respectively. Again,
to cite Wallerstein: 'When world contraction comes, the
squeeze is felt by core countries who proceed to fight each
other, each fearing "slippage". Now the semiperipheral
countries may be courted, as the outlets for core products

become relatively rare' [40].

The NICs are seen by the old industrialised states as their salvation during a period of high recession and inflation whereas the NICs themselves seek to turn such a period to their own advantage by laying claim more insistently to national and regional markets. In any event, whether 'external' or 'national' interests are victorious is related not only to international pressures but also to 'internal' politics. The balance between bureaucratic, managerial and comprador fractions within the Nigerian bourgeoisie depends, then, on domestic pressures, regional ambivalence and global situation as well as on the coexistence between extractive and industrial modes of production. And it is the intensity of these pressures, combined with the apparently 'natural' (and certainly inextinguishable!) ebullience of Nigerian politicians, especially at their rebirth, that has generated what Ake calls the 'overpoliticisation of social life in Nigeria' [41].

Foreign policy, especially if successfully crafted, may provide some escape or diversion from such contradictions, yet the structural constraints — both internal and global — projected to the end of this century will limit such a pursuit of 'glory' [42]. Pressures for 'reindustrialisation' at the centre will affect the prospects for growth and development in both the semi-periphery and the periphery. Such pressures will also undermine the position of transnational managerial and comprador elements within the Nigerian and other semi-peripheral bourgeoisies and strengthen the claims of the bureaucratic fraction for more protectionist policies. These ongoing issues hold implications for the balance between modes of production as well as between social forces; both are central factors in determining Nigeria's foreign policy direction in the future as they have been in the past. As Evans cautions in the case of Brazil, the triple alliance is not immutable:

> The present version [of dependent development] assumes no irreconcilable differences between local industrialists and the multinationals or between the state and the multinationals. The contradictions between the global rationality of the multinationals and the interests of the local bourgeoisie and the state are seen as potentially resolvable, provided the overall conditions under which the alliance operates are not too unfavourable to continued capital accumulation in the semi-periphery [43].

Given neo-mercantilist pressures in the North, state-corporate relations may be much warmer in the semi-periphery than in the metropole, in the short term at least.

NIGERIA PORTRAYED AND PROJECTED

Divergent views about Nigeria's development policy and political economy can be projected into the mid-term future:
Will growth lead to development? Will industrialisation lead
to influence? The outcome of these debates and trends is in
part, of course, a function of global as well as national
factors, especially the prices of oil and gas and the prospects for industrial development in the semi-periphery.

But external changes are mediated through transnational
'alliances' and internal contradictions. At the present
time, the major issues revolve around agricultural development, more 'national' (bureaucratic) versus more 'transnational' (managerial and comprador) fractions, and the
political process. These are associated with, or derived
from, the realist, radical and idealist modes of analysis,
respectively. The resolution of these issues will largely
determine the picture of Nigeria at the beginning of the
twenty-first century.

First, until the 1970s Nigeria could largely feed itself,
even exporting considerable amounts of primary commodities.
However the oil boom, combined with population pressure,
diverted attention away from the produce of the land and towards the flow from oil wells. The rapid rise of income for
some led to accelerated taste transfer, reflected in dramatic increases in the importation of rice and wheat [44],
automobiles and electrical gadgets. OPEC prices for 'sweet'
and light Nigerian crude have usually enabled the country
to extract premium 'rents' for its accelerating oil output.
But 'high-life' led to a new vulnerability: the government
could hardly afford to stem the tide of imports in 1978 or
1981 when the oil market went soft. Moreover, the demise of
agricultural production left the country more vulnerable to
vagaries in the price and supply of food as well as of oil
[45]. Nigeria's balances of trade and payments now reflect
Saudi Arabia's oil production and the United States' wheat
production and oil consumption. NICs like Nigeria may have
become increasingly 'interdependent' in the world of OECD
members yet they continue to be more 'dependent' than most
industrialised economies because their systems remain essentially outward looking.

Second, the competition between more national and more
comprador elements within the indigenous bourgeoisie is
likely to intensify as the growth rate declines, land becomes scarce and policy choices narrow. The Mohammed/

Obasanjo military regime encouraged more national bureaucratic fractions to expand their industrial and service activities, partially because they sought to encourage 'southern' Nigerian entrepreneurs. The civilian Shagari administration has returned somewhat to the traditional corporate-northern (Nigerian) coalition in which managerial and comprador elements are encouraged. Some of the limits placed on foreign investors under the indigenisation programmes have been eased under the National Party of Nigeria (NPN) government so that Nigeria is now once again a more extroverted political economy than at the end of the 1970s [46]. This trend towards renewed and enlarged transnational linkages, especially in the fields of agribusiness and manufacturing, is likely to continue under civilian rule unless (1) oil revenue declines significantly for a considerable period of time or (2) protectionist pressures in the US, EEC and elsewhere produce a withdrawal of foreign investment, technology and personnel.

And third, 'radical' elements within political parties, various state governments or trade unions may yet, as already indicated, pose a threat to the established transnational nexus. Nigeria's 'indigenisation' policy represented one attempt to meet 'nationalist' pressures but 'state capitalism' is unlikely to satisfy demands for more 'socialist' measures. Such demands may also intensify if the logic of growth at the semi-periphery is eroded by continued inflation and recession in OECD metropoles. Protectionist pressures in the North might curtail foreign investment and involvement in the semi-periphery undermining the position of the managerial and comprador bourgeoisies and reinforcing the claims of more nationalist and radical elements. Wallerstein has cautioned about the tension in the semi-periphery between fractions favouring less versus more integration, a tension that is likely to be exacerbated by global trends in the 1980s:

The semiperipheral states in the coming decades will be a battleground of two major transnational forces. One will be the multinational corporations who will be fighting for the survival of the essentials of the capitalist system: the possibility of continued surplus appropriation on a world scale. The other will be a transnational alignment of socialist forces who will be seeking to undermine the capitalist world economy ... forcing relatively drastic redistributions of world surplus and cutting the long-term present and potential organisational links between multinationals and certain strata internal to each semi-peripheral country [47].

Nigerian decisions may be compelled in the 1980s, then, to
revive or redefine 'nonalignment' as an economic as well as
a strategic doctrine, otherwise external pressures may
affect internal class formations and relations [48]. However while the prospects for socialism in Nigeria are still
slight, the balance between more national and more international capitalisms is likely to become more central and
controversial.

The next decade is likely to be an exciting as well as a
challenging one for Nigeria as its process of semi-
industrialisation proceeds. Crucial 'macroeconomic' factors
are the costs of food and capital imports and the value of
oil and gas exports, whereas salient 'microeconomic' factors
include the balance between national and comprador fractions
within the indigenous bourgeoisie and the relationship
between more (conservative) capitalist and more radical
(socialist) forces within the domestic polity. It is such
growing contradictions that have led to the 'overpoliticisation' that Ake has lamented. The treatment of apparently
'internal' political paranoia will have fundamental implications for the direction of foreign policy and position in
the world system:

Our problems are rooted in our history and in the concrete economic and social structures which it has evolved.
By the very nature of the problems they cannot be finally
solved without, at the very least, breaking our exploita-
tive dependence on the West, and doing away with the
existing relations of production ... the contradictions
of the present system are creating the conditions that
will change it [49].

This book is intended to offer alternative descriptions,
explanations and projections of these conditions and contradictions especially as they relate to Nigeria's external
relations and foreign policy.

NOTES AND REFERENCES

1. Andrew Young, 'The United States and Africa: Victory for Diplomacy', Foreign Affairs, 59 (3), 1981, p. 654.
2. Claude Ake, 'Off to a Good Start But Dangers Await ...', West Africa, 3330, 25 May 1981, p. 1163.
3. G. O. Okunzua, 'No Need to Worry Over Money in 1981: New Year Predictions', Sunday Times (Lagos), 28 December 1980, p. 11.
4. Sonni G. Tyoden, 'State, Class and Capital Accumulation in the Periphery', Nigerian Political Science Association, Kano, April 1981, p. 20.
5. Typical of such recognition are two essays by Jean Herskovits, 'Nigeria: Africa's New Power', Foreign Affairs, 53 (2), January 1975, pp. 314–33, and 'Dateline Nigeria: a Black Power', Foreign Policy, 29, Winter 1977–8, pp. 167–88. Cf. the critiques of this widely held position in Chapters 6 and 11.
6. Peter Evans, Dependent Development: the Alliance of Multinational, State and Local Capital in Brazil (Princeton University Press, 1979) p. 11.
7. See A. Bolaji Akinyemi, 'Mohammed/Obasanjo Foreign Policy' in Oyeleye Oyediran (ed.), Nigerian Government and Politics under Military Rule, 1966–1979 (London: Macmillan, 1979) pp. 150–68.
8. See B. C. Sullivan, 'Structural Dependency: the Nigerian Economy as a Case Study', Journal of Asian and African Studies, 14 (1–2), January and April 1979, pp. 44–55.
9. On this 'tradition' in Nigerian foreign relations see Douglas G. Anglin, 'Nigeria: Political Non-alignment and Economic Alignment', Journal of Modern African Studies, 2 (2), June 1964, pp. 147–63.
10. Evans, Dependent Development, p. 313.
11. On these decisions see Chapter 5 and Olatunde J. B. Ojo, 'Nigeria and the Formation of ECOWAS', International Organisation, 34 (4), Autumn 1980, pp. 571–604.
12. Oye Ogunbadejo, 'Nigeria's Foreign Policy Under Military Rule, 1966–79', International Journal, 35 (4), Autumn 1980, p. 765.
13. On the semi-periphery see Timothy M. Shaw, 'The Semi-periphery in Africa and Latin America: Sub-imperialism and Semi-industrialism', Review of Black Political Economy, 9 (4), Summer 1979, pp. 341–58, and 'Dependence to (Inter)Dependence: Review of Debate on the (New) International Economic Order', Alternatives, 4 (4), March 1979, pp. 557–78. See also Evans, Dependent Development, especially pp. 33–54 and 290–314.

14. See ECA/OAU, <u>Plan of Action for the Implementation of the Monrovia Strategy for the Economic Development of Africa to the First Economic Summit of the Assembly of Heads of State and Government of the OAU, Lagos, April 1980</u> (Addis Ababa: ECA, 1980; E/CN.14/781/Add. 1) especially pp. 1–16.
15. Despite the tenuousness of Nigeria's position at the semi-periphery — 'Nigeria is not only one of the least industrialised countries in the group but also one whose primary qualification for semi-peripheral status is its oil wealth. Brazil and Nigeria represent opposite poles within the range of third world countries that might be considered members of the "semi-periphery" ' (p. 299) — Evans indicates that the Nigerian state (and some of its bourgeois leading fractions) has cooperative links with transnational agencies: 'Despite external trade relations and an internal economic structure that resemble classic dependence more than dependent development, the Nigerian state is already thoroughly immersed in concrete alliances with the multinationals' (<u>Dependent Development</u>, p. 311).
16. See, for example, Olajide Aluko, 'Nigeria, the United States and Southern Africa', <u>African Affairs</u>, 78 (310), January 1979, pp. 91–102.
17. On this 'dialectic' see Chapter 2.
18. For more on the US-Nigerian 'alliance' of the late 1970s see Chapter 3.
19. Young, 'The United States and Africa', p. 655.
20. Ojo, 'Nigeria and the Formation of ECOWAS', p. 601.
21. Evans, <u>Dependent Development</u>, p. 309.
22. Ibid., p. 308.
23. See Timothy M. Shaw, 'Dependence with Growth: the Political Economy of Petroleum in Nigeria', <u>Workshop on the Effects of Commodity Dependence on Development in African Countries</u>, Centre for African Studies, Dalhousie University, March 1981.
24. <u>Globe and Mail</u>, 25 August 1981, and <u>Standard Chartered Review</u>, October 1981, p. 33.
25. See Chapters 6, 7 and 8.
26. See comparison between orthodox and radical modes of analysis in Chapter 11.
27. Young, 'The United States and Africa', pp. 655–6.
28. See Chapter 11 and Bibliography.
29. See Chapters 5 and 10 and Bibliography.
30. Typical of this genre see Ibrahim A. Gambari, 'Nigeria and the World: a Growing Internal Stability, Wealth and External Influence', <u>Journal of International Affairs</u>, 29 (2), Fall 1975, pp. 155–69, and Joseph Wayas,

Nigeria's Leadership Role in Africa (London: Macmillan, 1979); cf. critique in Chapters 6, 10 and 11.

31. See Bibliography, Ogunbadejo, 'Nigeria's Foreign Policy Under Military Rule 1966-79', and Olajide Aluko, Essays in Nigerian Foreign Policy (London: Allen & Unwin, 1981).

32. See Chapter 10.

33. For more on this important concept and category see Immanuel Wallerstein, The Capitalist World-Economy (Cambridge University Press, 1979) pp. 21-34, and Evans, Dependent Development, passim, especially pp. 33-54.

34. On this see Chapter 11.

35. See Gavin Williams' 'Introduction' to his collection on Nigeria: Economy and Society (London: Rex Collings, 1976) pp. 1-7, and Segun Osoba, 'The Deepening Crisis of the Nigerian National Bourgeoisie', Review of African Political Economy, 13, May-August 1978, pp. 63-77. See also Gavin Williams, 'Postface', in his collection on State and Society in Nigeria (Idanre, Ondo: Afrografika, 1980) pp. 10-21.

36. Wallerstein, The Capitalist World-Economy, p. 106. On the nature and limits to this 'radicalism' in Nigeria see Chapters 1, 2, 6, 8 and 11.

37. See Oyediran (ed.), Nigerian Government and Politics under Military Rule 1966-1979 and Chapters 7 and 8.

38. See Evans, Dependent Development, pp. 320-9, and Timothy M. Shaw, Towards an International Political Economy for the 1980s: from Dependence to (Inter) Dependence (Halifax: Centre for Foreign Policy Studies, 1980).

39. Wallerstein, The Capitalist World-Economy, p. 99.

40. Ibid., p. 89.

41. Ake, 'Off to a Good Start But Dangers Await ...', p. 1163.

42. On these see Timothy M. Shaw (ed.), Alternative Futures for Africa (Boulder: Westview, 1982) passim.

43. Evans, Dependent Development, p. 52.

44. See Barry B. Hughes and Patricia A. Strauch, 'The Future of Development in Nigeria and the Sahel: Projections from the World Integrated Model (WIM)', in Shaw (ed.), Alternative Futures for Africa, pp. 179-99, especially pp. 186-91.

45. Ibid. Hughes and Strauch project that to eliminate malnutrition in Nigeria by the year 2001 would require an eventual annual food trade deficit by the end of the century of $11 billion (p. 188).

46. See Chapter 2; cf. Chapter 8.

47. Wallerstein, The Capitalist World-Economy, pp. 117-18.

48. See Timothy M. Shaw, 'The Political Economy of Non-
    alignment: from Dependence to Self-reliance', <u>Interna-
    tional Studies</u>, 19 (3-4), July-September 1980, pp. 475-
    502.
49. Ake, 'Off to a Good Start But Dangers Await ...',
    p. 1163. For more on Nigeria's problems and development
    strategies to deal with them see Claude Ake, <u>A Politi-
    cal Economy of Africa</u> (London: Longman, 1981) pp. 114-16
    and 143-72.

Part I
Alternative Perceptions of Nigerian Foreign Policy

Part II

2 Nigeria in World Politics: Contemporary Calculations and Constraints

TIMOTHY M. SHAW

In a world economy that is basically reliant on oil,
Nigeria's economic and strategic importance is enormous ...
Increasingly, Nigeria's wealth and position has immensely
enhanced her political and strategic importance in Africa
and world politics. A strong member of OPEC, a pioneer
and stabilising force in the OAU, a member of the British
Commonwealth of Nations, a dynamic member of the Non-
Aligned Nations, a co-founder of ECOWAS, Nigeria is slowly
but assuredly emerging as a major factor in the global
power calculus.

Nigerian Development Plan Advertisement [1]

Clearly, the record of the military in the field of the
country's foreign relations is, in varying degrees, much
better than that of the Balewa regime. But then, this
could be explained to some extent by way of Lagos'
increased capability for influence. Its oil wealth, particularly in the years after the civil war, provided Nigeria
with the economic base, and thus the confidence, to give
more substance to its foreign policy of nonalignment.

Oye Ogunbadejo [2]

[On] the subject of my inaugural lecture—'Necessity and
Freedom in Nigerian Foreign Policy'—I shall say a few words
why I have chosen it ... The first is the lack of purpose
and consistency in our foreign policy since the mid-
seventies. The second has been the tendency of the Nigerian
government and some powerful sections of the public to
overestimate our ability to influence external events,
and perhaps shape world events in our own image. An
example of this was the recent statement of the Minister
of External Affairs, Professor Ishaya Audu, that Nigeria
was 'longing to become a world super-power soonest'. The
third is the psychological trait among Nigerian leaders
and some sections of influential opinion-moulders that we

23

have a great deal of freedom of manoeuvre in the conduct
of our external relations.

Olajide Aluko [3]

There are three important interrelated issues presently
identifiable in the continuing debate about Nigerian foreign
policy. First, as reflected in the official and Aluko cita-
tions above, does Nigeria have the 'power' to exert a significant influence in contemporary international affairs?
Second, as indicated in all three opening quotations, but
especially in that of Ogunbadejo, is Nigerian policy effective, at either global, continental or regional levels?
And third, given Nigeria's political economy and development strategy, what should be the orientation or direction
of its foreign policy in the mid-term future?

In the world of the 1980s — a world characterised by a
return to *realpolitik* in which a select group of Newly
Influential or Newly Industrialising Countries (NICs) [4]
have begun to play a significant role — it is considered
almost axiomatic by Nigerians and non-Nigerians alike that
Nigeria is Africa's major or great power. As suggested
elsewhere in an article with Orobola Fasehun, the bases of
this greatness have been seen to shift from the 1960s to
the 1980s from population and pluralism to petroleum and
presidentialism [5]. But, in a curious expression of consistency, neither before or after the oil boom nor before
or after military rule has much scepticism been expressed
about the limits of Nigerian power.

In an attempt to understand, and maybe to advance, the
debate over the capabilities and constraints on Nigerian
foreign policy, this chapter identifies different levels
of interaction, various types of role conception and alternative modes of analysis. It does so not only for intellectual reasons but also as a way of clarifying policy options
and limitations for both Nigerian decision-makers and also
extra-African policy-makers concerned with Nigeria. And in
a final section, contradictions between levels and policies
will be identified as a means to identifying some choices
and constraints.

NIGERIA: AFRICA'S GREAT POWER?

Undeniably, Nigeria is *primus inter pares* in Black Africa.
But in a complex, as well as unequal, world order its power,
like that of all other actors, is limited. If Nigeria is to
be an effective leader of Africa it surely needs to recognise and not to ignore these constraints lest its credibility

be eroded. Olajide Aluko has cautioned against two particular errors based on economic and psychological miscalcula-
tions or misperceptions, namely:

> to cast for Nigeria a role in world affairs that is clearly
> beyond our means ... [and] the psychological error made by
> most Nigerians in and outside government that because of
> the size, population, and the agricultural and mineral
> resources in the country we are destined to lead Africa
> [6].

Nigeria's self-perception of a larger-than-life role on the
world stage cannot be deduced from the formal conception of
foreign policy presented in the 1979 second federal constitution:

> The state shall promote African unity as well as total
> political, economic, social and cultural liberation of
> Africa and all other forms of international cooperation
> conducive to the consolidation of universal peace and
> mutual respect and friendship among all peoples and states,
> and shall combat racial discrimination in all its manifes-
> tations [7].

And the earlier, interim formulation of national interest by
the military-appointed Adedeji Review Panel on Nigerian
Foreign Policy of 1976 is also misleading because of its wel-
come but ineffective concern for self-reliance:

(1) The defence of our sovereignty, independence and
territorial integrity;
(2) The creation of the necessary political conditions
in Africa and the rest of the world which would
facilitate the defence of our sovereignty, independence and territorial integrity;
(3) The creation of the necessary economic and political
conditions in Africa and the rest of the world which
would foster Nigeria's national self-reliance and
rapid economic development;
(4) The achievement of collective self-reliance in Africa
and the rest of the developing world;
(5) The promotion and defence of social justice and
respect for human dignity;
(6) The promotion and defence of world peace [8].

Neither of these contemporary formulations really provide
much of a framework either to guide Nigerian foreign policy-
makers or to enable non-Nigerian interests to predict

Nigerian behaviour. Nevertheless, despite the deficiencies
of formal definitions, the debate over Nigerian foreign
policy is a lively one, especially amongst Nigerian scholars
and practitioners: a considerable contrast to the moribund
nature of foreign policy analysis in most of Africa [9].
This chapter attempts to capture (and, hopefully, to contribute to) the characteristic intensity of the Nigerian
'palaver' over foreign policy.

LEVELS OF ANALYSIS AND INTERACTION

Turning first to different levels of analysis and interaction, under the military, Nigeria's policy became more and
largely Afrocentric. The inheritance from the first civilian
republic of Balewa was one of essentially pro-Western 'non-
alignment' in which links with the ex-colonial power remained
central. Ogunbadejo laments that

> ... when the military intervened in January 1966, Nigeria's
> foreign policy remained what it had been when the country
> attained its independence from Britain in 1960; it was
> openly pro-West and lacked any initiative, creativity, or
> leadership of any consequence in African affairs [10].

Under successive military regimes — in part forced or
facilitated by the civil war and the oil boom — Nigeria
moved towards a more balanced form of nonalignment as well
as towards a more African-oriented focus. This Africa-first
policy is reflected in three different ways, over three
different issues — liberation, mediation and integration.
    First, Nigeria has been increasingly concerned about the
achievement of majority rule in Southern Africa. In the
post-Portuguese coup period under the Mohammed and Obasanjo
leaderships, Nigeria became a close associate of the five
Front Line States of Southern Africa; no major diplomatic
initiatives occurred without Nigeria's involvement if not
Nigeria's consent. Its most dramatic and effective action
occurred when Murtala Mohammed recognised the MPLA government in Angola in 1976 so affecting the diplomatic impasse
in the OAU. This recognition was mistakenly interpreted as
an indication that the post-Gowon leadership was radical.
Rather, it was an attempt to lead Africa in a decisive way
(i.e. to resist extra-continental intrusions, especially if
they served to radicalise) and to oppose South African
intervention in Angolan affairs. Nigeria not only opposed
South Africa on principle because of apartheid; Nigeria
also opposed its Angolan adventure because of its earlier

interference in Nigeria's own civil war. Since then Nigeria
has provided aid and assistance to the Zimbabwe regime
(₦10m. at independence alone in part to fund the nationalisation of the South African-owned press) and demanded early
decolonisation in Namibia. Nigeria's Southern African policy
is a central feature of its post-Balewa Afrocentricity;
another is its role as continental mediator.

Second, Nigeria has continued to serve as a mediator in a
variety of African disputes. President Shagari has followed
in the footsteps of Balewa, Gowon and Obasanjo in serving as
a PanAfrican mediator, in particular in the Sahara and Chad
disputes in West Africa. However whilst the new civilian
regime has attempted to bring Nigerian power to bear in
these international disputes, it has, as one might expect,
been more 'interventive' than the soldiers in expressing
its disapproval of military involvement in the domestic
affairs of other African states, breaking relations with
both Liberia (over the Doe coup) and Libya (over Gaddafi's
alleged take-over of N'Djamena in violation of the August
1979 Lagos Accord on National Reconciliation in Chad).

Finally, at its immediate, regional level, Nigeria has
been an advocate of cooperation and integration, being a
leading actor in the founding of ECOWAS in 1975. Although
ECOWAS headquarters is in Lagos and Nigerian industries
stand to gain regional markets and cheap labour from the
Community, Nigeria is very aware of its image of regional
power in West Africa and has contributed aid and investment
as a means to relieve fears of its dominance (see Chapters
3 and 6). To emphasise the civilian regime's commitment to
ECOWAS and good neighbourliness, President Shagari's first
state visits in early 1980 were to Benin and Niger. But
over-reaction by the new administration (noted in the
previous paragraph) to the anti-Tubman coup in Liberia,
plus associated threats and pressures over events in Ghana
and Chad, have revived fears of Nigerian dominance throughout the region. Lagos has always been selfconscious about
its image at different levels of international interaction.

NATIONAL ROLE CONCEPTIONS

Turning, second, to Nigerian national role conceptions,
these are also concentrated at the African level, reflective of official policies and self-perceptions. If Kal
Holsti's typology is adopted, then at the continental level
Nigeria has continued to be a 'status quo mediator'. In
Southern Africa it has become more clearly, as already
indicated, a 'liberation supporter' whereas in West Africa,

despite a certain reluctance, it has maintained the role, in
both formal and informal ways, of being 'regional leader'.

Before turning to alternative modes of analysis for
Nigerian foreign policy and to identifying contradictions
amongst levels and roles, one further type of interaction
and goal should be identified. Nigeria also interacts inten-
sively with the major industrial powers, especially with the
US (see Chapter 3), Japan and the EEC, and it is very concerned with industrialisation as a means to development (see
Chapter 5). Nigeria was incorporated into the world system
in the nineteenth century to provide raw materials for
Europe's industrial revolution. Since the discovery of oil
it provides hydrocarbon feedstock to the world whilst trying
at the same time to industrialise itself. But the switch
from exporting palm oil to exporting fuel oil has led to new
problems, not only of rapid growth and inflation, but also
to dependence on one commodity — at least until liquefied
natural gas (LNG) is produced and exported — and on a few
markets — the US and the Netherlands primarily [11]. Moreover, great expectations have been raised about a continuing
flow of capital and consumer imports.

Nigeria rapidly depleted its foreign reserves in the boom
years from 1976 to 1978 but with military-imposed restrictions its balance of trade surplus yielded foreign reserve
holdings of more than ₦3 billion from 1979 onwards. Dependence on oil revenue is important not only to cover imports
but also to provide tax revenue for infrastructural development, the basis of Nigerian external capabilities or power
(see Chapters 6 and 10). Petroleum profits tax and mining
rents and royalties now constitute more than 50 per cent of
the federal government's revenue; company taxation and
import/export duties cover most of the rest [12]. Income
tax provides an infinitesimal amount of revenue. Nigeria is
a very *laissez faire* capitalist economy; its foreign policy
cannot but reflect its capitalism as well as its nationalism.

Dependence on oil and associated dependence on Western
corporations, investments, technology, skills, etc., constitute central features (albeit often forgotten ones) of
Nigeria's political economy [13]. Together they constrain
its range of foreign policy choices and affect its performance in Africa and elsewhere. Nigeria has become an advocate of Third World collective interests in North-South and
EurAfrican forums at the same time as becoming a relatively
privileged oil exporter itself. Its position as a NIC within
the global capitalist system — as well as fears of its
dominance throughout Africa — constrains its leadership of
the Nonaligned Coalition and presents ambiguities, if not

contradictions, in its national role conceptions in Africa
(see Chapter 11).

Before turning in conclusion to pointing out some of these
contradictions, I would like to note first, the two major
state visits that President Shagari has undertaken outside
of Africa since assuming office — to the US and the UK —
and second, the first major international conference to be
held in Lagos under his auspices. Shagari's visits to the
US (October 1980) and UK (March 1981) symbolise (1) the
renewal after a period of difficulties of Nigeria's traditional ties with these two central states in the Western
alliance and (2) the recognition of growing interdependence
amongst these three OECD or NIC states: the exchange of oil
for food with the US and markets for investment with the UK
(with the prospect of a major £600m. arms deal). Despite
the election of conservative regimes in both countries, the
Shagari administration (which is also quite conservative!)
has reinforced these particular North-South ties.

The military regime hosted two symbolic meetings in 1977:
the lavish FESTAC spectacle and an OAU/UN anti-apartheid
conference. By contrast, in April 1980 the civilian government hosted the first African economic summit from which
emerged the Lagos Plan of Action on establishing an African
Common Market before the end of the century. Like Nigeria's
concern for political and racial decolonisation in Southern
Africa, the Lagos economic summit reflected its concern for
economic decolonisation. For Shagari the Lagos summit was
'the signal for the commencement of Africa's struggle for
economic interdependence ... without economic power political interdependence is meaningless, incomplete and insecure'.
And, introducing the Lagos Plan of Action to the UN he
warned that

> in spite of the enormous natural wealth and resources of
> Africa, our continent remains the least developed and our
> peoples the most deprived. These degrading disabilities
> mock our political independence ... I call upon this
> august assembly to launch a decade of reparation and
> restitution ... as a master plan for the economic recovery
> of Africa [14].

Meanwhile Nigeria's own economy is quite distinguishable
from the continent's general condition [15]: it is amongst
the fastest growing in Africa, with an annual trade balance
in 1979 of ₦3.3b. on total external trade of $18 billion.
However, the importation of food as well as consumer and
capital goods has accelerated once again and major infrastructural projects like the iron and steel complexes,

fertilizer factory and the proposed Bonny LNG plant remain
incomplete. Yet the latest, fourth five-year plan is very
optimistic, as befits a NIC: GDP is expected to rise over
the period by 7.2 per cent per annum to reach ₦51 billion
in 1985 up from ₦36 billion in 1980. However the balance of
trade is expected to decline from ₦2822 million in 1980 to
a negative figure in 1985 as imports continue to expand.
And the new plan anticipates heightened not reduced dependence on foreign skilled (as well as unskilled) labour [16].

CONTRADICTIONS AND CONSTRAINTS

In conclusion, I would like to turn to six central issues
or contradictions that may disturb Nigeria's growth pattern
over the short-term future, recognising the underlying
strengths and difficulties of its oil, and maybe gas, based
economy. First, Nigeria is becoming a very unequal society,
with rapid urbanisation, differentiation and alienation: is
growth going to continue to be sought at the expense of
development? And if so, what social tensions are likely to
emerge and how might they be contained: through reform,
revolution and/or repression? Second, Nigeria is becoming
very dependent on food imports, especially wheat, despite
its history of feeding itself: is it able or willing to
spend foreign exchange on wheat? If not, how will it revive
its agricultural industry: peasant farmers or agribusiness?
The present regime seems determined to introduce large-scale
agriculture whatever the cost; the fourth national plan
reveals that 'the Federal Government would place emphasis on
encouraging private entrepreneurs to establish large-scale
farms ... agricultural production and processing has been
transferred from Schedules II to III of the Nigerian Enterprises Promotion Act which means that foreigners can now
own up to 60 per cent of the equity in an agricultural
enterprise' [17].

Third, revealed in part by who owns land and capital,
houses and shares there is a growing tension within the
Nigerian bourgeoisie between more national and more transnational fractions: are Nigerian industry, agriculture and
services to be owned mainly by nationals or multinationals
[18]? And if by Nigeria, then by individual citizens or by
the federal or state governments? Fourth, many multinationals
operating in Nigeria also have branches in South Africa, an
apartheid regime that the Nigerian government is anxious to
overthrow. Should Nigeria ignore or challenge those companies
who 'play both sides of the street'? Nigeria nationalised BP
in July 1979 to put pressure on the British before the

Lusaka Commonwealth meeting on Zimbabwe; but in February 1981 it compensated BP by $134m. in oil and allowed it to resume its Nigerian operations at the same time as the UN was discussing oil sanctions against South Africa and actions against multinational energy corporations that supply the apartheid state (as well as against sportspersons who play games with it).

Fifth, Nigeria is a country divided not only by region and tribe and class but also by religion: how should the non-sectarian Nigerian regime deal with, say, Libya or Israel? Already Senator Jaja Wachuku has called, at some personal cost, for the recognition of Israel; meanwhile, an adviser to the Governor of Kaduna State, Dr Bala Usman laments Nigeria's confrontation with Libya on the grounds that it advances French imperialism in Africa [19].

Finally, sixth, Nigeria's interests and influence tend to be concentrated at the regional level: is its role in West Africa to be that of regional leader or regional dominator? And if Nigeria has a decisive impact on regional cooperation and conflict is this exerted on behalf of itself or on behalf of extra-regional interests; i.e. is Nigeria a 'sub-imperial' power [20]? Nigeria is the only NIC in ECOWAS and it has been very active over political change in Chad, Ghana, Liberia and Sahara; does it advocate regional economic cooperation and conflict resolution for itself and West Africa or Western countries and corporations? In short, is Nigeria's Afro-centric policy one it claims for its own national interests or a role it plays for extra-continental interests?

Notwithstanding this ambiguity or uncertainty, let me conclude by returning to two of the leading students of Nigerian foreign policy cited at the opening of this chapter, both of whose comments are particularly relevant to Nigeria's African role. Overall, Ogunbadejo remains rather optimistic and complimentary about the direction of Nigerian foreign policy:

> There is an element of continuity in Nigerian foreign policy in that all the various regimes subscribed to 'non-alignment' at the international level and good neighbourliness in Africa. What varied was the way successive regimes interpreted these cardinal principles and the extent to which other intra- and extra-Nigerian events shaped the execution of these policies ... The Mohammed regime steered Nigeria's foreign relations onto a more militant path and redressed the lopsided nature of the country's non-aligned policy [21].

By contrast, in focusing on inputs rather than outputs, constraints rather than rhetoric, Aluko remains pessimistic and

critical, arguing that Nigeria both overestimates its power
and overstretches its scarce resources:

> The catalogue of errors in our foreign policy is long ...
> The first is the failure of our leaders especially the
> post-1975 ones to appreciate severe external and internal
> constraints on their freedom of choice and therefore strike
> a foreign policy that will be Nigeria-centred, that is
> that will be self-seeking in the sense that its primary
> preoccupation should be the promotion of the country's
> security and the well-being of the people [22].

NOTES AND REFERENCES

1. Advertisement on 'Nigeria's Fourth National Development
   Plan', Financial Times (London), 17 March 1981, p. 5.
2. Oye Ogunbadejo, 'Nigeria's Foreign Policy Under Military
   Rule 1966-79', International Journal, 35 (4), Autumn
   1980, p. 765.
3. Olajide Aluko, 'Necessity and Freedom in Nigerian Foreign
   Policy', inaugural lecture, University of Ife, 17 March
   1981, pp. 9-10.
4. On these see Timothy M. Shaw, 'Towards an International
   Political Economy for the 1980s: from Dependence to
   (Inter)Dependence' (Halifax: Centre for Foreign Policy
   Studies, 1980).
5. See Timothy M. Shaw and Orobola Fasehun, 'Nigeria in the
   World System: Alternative Approaches, Explanations and
   Projections', Journal of Modern African Studies, 18 (4),
   December 1980, pp. 551-73.
6. Aluko, 'Necessity and Freedom in Nigerian Foreign Policy',
   pp. 31 and 33.
7. 'Nigerian Constitution' in Colin Legum (ed.), Africa
   Contemporary Record: Annual Survey and Documents, Volume
   12, 1979-1980 (New York: Africana, 1981), section 19,
   p. C66. See also the section on 'Nigeria — Return to
   Civilian Rule', pp. B582-B613.
8. Report of the Committee on the Review of Nigeria's
   Foreign Policy, Including Economic and Technical
   Cooperation, under the Chairmanship of Professor Adebayo
   Adedeji (Lagos, May 1976) p. 59, cited in Aluko,
   'Necessity and Freedom in Nigerian Foreign Policy',
   p. 13.

9. For a lament on the state of African foreign policy studies see Timothy M. Shaw, 'Class, Country and Corporation: Africa in the Capitalist World System' in Donald I. Ray et al. (eds.), Into the 80s: Proceedings of the 11th Annual Conference of the Canadian Association of African Studies, Vol. 2 (Vancouver: Tantalus, 1981), pp. 19-37.

10. Ogunbadejo, 'Nigeria's Foreign Policy Under Military Rule 1966-79', p. 751.

11. On Nigeria's new dependence, having diversified products and markets between its palm oil and fuel oil periods, see Timothy M. Shaw, 'Dependence with Growth: the Political Economy of Petroleum in Nigeria', Workshop on the Effects of Commodity Dependence on Development in African Countries (Centre for African Studies, Dalhousie University, March 1981).

12. Taken together, payments from the oil industry now provide 90 per cent of the federal government's revenue and 95 per cent of Nigeria's foreign exchange. See ibid.

13. On these see Timothy M. Shaw, 'Nigeria's Political Economy: Constitutions, Capitalism and Contradictions', ODI Review, 2, 1980, pp. 76-85.

14. West Africa (3299), 13 October 1980, p. 2011.

15. On Africa's unpromising prospects and on Nigeria's promising projections see Timothy M. Shaw (ed.), Alternative Futures for Africa (Boulder: Westview, 1982), especially chapter 7 on 'The Future of Development in Nigeria and the Sahel: Projections from the World Integrated Model (WIM)', by Barry Hughes and Patricia Strauch.

16. See Outline of the Fourth National Development Plan, 1981-1985 (Lagos: Federal Ministry of Planning 1981) pp. 9 and 91.

17. Ibid., pp. 20-1. Nigeria is counting particularly on North American grain and skills to sustain its 'green revolution', with attention focused especially on the Nigerian-US Joint Agricultural Consultative Committee: 'To reverse agriculture's downward trend and achieve self-sufficiency, Nigeria is counting on US companies to provide technology, goods and investment in farming ventures' (Robert Hecht, 'US Looks for Increased Involvement in Nigeria's Agriculture', African Economic Digest, 27 February 1981).

18. On a similar division within Zambia's political economy, see Timothy M. Shaw, 'Dilemmas of Dependence and (Under) Development: Conflicts and Choices in Zambia's Present and Prospective Foreign Policy', Africa Today, 26 (4), Fourth Quarter 1979, pp. 43-65.

19. See Yusufu Bala Usman's open letter, 'Debate on Libya Warms Up', <u>West Africa</u>, 3318, 2 March 1981, pp. 421-3.
20. On the general question of regional dominance in Africa since the mid-1970s see Timothy M. Shaw, 'Foreign Policy, Political Economy and the Future: Reflections on Africa in the World System', <u>African Affairs</u>, 79 (315), April 1980, pp. 260-8 and 'Kenya and South Africa: 'Sub-imperialist' States', <u>Orbis</u>, 21 (2), Summer 1977, pp. 357-94.
21. Ogunbadejo, 'Nigeria's Foreign Policy under Military Rule, 1966-79', p. 763.
22. Aluko, 'Necessity and Freedom in Nigerian Foreign Policy', p. 30.

3 Nigerian–American Relations: Converging Interests and Power Relations

DANIEL C. BACH

> Americans too often see Nigeria in strategic terms — a
> bulwark against Soviet expansion in Africa and as a pos-
> sible regional manager, much like that of Brazil or Iran.
> Nigerians also assume that this was to have been the role
> that the United States had hoped Zaire would play in
> Africa but the latter's instability and lack of influence
> in African diplomatic circles has precluded such a role.
> Consequently, in a search for a more useful ally, Nigeria
> has emerged as the only other choice and a major source
> of oil as well ... [The Nigerians] concede that this some-
> what coincides with Nigeria's own interest which has as
> the cornerstone of its foreign policy a commitment to a
> free and stable Africa [1].

The close relationship established between Nigeria and the
United States after Jimmy Carter's election as President in
January 1977 was in many respects symptomatic of a more
comprehensive evolution of Nigeria's status in the international system. Unlike the arguments of some authors, the
Nigerian civil war which ended in January 1970 did not
weaken the ideological, cultural, economic and financial
links which existed between Nigeria and the Western countries in the early 1960s. The substantial military aid which
the Soviet Union and some East European countries gave to
the federal government during the thirty-month conflict did
not provoke any real reorientation in Nigeria's foreign
policy. Thereafter, Nigeria, though frequently proclaiming
itself nonaligned, in effect retained particularly close
relations with the Western group of states [2]. As indicated
below, important changes did occur in Nigeria's foreign
policy but these related only to the modalities of its
integration into the Western bloc. Indeed, during the 1970s
Nigeria acquired a limited yet real capacity to negotiate
and redefine the forms of its incorporation into the international capitalist system (see Chapters 5 and 7). This

35

capacity was due (1) to the size of the country's internal
market, (2) to the federation's oil resources, and (3) to
the government's increasing control and authority over
Nigerian society [3]. With respect to foreign policy, changes
were revealed as much through the 'Nigerianisation' of
foreign companies' assets as through the dynamics of political relations between Nigeria and both its African and extra-
African environments.

Any study of the various dimensions of US-Nigerian relations raises issues related to the general debate between
'developmental' and 'dependency' schools in the analysis of
Nigerian foreign policy [4]. Do Nigerian-American relations
rest upon Nigeria being acknowledged by the Carter administration as a leading 'broker' in US-African relations, a
situation implying American recognition and encouragement
of Nigeria's emerging influence on the African continent?
Or, alternatively, is Nigeria increasingly a 'client-state'
of the United States, a growing dependency?

These are major questions that provide the framework of
analysis for this chapter. I will first consider the process
of convergence in US-Nigerian relations based on (1) a joint
concern for Southern Africa's future stability, and (2) on
an American wager with respect to the inauguration of a
'Pax Nigeriana' on the African continent. I shall then discuss bilateral economic and ideological relations between
Nigeria and the United States.

LIBERATE SOUTHERN AFRICA IN ORDER TO STABILISE IT

One of the basic priorities of the new Carter administration
after January 1977 was to defuse the dangers of a violent
international confrontation in Southern Africa. This priority was the centrepiece in the *rapprochement* between the
US and Nigeria as pursued by Andrew Young, an active parti-
cipant in the civil rights movement of the 1960s in the
American south. Early in February 1977, Young travelled
briefly to Nigeria to attend the second World Black and
African Festival of Arts and Culture (FESTAC). On that
occasion, he favourably impressed many Nigerians by his
unorthodox declarations (such as considering the presence
of Cubans in Angola to be a stabilising factor), his personal initiatives (such as meeting Agostinho Neto despite
the lack of diplomatic relations between the US and Angola)
and his public commitment to a solution of the conflicts of
Southern Africa in accordance with the interest of the
majority of the population. In order to establish close
relations with the Nigerian leadership, Young undertook to

secure from the American Congress the repeal of the Byrd
amendment which authorised American imports of Rhodesian
chrome. The March 1977 revocation of this measure symbolised
the new orientation in American policy towards Southern
Africa.

Andrew Young's appointment as US Ambassador to the United
Nations gave institutional legitimacy to his good personal
contacts with Nigerian decision-makers. Henceforth, Nigeria
became frequently consulted over and closely associated with
Anglo-American initiatives to solve the Rhodesian problem.
Thus, together with the British Foreign Secretary David Owen,
Young flew to Lagos in August to present a revised version
of the Anglo-American plan to General Obasanjo who subsequently undertook to gain support for it among the Front
Line States; after visiting Tanzania, Zambia and Mozambique,
the Nigerian Head-of-State arrived in New York in late
September 1977. There Obasanjo attended the UN General
Assembly where he declared himself prepared to send troops
to Rhodesia as part of a UN ceasefire [5]. When three years
before General Gowon had wished to meet President Nixon
during a similar visit to the UN, this had been refused in a
humiliating fashion. In sharp contrast, Obasanjo was now
received with pomp and honour in New York, in Washington and
at Howard, the black American university.

The new pace in US-Nigerian relations was confirmed a few
weeks later when the US provided decisive support for
Nigeria's election to the Security Council — a decision
secured despite the previous nomination of Niger for the
seat by the Organisation of African Unity (OAU). From
January 1978 onwards, Nigeria's membership of the Security
Council favoured its assertive role as a privileged inter-
locutor of Western countries and especially of the Carter
administration, which remained concerned that Nigeria should
adopt an attitude of neutrality, if not of support, towards
important US moves in Southern Africa. Significantly, it was
while visiting Nigeria in April 1978 that Jimmy Carter
announced that the Western countries' five-nation 'contact-
group' on Namibia intended to get in touch again with South
Africa and table new propositions for a solution to the
Namibian problem [6]. And in August 1978, secret discussions
were held in Lusaka between Joshua Nkomo and Ian Smith under
the aegis of a Nigerian observer: the former Foreign
Minister, Joseph Garba.

However, during the ensuing months, the Anglo-American
initiative on Rhodesia appeared to be a failure. At the
same time, the Carter administration faced difficulties in
its relations with the Congress which, sensitive to the
influence of pro-South African and pro-Rhodesian lobbies,

appeared inclined to support 'internal solutions' in Rhodesia
and Namibia. Yet no serious disruption of US-Nigerian relations occurred, although in 1979 the Nigerian Embassy in
Washington let it be known on two occasions that Nigeria
might consider the adoption of an 'appropriate response'
were the US to lift economic sanctions against Rhodesia. In
actual fact such declarations were directed not so much at
the American presidency or administration as towards
Nigeria's public opinion and the US Congress [7].

In spite of a somewhat radical external image, Nigerian
policy towards African countries under colonial or racial
rule did not intend to change existing socio-economic structures but merely to ensure the transfer of power to the
(black) majority. Consistently, Nigerian leaders have shown
little sympathy for the political and ideological options
of countries like Tanzania, Algeria, Angola or Mozambique.
When Nigeria threatened to apply pressure on Western policy
towards Southern Africa, it still pursued a strategy geared
towards stabilising and reducing existing conflicts. For
the extension of the struggle of the national liberation
movements appeared likely to provoke increasing radicalisa-
tion which could eventually represent a challenge to the
political status quo or the socio-economic arrangement prevailing in most African countries which, like Nigeria, had
become independent in close association with the colonial
power.

In Nigeria, *rapprochement* with the US provoked accusations
of subservience to American interests in Africa from the
press and in academic and trade union circles. However
federal government representatives in reply pointed to the
overall positive role of the new American stance in Southern
Africa. As early as in February 1977 they were quoted as
saying that it was necessary for the US to intervene in the
Rhodesian issue since Britain had failed to solve it [8].
Three years later, President Shehu Shagari justified US-
Nigerian relations in a similar fashion when he told the
American Vice-President, Walter Mondale, on the latter's
visit to Nigeria, that after Zimbabwe's independence
Namibia and South Africa 'must be free if the friendship
between Nigeria and the United States is to thrive' [9].

These statements were accompanied by threats of an oil
embargo or of economic sanctions; a regular feature of
Nigerian statements on relations with the US in particular
and the West in general [10]. However such public declarations did appear to be rather symbolic for they were voiced
in the context of a pre-existing convergence in the overall
policy options of the US and Nigeria in Southern Africa.
To a large extent, Nigeria's critical, but none the less

effective, association with American initiatives on Rhodesia
and Namibia contributed to the former's pre-eminence in the
UN and the OAU. And when Carter's Rhodesian policy ran into
difficulties during 1979, it did not appear as a challenge
to the credibility of Nigeria's policy.

By contrast, this was most definitely not the case with
the policy of Margaret Thatcher's Conservative government,
which appeared ready to support the regime of Bishop
Muzorewa in May 1979. In this instance the Nigerian government reacted initially by imposing an embargo on any new
contracts to British companies. Then on 31 July, just before
the opening of the Commonwealth summit in Lusaka, Nigeria
nationalised the assets of British Petroleum in Nigeria [11].
Nigerian policy in Southern Africa combined a willingness
to promote the independence of the region with a no less
important concern that its actions should help to legiti-
mise the emergence of a Nigerian leadership in sub-Saharan
Africa. Accordingly, it should be emphasised that in so far
as the solution of conflicts in Southern Africa was concerned, bilateral US-Nigerian relations reflected a more
general process of evolution related to the linkages of
both with the continent as a whole. Each of them could advance the other's interests in Africa.

TOWARDS A 'PAX NIGERIANA' ON THE AFRICAN CONTINENT?

Early in 1977 changes were made in US policy towards
Southern Africa to reflect a new approach to the continent
as a whole. According to the new Secretary of State, Cyrus
Vance: 'We proceed from a basic proposition: that our
policies must recognize the unique identity of Africa. We
can be neither right nor effective if we treat Africa
simply as one part of the Third World or as a testing
ground for East-West competition' [12].

This policy line took into consideration the limited
intervention capacity of the American executive following
its confrontation with the Congress during 1975 and 1976.
From the new attitude adopted towards the African continent resulted an assertion of the imperative of Africans
resolving their own conflicts. This was a considerable contrast to Gerald Ford's interventionist policies under which
several crises in Africa had tended to acquire extra-
continental dimensions.

Beyond its natural tendency to support the restoration
in Africa of a 'status quo ante' favourable on the whole to
Western interests, the US approach under Carter gave particular importance to the configuration of forces on the

African continent in general and in particular to Nigeria's
developing influence. After 1973 the oil 'crisis' favoured
the growth of Nigeria's regional weight. The federal government negotiated successfully in the name of the group of the
African, Caribbean and Pacific (ACP) countries, the first
Lomé convention with the European Economic Community of West
African States (ECOWAS). This new organisation, which was
born in Lagos in May 1975, resulted from a series of joint
Nigerian-Togolese initiatives which successfully overcame
initial opposition from the French-speaking countries of the
region and also from France itself. In several respects,
ECOWAS featured as an expression of Nigeria's increasing
regional influence [13].

Nigeria's new weight in African affairs was directly felt
by the US when the federal government decided to recognise
the MPLA as the sole government of Angola on 25 November
1975. This stance constituted a radical change as until then
Nigeria favoured a postponement of Angola's accession to
independence and the formation of a national unity government. As a result of this new stance, Nigerian policy came
into direct conflict with that of the Ford administration,
soon paralysed by a Congressional decision to embargo all
military and financial aid to those Angolan movements
fighting against the MPLA — the Clark amendment [14].
During this period Nigeria first provided the MPLA with
military and financial aid and then proclaimed itself ready
to send troops to Angola if necessary [15]. A few weeks
before the Addis Ababa OAU summit in January 1976, Nigeria
launched an important diplomatic offensive to secure diplomatic recognition of the MPLA by African states. This was at
the heart of a serious clash with the US when, on the eve
of the OAU conference, Nigeria published the contents of a
letter which President Ford had sent to all the African
heads of states to press them not to recognise the MPLA.
The Nigerian communiqué which accompanied the release of
the letter considered it to be 'an attempt to insult the
intelligence of African nations' [16]. With a mere one-vote
majority the OAU summit decided against a recognition of
the MPLA which, however, took place a few weeks later. To
a large extent, the federal government's ability to neutralise American policy moves over Angola was a corollary of
the Congressional decision to paralyse the executive branch.
Yet, Nigeria's neutralisation of Washington's diplomatic
initiatives in Africa was a reality. On three occasions
during 1976 Nigeria also refused to receive the US Secretary of State, Henry Kissinger, to oppose his plans for a
solution to the Rhodesian conflict.

From 1977 onwards, US support for the development of
Nigerian influence on the continent was based on an acknowledgement of the 'stabilising character' of the federal
government's African policies. Twenty years after independence, the country's political and administrative structures,
its commitment to a development strategy geared towards the
construction of a national capitalist system, and the liberal
ideology instilled by higher educational institutions, all
illustrate the persistence of deeply rooted relations with
the West. Any interruption of such links would involve radical changes affecting the whole country. Indeed, a transformation of existing relations by decision-makers in power
would undermine the very basis upon which Nigerian society
has been built.

With respect to independent Africa, Nigerian policy has
been primarily concerned with the preservation or the restoration of the territorial status quo. Nigeria criticised
virulently the participation of Tanzanian troops in the fall
of the Amin regime in November 1978. The federal government
subsequently refused to grant diplomatic recognition to the
first regime of Professor Yusuf Lule. A few months later
Nigeria attempted to prevent further executions of corrupt
Ghanaian politicians by Flt. Lt. Jerry Rawlings' revolutionary regime which came into power on 4 June. Oil was used
as a weapon when Nigeria reduced from ninety to thirty days
the terms of payment for Ghana's imports, demanded the immediate settlement of outstanding bilateral debts and, under
the pretext of 'technical difficulties', actually interrup-
ted oil deliveries to Ghana [17]. And following Master
Sergeant Doe's coup in April 1980 the civil regime of President Shagari reacted in a comparable fashion when President
Tolbert and various other Liberian personalities were killed.
Nigeria refused to accept this take-over and considered the
new Liberian head of state *persona non grata* when he landed
at Lagos airport in order to attend the OAU economic summit
in April 1980 [18].

The Carter administration was inclined to support the
principle of African solutions to African conflicts, due not
only to its relations with the Congress but also to pressure from civil rights militants and academic specialists
on Southern Africa. Thus the US came to support the Nigerian
federal government's attempts to assert itself as the
'status quo mediator' on the African continent [19]. So in
March 1977, as the first Shaba crisis exploded, various
senior American officials including Andrew Young and the
US Ambassador to Nigeria, Donald Easum, requested Joseph
Garba to find an African solution to the conflict [20].
Subsequent Nigerian diplomatic moves towards Zaire were

publicly greeted by Cyrus Vance as an initiative which might
make it 'unnecessary for the US to send additional military
supplies to the Zaire government' [21]. In a similar manner,
the US supported Nigerian interventions in the Somali-
Ethiopia conflict. In particular, Washington adopted the same
position as that of the OAU *ad hoc* commission chaired by
Nigeria, which advocated the restoration of peace between
Somalia and Ethiopia on the basis of respect for colonial
boundaries. The US accordingly refused to accept Somalia's
annexation of the Ogaden despite Somalia's request for
Western aid and its fight against the Ethiopian regime, then
backed by Cuban troops and Soviet military instructors.

Nigeria's diplomacy was very active in these various Afri-
can conflicts, yet its capacity to solve them remained
limited (see Chapters 6 and 10). To be sure, in July 1980
Shagari's intervention during the OAU summit at Freetown
prevented a serious crisis within the Organisation which
Senegal and Morocco threatened to leave if the Sahraoui Arab
Democratic Republic was recognised [22]. But during 1977 and
1978 Nigeria approached the Soviet Union and the various
African countries involved in the conflict in the Horn of
Africa without success. Nigerian diplomacy was also unable
to prevent the outburst of the second Shaba crisis. Only
foreign interventions — by France and Morocco in 1977, and
by France and the US in 1978 — prevented the fall of the
Mobutu regime. Nigeria also failed in Chad in attempting to
solve the conflict during 1979. In April of that year, the
Chadian government demanded the withdrawal of Nigerian troops
sent to Ndjamena a month before, following the first Kano
conference. The Nigerian army had proved unable to fulfil its
mission, because it lacked discipline and was unprepared to
intervene outside its national boundaries [23]. Other variables included the increasing reluctance of France and
several African countries to support Nigerian attempts to
find a solution to the conflict in close association with
Libya [24].

The shortcomings of Nigerian diplomacy, plus changes in
the global situation, induced the US to adopt a policy of
direct intervention in several African conflicts from 1978
onwards. Following the second Shaba crisis, the US administration applied direct pressure on President Neto and his
Zairois counterpart, Mobutu, who sealed their reconciliation
a few months later [25]. The continuation of Soviet and
Cuban military support to Ethiopia, the overthrow of the
Iranian regime and Soviet intervention in Afghanistan resulted in the development of an American policy (1) of reinforcing its naval presence along the East African coast, and
(2) of securing port and air base facilities in the Indian

Ocean and North Africa [26].

However this American policy did not involve any fundamental reconsideration of Nigeria's role. Rather, Nigeria's continued association with the elaboration of US African policy resulted from a wager on the federation's increasing emergence as a regional power and as a privileged partner. By 1980 Nigeria did not possess the required military, financial and industrial capabilities to impose itself as an effective 'broker' in relations between African and non-African states. Nevertheless, in spite of this Nigeria retained a privileged position in the definition of Carter's African policy: throughout this period imports of Nigerian oil were at the centre of the economic relationship between the two countries.

OIL AS A FACTOR OF MIGHT WITHOUT POWER

The spectacular growth in Nigeria's oil production in the early 1970s resulted in a rapid increase in its share of American imports. During the period of the Arab embargo in 1974 and 1975, Nigeria was the United States' first crude oil supplier. After 1976, the high price of Nigerian oil (due to its low sulphur content) induced the US to purchase cheaper Saudi Arabian oil. Since then Nigeria has remained America's second supplier (see Table 3.1). Because of the importance of these imports, the US is Nigeria's first trading partner (accounting for 39.5 per cent of Nigeria's external trade in 1977).

Table 3.1 Origin of some American crude oil imports
(in '000 tons) (in provisional figures) [27]

	1970	1972	1974	1976	1978	1979
Saudi Arabia	2,059	8,633	21,546	60,464	56,484	66,200
%	*3.1*	*7.8*	*12.6*	*20.3*	*16.4*	*18.9*
Nigeria	2,376	12,075	34,289	53,775	46,834	51,800
%	*3.5*	*10.9*	*20.0*	*18.09*	*13.6*	*14.8*
Canada	33,018	42,062	38,927	18,292	12,103	13,200
%	*49.9*	*38.19*	*22.7*	*6.1*	*3.5*	*3.7*
Venezuela	13,989	13,319	15,697	16,660	13,123	14,300
%	*21.1*	*12.09*	*9.1*	*5.6*	*3.8*	*4.09*
Total of Imports	66,117	110,114	171,091	297,179	343,282	349,500

Source: OECD, *Statistiques Pétrolières* (1971–6); Comité Français du Pétrole, *Pétrole 77* (1978) and *Pétrole 79* (1980).

Nigerian oil supplies to the US have featured as a factor
either of strength or of weakness in the bilateral relationship, depending on the state of the international oil market.
Thus the 1976 conflict between Nigeria and the US over
Angola did not affect oil supplies from Nigeria. In the
world market at that time an excess of supply over demand
resulted in prices falling and OPEC had to order a cutback
in production; as a result Nigeria was in a weak position
vis-à-vis the United States, although the latter purchased
as much as 36 per cent of Nigerian oil exports in 1976 [28].
By contrast, during the 1973-4 and 1979-80 periods, sharp
increases in world prices enabled Nigeria to consider its
oil exports to Western countries as a way of influencing
their policies towards Southern Africa. However a Nigerian
oil embargo would also jeopardise the economic strategy of
the federal government. Indeed, the oil crisis had enabled
Nigeria to impose a redefinition of the modalities of the
country's incorporation into the international economic
system on foreign companies — as can be seen in the case of
US-Nigerian relations, for Nigerian oil was a factor of
might but not of power.

In January 1974 the Nigerian government compelled foreign
oil companies to sell 55 per cent of their capital to a public corporation, the Nigerian National Oil Corporation,
renamed the Nigerian National Petroleum Corporation (NNPC)
in 1977. In July 1979, when the international oil situation
was again favourable, the NNPC brought its share in the oil
companies' capital to 60 per cent. Various other measures
were also announced in order to reinforce Nigeria's control
over oil exploration activities. In effect, all these decisions related to a more comprehensive policy of regulating
the foreign companies' access to Nigerian resources which
began with the promulgation of the Nigerian Enterprises
Promotion Decree in 1972. The progressive implementation of
this decree between 1972 and 1979 forced foreign companies
based in Nigeria to sell between 40 per cent and 100 per
cent of their shares, depending on sector of activity and
size of the enterprise [29].

In 1970 individual Nigerians and the federal government
respectively controlled 10 per cent and 27 per cent of the
foreign capital invested in Nigeria; ten years later, some
500 million shares representing about $780 million had been
transferred to Nigerian owners in spite of the reluctance
of some foreign companies [30]. The federal strategy, which
aimed at the stimulation of Nigerian capitalism, also resulted in massive intervention into the various sectors of the
national economy to support initiatives in the private sector. According to Nigeria's Third Development Plan (1975-80),

massive expenditures were planned for the construction of
steel mills, oil refineries, petro-chemical complex, paper
mills and over 13,000 miles of roads. In 1965 the public
sector represented about 35 per cent of gross investment in
the country and 9.2 per cent of GDP; by 1976 these propor-
tions amounted to 67.5 per cent and 38 per cent respectively
[31].

The immediate effect of these economic policies was to
increase Nigeria's economic and political vulnerability to
the United States. At the same time, Nigeria could not be
described as a powerless country as it controlled important
oil resources in a context of international scarcity.
Nigeria's ability to influence the African policy of Western
countries through economic sanctions remained unaffected as
the nationalisation of BP showed in July 1979. However the
effects of such measures were limited by the pre-existent
policy of Nigerianisation. In 1980 a large number of the
multinationals which operated in Nigeria through Nigerianised
subsidiaries maintained relations — sometimes very close
ones — with branches in South Africa in spite of the sanctions policy announced in Lagos by General Obasanjo in
August 1977 during the UN World Conference for Action against
Apartheid. The Nigerian Head of State had then committed his
country to veto the award of contracts to any foreign company conducting business with South Africa [32]. In effect
the federal government adopted sanctions against such companies on two occasions only.

In April 1978 sanctions were decided against the Nigerian
branches of Barclays Bank following a public announcement by
one of the company's London directors of a subscription to
South African Defence Bonds. The Nigerian government subsequently increased its share in the bank's assets from 60
per cent to 80 per cent and ordered the withdrawal of all
government funds from the bank [33]. The previous Nigerianisation of a majority of the shares in Barclays Nigeria made
its expulsion from Nigerian territory impossible. As far as
the decision to withdraw all public funds was concerned, it
primarily affected the Nigerian state itself since it already
owned 60 per cent of the bank's capital. Similar problems
reappeared in July 1979 when the federal government increased
from 60 per cent to 100 per cent Nigeria's share in the capital of BP Nigeria [34]. As with Barclays, these measures
could not affect the activities of the London-based company
in South Africa. Sanctions against its Nigerianised branch
were of limited impact as they primarily affected the
Nigerian owners of the company's capital. In Nigeria BP,
renamed African Petroleum (AP), retained close links with
its London-based parent company from which it continued to

purchase oil products. When asked to justify such a situation, a Nigerian director of AP mentioned the necessity of safeguarding the interest of Nigerian shareholders [35]. Thus the widespread implementation of the South African policy guidelines defined by the government in 1977 proved impossible as this would have threatened the very basis of Nigerian society. The bureaucrats, the military and the politicians in Nigeria did not seek to prevent foreign capital from entering the Nigerian market; they were simply eager to benefit from it and to control its penetration.

Besides these political effects, the Nigerianisation policy involved others such as a sharp decline in the inflow of foreign capital which was not matched by an increase in Nigerian private investment. American investors in particular remained reluctant about the Nigerian market despite the establishment of special political relations between the US and Nigeria after 1978 and the frequent Nigerian appeals for investment on the basis of joint ventures. While in 1972 Nigeria received over 20 per cent of the total foreign investment entering Africa, the implementation of the Nigerian Enterprises Promotion Decree resulted in a sharp decrease in the net inflow of capital from 1974 as indicated in Table 3.2

Table 3.2   Net inflow of foreign capital into Nigeria
            (in million naira) [36]

1970	1971	1972	1973	1974	1975	1976	1977
121.6	319.6	248.3	192.6	48.3	475.4	46.3	197.6

Source: Business Times, 17 June 1980

From 1977 until 1980, as the Nigerianisation programme was being progressively implemented, the net inflow of capital into Nigeria came to a halt according to a Financial Times survey [37]. American investors still had serious reservations about the Nigerianisation decrees. Some companies like Citibank and IBM preferred to withdraw from the Nigerian market rather than comply with the new guidelines. Others adopted a disinvestment policy in spite of the improvement in political relations between the US and Nigeria. In 1970 American investments represented 22.9 per cent of cumulative foreign capital in Nigeria; by 1977 this proportion had fallen to 11.3 per cent [38]. American

companies figured prominently among those 'sensitive'
foreign investors who, according to a senior official from
the Central Bank of Nigeria, 'tended to confuse the decree
with nationalisations comparable to the Soviet confisca-
tions of 1918, the Latin American take-overs in the 1930s
and the Iranian oil nationalisations in the 1950s [39].
Early in 1979, a survey based on interviews with the directors of major international banking institutions confirmed
that they considered Nigeria to be a 'high-risk' country in
spite of its low rate of indebtedness [40].

The decline of private foreign investment, combined with
the adverse effects of the international oil recession on
Nigeria's public finances, compelled the federal government
to resort to borrowing on the Eurodollar market in January
1978 (one billion dollars) and in January 1979 (750 million
dollars) [41]. Other loans from German banks and from the
World Bank were also called upon in order to complete
specific projects of the overambitious Third Development
Plan. During this period regular economic discussions also
started between Nigeria and the US. After several meetings
of experts from the two countries, Andrew Young flew to
Lagos in September 1979 as the head of a twenty-four member
commercial delegation which included the chairman of the
Export-Import Bank and his counterpart from the Overseas
Private Investment Corporation [42]. One year later, important cooperation agreements were signed which were designed
to associate the US administration and private companies
with the implementation of the 'green revolution', now an
urgent necessity for Nigeria. According to various studies,
a continuation for the next decade of Nigeria's slow, 1 per
cent growth rate in agriculture would compel it to import
40 per cent of its food requirements by 1990 [43].

The political and legal guarantees offered to private
American investors by the Nigeria-US agreements of September
1980 constituted a most innovative feature. Various joint
bilateral consultative structures were installed which
reflected a possible attempt to broaden in the economic and
financial fields the special political relations already
established between Nigeria and the US [44]. While the
latter were interested in counter-balancing their reliance
on Nigerian oil with Nigeria's technological and agricultural dependency on the US, the Nigerians conceived their
rapport with their US partner in terms of increased foreign
private investment.

THE IDEOLOGY OF EXCHANGE: ACCULTURATION AND MUTUAL
IDENTIFICATION

The close association of activists from the civil rights
campaigns in the American south with the definition of
Carter's African policy had a decisive impact on relations
between Nigeria and the US. As already noted, in February
1977 an important American delegation attended the FESTAC
celebrations in Lagos. By so doing, the Americans expressed
a symbolic allegiance to African culture, Nigeria being
celebrated implicitly as its depository. Nigeria's technological dependency on the US also appeared to be exorcised
by this recognition of Nigerian Africanity. In August 1977,
when Andrew Young attended the Lagos UN Conference against
Apartheid, he asserted a parallel between the situation of
the blacks in Southern Africa and those in the south of the
US [45]. Through such comparisons, it was implied that a
resolution of conflicts in Southern Africa would occur
through legal and peaceful means as in the US south which
justified, and lent support to, the Carter administration's
policies. Thus a process of transfer benefiting the American
system as a whole was conducted on the basis of an evocation
of socio-cultural situations and historical experiences
(slavery and colonisation) common to black Americans and
Africans.

Andrew Young declared during General Obasanjo's visit to
Washington in September 1977, 'it is entirely appropriate
that US black leaders should pay tribute to a nation
[Nigeria] that certainly today is a friend and brother not
only to black Americans but to all Americans' [46]. Yet this
assertion of a privileged relationship between American
blacks and Nigerians extending to the profit of society as
a whole should not be considered to be a one-sided process.
For under Carter Nigeria was associated with US African
policy and this decisively affected relations between the
two countries. When confronted with serious disagreements
between the US and Nigeria, Andrew Young or Mohammed Ali
could point to their own marginality *vis-à-vis* the American
system, the orientation of which they did not hesitate to
criticise whenever necessary [47]. Their pronouncements on
such occasions could be disavowed by the White House or the
State Department, but their positive effects in Africa
remained.

The importance of such bilateral understanding appeared
clearly after Andrew Young's resignation as US Ambassador
to the UN in August 1979. During a brief visit to Lagos a
month later he sought to ensure the continuity of US-
Nigerian relations. The implementation of Nigeria's new

federal Constitution, largely inspired by the American model, provided another political and ideological dimension to the bilateral relationship. This was soon reinforced by an increasing number of visits paid to each other by members of the two countries' representative institutions. In Nigeria, American academics and experts also featured prominently at conferences organised by universities, states or federal institutions in order to enhance the functioning of Nigeria's new system of government. With much pride, some Nigerian leaders insisted that it was in Nigeria that the American Constitution was for the first time being introduced outside its frontiers. When Vice-President Walter Mondale visited Nigeria in August 1980 the President of the Senate, Joseph Wayas, expressed the hope that the new Nigerian House of Assembly would become a 'citadel of democracy' comparable to the US Congress [48]. Thus there emerged a clear identification of the Nigerian élite with the values of American society either in its global form or solely in its Afro-American component.

LIMITS TO THE NIGERIAN-AMERICAN ALLIANCE

The evolution of US-Nigerian relations under Jimmy Carter's presidency was closely related to a transformation in the modalities of Nigeria's incorporation into the international system during the 1970s. Such changes as those which have been described can only be inserted with great difficulty into the theoretical alternatives presented by the models of extroversion and dependency (see Chapters 2, 6, 8 and 11). The dynamics of Nigeria's foreign policy are neither an illustration of the 'vicious circle' nor of the 'virtuous circle' of development [49].

In the early 1970s the increase in oil prices and the consolidation of the powers of the Nigerian federal government over its own society conferred on Nigeria a limited but none the less real capacity to redefine the forms of its insertion into the international system. This new capacity was revealed after 1972 (1) through the implementation of a policy of Nigerianisation and (2) through the adoption of a policy of greater political independence *vis-à-vis* the Western countries, whose relations with sub-Saharan Africa Nigeria sought to influence. The first and foremost expression of this strategy occurred with the unexpected reversal of Nigerian policy during the Angolan civil war. In this case, both the ideological orientations of the nationalist parties and the intervention of South Africa in the conflict (already known several months prior to the recognition) were

less important than Nigeria's willingness to assert its pre-
eminence in front of both Western and African countries.
   Among the Western states, only the US attempted to integrate into its African policy Nigeria's determination to
influence relations between extra-African countries and the
continent. This orientation of the Carter administration
resulted from the *ad hoc* evolution of the US political
system which took into account Nigeria's ability to hamper
the implementation of the Africa policy of the Ford administration in 1976. Obviously Nigeria did not act as a propa-
gator of US policy, but their mutual objectives in Southern
Africa were a factor of convergence. While Nigeria sought
to expand its influence, the US was concerned to help stabilise the African continent, a goal which the underlying
values of Nigerian society appeared likely to favour.
Given the nature of the Nigerian political context, the
implementation of a 'pax Nigeriana' could only affect positively the preservation of close relations between the West
and Africa. However Nigeria's inability to control effectively the evolution of its international environment and
the renewed involvement of extra-African powers on the
African continent, led the US to undertake a series of
direct interventions during 1978-80. These activities have
not aimed at undermining Nigerian influence but rather at
relieving its shortcomings. They were undoubtedly a specific
factor in the Carter administration's policy of Ronald
Reagan, one that reflects a general obsession with building
up military power and resistance against the Soviet Union.
   Since Reagan's accession to the presidency, the Namibian
issue has featured as an epitomy of overall US African
policy, just as the Rhodesian crisis did under Carter's
presidency. In June 1981, the new US Assistant Secretary of
State for African Affairs, Chester Crocker, insisted that
policy over Namibia had yet to be 'reviewed at the highest
level' [50], but this no-policy claim appeared somewhat
rhetorical in view of existing commitments made by the in-
coming administration on related issues in Southern Africa.
Throughout the region its primary concern was with Soviet
influence seen to be manifested through the continuing presence of Cuban troops in Angola or the possible coming into
power of the 'Marxist-oriented' SWAPO in Namibia. Besides
this, as a result of its strong anti-communist bias, the new
US administration has tended to consider South Africa to be
a natural 'ally'. In March 1981 a high-level delegation of
South African military officials (including the Chief of
South African military intelligence) was received in
Washington and in New York — where the Head of the US mission to the UN denied knowledge of her visitors' identity

[51]. Also in March, the Reagan administration announced its
intent to seek the abrogation of the Clark amendment which
prohibited overt or covert aid to rebel forces in Angola.

In mid-May, South Africa's Foreign Minister, Roelof 'Pik'
Botha, was received by the new president in the course of an
official visit which confirmed US attempts to promote a reintegration of South Africa into the Western world. Briefing
papers leaked to the press emphasised this point: the US
would seek South Africa's cooperation for an 'internationally
acceptable settlement' in Namibia. And as a counterpart,
Washington would 'work to end South Africa's polecat status
in the world and seek to restore its place as a legitimate
and important regional actor with whom we can cooperate
pragmatically' [52]. The US administration, journalists were
officially told after the Botha-Reagan discussions, was
pursuing a policy of 'constructive engagement' with the
South Africans and not one of 'confrontation' as prevailed
under Jimmy Carter [53]. Crocker's visit to South Africa in
June was yet another sign of the increasing acknowledgement
by the US of South Africa as a privileged partner in the
definition of its strategy over Namibia within the five-
nation Western contact group. This evolution adversely affected Nigeria's association with US policy over Southern
Africa.

Shehu Shagari warned during his visit to Britain in March
1981 that Nigeria was committed to the independence of
Namibia and the eradication of apartheid in South Africa.
But the president also added that resorting to the treatment
of oil shipments to the US as a political weapon would only
occur 'if absolutely necessary' [54]. Such a moderate statement contrasted with Shagari's earlier pledge to secure the
independence of Namibia by the end of 1981. When the president had made this pledge in October 1980 the Iran-Iraqi war
had curtailed Western oil supplies and conferred a position
of strength on Nigeria: then Shagari had excluded any
increase in Nigerian oil production to meet shortcomings
which might result from the continuation of the Gulf conflict. Instead he announced Nigeria's intention to 'use any
means at our disposal including oil' to secure Western support for the liberation of Southern Africa [55].

However by July 1981 Nigeria was selling about half of its
oil exports to the US and this clearly had become a con-
straining factor of dependency considering the current oil
recession. While oil prices still remained at an average of
$40 per barrel, successive cutbacks had reduced Nigerian
production from 2.1 million barrels per day (bpd) in January
down to 815,000 bpd in late July. This meant a sharp and
unexpected decline in revenue: the Nigerian budget for 1981

had been based on an expectation of average production of
1.9 million bpd at $36 a barrel [56]. As Crocker was stopping
in Lagos during April to discuss Nigerian views on Namibia,
for the first time in several years an oil company — the
American Atlantic Richfield Corporation (ARCO) — had noti-
fied the Nigerian government of its intent to terminate two
oil supply contracts for about 60,000 bpd, owing to the continued high price of Nigerian oil [57]. In these circumstances, Nigeria had had to rule out any consideration of
using oil as a weapon to pressurise the US over Namibia or
South Africa. On this very issue, Chester Crocker sternly
commented that the US had 'economic interests throughout
Africa and we are not going to be forced by anybody to
choose between them' [58]. Nigeria's reaction came on 30
June, when for the first time Shehu Shagari directly and
publicly criticised the Reagan administration for concluding
a military pact with South Africa which both 'ignored world
opinion' and 'decided to classify black Africa in geo-
political terms as belonging to the communist bloc' [59].
Barely six months after Ronald Reagan's election, renewed
bilateral tension appeared to be slowly building up, and
pointing to a deterioration in US-Nigerian relations which
might come to equal their 1976 crisis over Angola.

NOTES AND REFERENCES

This essay was originally published in French in *Politique
Africaine*, 1 (2), April 1981, pp. 7-26.

1. Nigerian viewpoint summarised in Nigerian Institute of
   International Affairs (NIIA) and Rockefeller Foundation,
   *Nigerian-American Relations: a Report of a Nigerian-
   American Dialogue*, 9-12 October 1978, Bellagio (Lagos:
   NIIA, n.d.) pp.7-8.
2. See Olatunde J. Ojo, 'Nigerian-Soviet Relations: Retro-
   spect and Prospect', *African Studies Review*, 19 (3),
   December 1976, pp. 43-63, and Oye Ogunbadejo, 'Ideology
   and Pragmatism: the Soviet Role in Nigeria', *Orbis*, 21
   (4), Winter 1978, pp. 803-30.
3. The consolidation of federal government powers is ana-
   lysed by A. Akinsanya, 'The Machinery of Government
   during the Military Regime in Nigeria', *Africa Quarterly*
   (New Delhi), 17 (2), October 1977, pp. 32-54, and
   A.-D. Yahaya, 'The Struggle for Power in Nigeria, 1966-
   1979' in Oyeleye Oyediran (ed.), *Nigerian Government*

and Politics under Military Rule (London: Macmillan, 1979) pp. 259–75. On the effects of the oil boom see Richard Joseph, 'Affluence and Underdevelopment: the Nigerian Experience', Journal of Modern African Studies, 16 (2), June 1978, pp. 221–39.

4. The first 'developmental' approach underlies the articles of Jean Herskovits, 'Dateline Nigeria: a Black Power', Foreign Policy, 29, Winter 1977–8, pp. 167–88, and Ibrahim Gambari, 'Nigeria and the World: a Growing Internal Stability, Wealth and External Influence', Journal of International Affairs, 29 (2), Fall 1975, pp. 155–69. For a critical review of the literature on Nigeria's foreign policy by 'dependency' analysts see Chapter 11.

5. West Africa, 12 September 1977, p. 1855, and 17 October 1977, p. 2138.

6. Christian Science Monitor, 3 April 1978. See also Jimmy Carter, America's African Policy (Lagos: NIIA, 1978).

7. New Nigerian (Kaduna), 15 June 1979, and R. Deutsch, 'African Oil and U.S. Foreign Policy', Africa Report, 24 (5), September–October 1979, pp. 48–9.

8. Quoted in Africa Confidential, 18 February 1977, p. 3.

9. The Punch (Ibadan), 5 August 1980.

10. See West Africa, 4 July 1977, p. 1332; or Ishaya Audu, Nigeria's Minister of Foreign Affairs, in Financial Times, 30 September 1980, Shehu Shagari in Time, 6 October 1980, pp. 18–19, and Olajide Aluko, 'Nigeria, the United States and Southern Africa', African Affairs, 78 (310), January 1979, pp. 91–102.

11. The Observer, 8 July and 5 August 1979, Business Times (Lagos), 14 August 1979, and D. Ingram, 'Tory Policy in Africa', Africa Report, 25 (2), March–April 1980, pp. 4–8.

12. Cyrus Vance in West Africa, 1 August 1977, p. 1573. See also A. Lake, 'Africa in a Global Perspective', Africa Report, 23 (1), January–February 1978, pp. 44–8.

13. See Daniel C. Bach, 'The Politics of West African Economic Integration in the 1970s: a Comparison Between CEAO and ECOWAS', Journal of Modern African Studies (forthcoming).

14. N.C. Livingstone and M. Nordheim, 'The US Congress and the Angolan Crisis', Strategic Review, 5 (2), Spring 1977, pp. 34–43.

15. A. Bolaji Akinyemi, 'Mohammed-Obasanjo Foreign Policy' in Oyediran (ed.), Nigerian Government and Politics under Military Rule, pp. 155–67.

16. Text of the letter and the communiqué in Yusufu Bala Usman, For the Liberation of Nigeria (London: New Beacon Press, 1979), pp. 287–91.

17. Barbara Harrell-Bond, 'Diary of a Revolution Which Might Have Been, Part I', _American Universities Field Staff Reports_, 24, 1980, pp. 11-13.

18. See Amadu Sesay, 'The Master Sergeant's Coup in Liberia and its Impact on the Country's Relations with its Neighbours', _Politique Africaine_ (forthcoming).

19. Orobola Fasehun, 'Nigeria and the Ethiopia-Somalia Conflict' (Ife: Department of International Relations, 1980, mimeo) _passim_.

20. S. Feustel, 'Nigeria: Leadership in Africa', _Africa Report_, 22 (3), May-June 1977, p. 49.

21. _West Africa_, 28 March 1977, p. 632. See also the statement made by Dick Clark, Chairman of the Foreign Affairs Committee of the American Senate, _The Washington Post_, 24 March 1977.

22. _New Nigerian_, 5 and 11 July 1980.

23. On the behaviour and the equipment of Nigerian troops see AFP, _Bulletin d'Afrique_, 31 March 1979, and _Daily Times_, 1 June 1979.

24. After the refusal of the Chadian government to implement the Kano II agreements, Nigeria installed an embargo on oil deliveries; see _The Punch_, 30 May 1979, _AFP_, _Bulletin d'Afrique_, 29 May and 2 June 1979, and _Jeune Afrique_, 13 June 1979, pp. 14-16.

25. See _Washington Post_, 22 and 28 June 1978.

26. On these changes see _Washington Post_, 1 June 1978, and R. Deutsch, 'Carter's African Policy Shift', _Africa Report_, 15 (3), June 1980, pp. 15-18.

27. OECD, _Statistiques Pétrolières_ (Paris, 1971-6), 1970 to 1973 (pp. 26-7), 1974 (pp. 30-1) and 1975 (pp. 45-6); Comité Français du Pétrole, _Pétrole 77_ (Paris, 1978), pp. 290 and 343, and _Pétrole 79_ (Paris, 1980), p. E55.

28. Federal Office of Statistics, _Nigeria Trade Summary, 1976_ (Lagos, n.d.) p. 253; see also Chapter 7.

29. See P. Collins, 'The Political Economy of Indigenisation: the Case of the Nigerian Enterprises Promotion Decree', _The African Review_, 4 (2), 1974, pp. 491-508.

30. Akin Iwayemi, 'The Military and the Economy', in Oyediran (ed.), _Nigerian Government and Politics under Military Rule_, p. 57, and _Sunday Tribune_ (Ibadan), 13 July 1980.

31. Quoted from J. F. E. Ohiorhenuan, 'Nigerian Economic Policy under Military Rule' (Ibadan, 1980, mimeo), p. 80.

32. United Nations, Centre against Apartheid, _Notes and Documents_ (77-77310), September 1977, p. 11.

33. _West Africa_, 3 April 1978, p. 636.

34. _Financial Times_, 1 October 1979.

35. New Nigerian, 21 October 1980.
36. Business Times, 17 June 1980.
37. Financial Times, 29 September 1980.
38. Business Times, 17 June 1980.
39. ibid.
40. International Insider, 25 February 1979.
41. New York Times, 7 December 1978.
42. New Nigerian, 14 September 1979, and Business Times, 11 September 1979.
43. See The Sun (Baltimore), 1 January 1978, New Nigerian, 5 August 1980 and The Punch, 21 July 1980; see also Okello Oculi, 'Dependent Food Policy in Nigeria', Review of African Political Economy, 15-16, May-December 1979, pp. 63-74
44. New Nigerian, 23 July 1980, and West Africa, 6 October 1980, p. 1987.
45. United Nations, Centre against Apartheid, Notes and Documents (77-77651), December 1977, pp. 14-15.
46. Interlink: American-Nigerian Journal, 52, 1977, p. 8.
47. Mohammed Ali, who came to Lagos to invite Nigeria to boycott the Moscow Olympic Games, renounced his mission, and, in the course of a rowdy press conference, started to criticise American policy on Southern Africa; see New Nigerian, 6 and 8 February 1980.
48. New Nigerian, 28 July 1980. After his visit to the US in September 1980, Shehu Shagari insisted in an appreciation letter to President Carter that 'your country and mine are two great democracies which have a lot in common'; New Nigerian, 24 October 1980.
49. See J. Coussy, 'Extraversion Economique et Inégalités de Puissance', Revue Française de Science Politique, 28 (5), October 1978, p. 872.
50. West Africa, 20 July 1981, p. 1643.
51. Washington Post, 1 April 1981.
52. Washington Post, 29 May 1981.
53. ibid.
54. Newsletter Nigeria (London), 13 April 1981, p. 10.
55. New Nigerian, 6 October 1980.
56. Daily Times, 18 June 1981; and West Africa, 6 July 1981, p. 1542 and 13 July 1981, p. 1569.
57. Daily Times, 21 April 1981; and AFP, Bulletin d'Afrique, 15 April 1981.
58. The Times, 22 April 1981.
59. Daily Times, 2 July 1981.

4 The Administration of Nigeria's Foreign Service, 1960-80

SOLA OJO

In this chapter, the term 'Nigeria's foreign service' refers to the Ministry of External Affairs (MEA) in Lagos and Nigeria's diplomatic missions abroad. The MEA, like its counterparts in other parts of the world, is supposed to be 'the brains of foreign policy where the impressions from the outside world are gathered and evaluated, where foreign policy is formulated and where the impulses emanate which the diplomatic representatives transform into actual foreign policy' [1]. On the other hand, Nigeria's embassies and high commissions are meant to be the eyes, ears and mouth, the fingertips as it were, the itinerant incarnations of the MEA. In short, they are the outlying fibres of the nerve centre.

The MEA has come a long way from what it was at the time of independence in 1960. However this is hardly surprising. For the need to make the MEA responsive to the scope and complexity of contemporary international relations has constantly led to the expansion of, and structural changes within, the ministry and its overseas establishments. From a few inherited offices in October 1960, MEA now has seventy-nine diplomatic and consular missions abroad. Similarly, the ministry's personnel has increased from a handful in October 1960 to 2371 by July 1980. This chapter aims at examining these developments, providing some background to the analysis of bureaucratic politics in Nigeria presented in the next chapter.

It proceeds, first, by looking at the background of the ministry, since this had a significant impact on the MEA particularly during the first decade after independence. Second, it identifies the functions assigned by government to the ministry. Third, the chapter examines how the ministry is structured and organised to carry out these functions effectively. Fourth, issues such as recruitment, training and deployment of staff which are crucial to the effective formulation and implementation of the country's

foreign policy are also dealt with. And finally, it concludes with a number of suggestions on reforms needed to
improve both the image and performance of the foreign service.

BACKGROUND

Although the Ministry of Foreign Affairs and Commonwealth
Relations — as the MEA was then known [2] — was formally
established in 1960, the existence of units which can be
regarded as the ministry's precursor predated independence.
An External Affairs Department was established within the
colonial Chief Secretary's Office in April 1956. This
department's functions were, however, purely administrative
as the formulation and implementation of the colonial territory's external relations were the prerogative of the
British government. The department handled matters affecting the welfare of Nigerians abroad, administered foreign
consulates in Nigeria and prepared reports for the United
Nations (UN) Trusteeship Council. In 1957 it was transferred
to the newly created Office of the Prime Minister. Antici-
pating the accession of the country into independent state-
hood, the department was reconstituted and elevated into a
separate semi-autonomous unit in 1959. It was this unit —
without much further reorganisation — that was transformed
into the Ministry of Foreign Affairs and Commonwealth Relations at independence in October 1960 [3].

Abroad, Nigeria then had five offices which performed some
of the functions of a diplomatic mission. These were the
Office of the Nigerian Commissioner in London, established
in 1955; the Students' Liaison Office in Washington; the
Pilgrims' Offices in Khartoum and Jeddah; and the Vice-
Consulate and Labour Office in Fernando Po. A few Nigerians
were attached to British embassies for training, and this
group was later to form the nucleus of the new ministry's
personnel. There were, however, other units within the
colonial administration whose functions impinged upon the
management of Nigeria's external relations. These were the
departments of Finance, Commerce and Industry; Education,
Labour; and Social Service. This established overlapping of
responsibilities was to have very significant implications
for the management of the country's external relations
after independence.

FUNCTIONS OF THE NIGERIAN FOREIGN SERVICE

One of the consequences of the evolutionary process of form-
ing Nigeria's foreign service was the lack of a proper de-
lineation of functions between the MEA and other arms of
government. This caused much confusion and unhealthy inter-
ministerial rivalry, particularly in the early 1960s. In
response to this situation, the federal government in a
notice issued in April 1965 [4] spelt out the functions the
MEA was expected to perform. These were:

(1) establishment and administration of diplomatic and
    consular posts;
(2) training of Nigerians for overseas representation;
(3) diplomatic mail;
(4) protocol and ceremonial in so far as it affects the
    diplomatic corps and foreign visitors;
(5) consular matters affecting Nigerians abroad;
(6) collection and collation of information about other
    nations; and
(7) coordination of any arrangements for international
    conferences in Nigeria.

In 1975 these functions were further elaborated with additional responsibilities assigned to the ministry [5]. Apart
from the above-mentioned functions, the MEA was charged with
the conduct of government business relating to foreign and
Commonwealth affairs; passports and travel certificates;
pilgrimage arrangements; relations with the diplomatic corps
in Nigeria; repatriation of destitute Nigerians; and sea-
men's identity certificates.

Although the 1975 statement defined the functions of the
MEA more clearly than ever before, it still failed to resolve some of the controversies over the overlapping of
responsibilities between the ministry and other 'home'
ministries, such as Information, Economic Development, Education, Trade, and Industry. It was not until the late 1970s
that some of the issues that aroused these controversies —
such as the control of external publicity — were resolved
and streamlined. The government specifically assigned the
MEA the responsibility for external publicity, implementation of policy abroad on behalf of home ministries (both
federal and state), for international economic and financial
institutions and matters, and for the Nigerian Institute of
International Affairs (NIIA) [6].

ORGANISATION OF THE MINISTRY IN LAGOS

There has been no fixity in the organisational structure of the MEA in Lagos. It has changed over the years in response to constitutional changes, to the expansion of the ministry's activities arising from the phenomenal increase in the country's participation in the international arena, and to deliberate internal soul-searching aimed at improving its performance.

Until Jaja Wachukwu took over from the Prime Minister as Minister of Foreign Affairs in 1961 there had been no major changes in the organisation of the MEA from the colonial inheritance. There had been just two units added to those that existed before 1960. These were units that dealt with Commonwealth and non-Commonwealth countries respectively. So at the end of 1960 the ministry was organised into nine sections: Economic Division, Protocol, Administrative, Passport Office, Overseas Communication, Afro-Asia, Western European, International and Research (see Figure 4.1).

Wachukwu's reforms involved the reorganisation of the ministry along clearer functional and geographical lines. The geographicals concentrated on good relations with specific areas of the world, while the functionals were assigned titles which at once identify their particular concerns. Wachukwu created new departments and upgraded some others. Specifically, he split the Afro-Asia Division into separate divisions for Africa and Asia. The International Division was divided into three branches: Economic, UN and International Cooperation. A Language Bureau and a Division of Information were also established [7]. Finally, the NIIA was established in 1962, though it was not formally inaugurated until May 1963. It was, among other things, set up to provide 'information and advice to the Government of the Federation on matters concerning international relations' [8].

These reforms did not, however, resolve all of the contradictions in the way the country's external relations were managed. For instance, the vexed issue of the overlapping and duplication of responsibilities between the ministry and other ministries and regional governments was not resolved. The Ministry of Information still continued to dispute responsibility for external publicity with the MEA. Furthermore, although the Economic Division of the MEA was expected to coordinate all foreign aid and assistance programmes and to conduct relations with international financial organisations, these did not involve other economic areas of foreign trade, federal and regional economic missions overseas or international labour activities [9]. Moreover, the

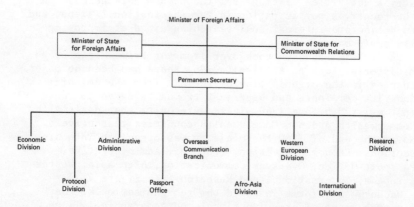

Source: Federation of Nigeria, *Office Directory*, 1 January 1961 (Lagos:
          Federal Government Printer, 1961) pp. 8–9.

Figure 4.1   Ministry of Foreign Affairs and Commonwealth
              Relations, 1961

Source: Federation of Nigeria, <u>Office Directory</u>, 1 January
        1961 (Lagos: Federal Government Printer, 1961)
        pp. 8–9.

ministry still lacked adequate qualified personnel to employ
in its divisions.
   Another important administrative innovation was introduced in the ministry of 1968. This was the creation of two
Deputy Permanent Secretaries to whom the heads of divisions
were responsible. However these division heads could bypass
the two deputies as they also had direct access to the
Permanent Secretary. This system was very difficult to
operate and it produced very unsatisfactory results. At a
meeting of all heads of missions with senior officials at
headquarters at the end of 1969 to discuss the structure of
the ministry, it was agreed to reduce the number of deputies
to one. However heads of divisions would still have access
to the Permanent Secretary, but with a new proviso that they
should approach the Permanent Secretary through the Deputy
on very important issues [10].

After independence there was a phenomenal increase in both the ministry's personnel and its overseas establishments, particularly in the early 1970s. From thirty-nine overseas establishments during the 1965-66 fiscal year, the number of missions had increased to forty-seven by January 1970; and this number had risen to seventy-eight by December 1973. The increase was an inevitable and direct consequence of the expansion of Nigeria's participation in world affairs. The active interest in African affairs shown by the Gowon regime and the increasing participation of the country in many international organisations such as the UN system and OPEC resulted in the expansion of both missions and personnel. This expansion, coupled with the experiences of the civil war resulted in an urgent need to review the administrative structure of the foreign service in order to provide 'a more effective structure for executing the increased responsibilities and new demands on the Foreign Service and the Headquarter's machinery' [11].

In response, a wide-ranging reorganisation of the ministry took place in the middle of 1972 under the personal direction of Joe Iyalla, the then Permanent Secretary, with the full support of his political head, the Commissioner for External Affairs, Dr Okoi Arikpo. The rationale was:

(1) to ensure rational interchangeability between officers serving as heads of mission and in other capacities abroad, and senior officers of the ministry at the headquarters;
(2) to achieve an appreciable devolution and delegation of responsibility from Permanent Secretary downwards;
(3) to ensure adequate performance at all levels of the ministry's functions and responsibilities; and
(4) to ensure that officers at headquarters have sufficient authority, experience and seniority to deal knowledgeably with Nigeria's principal representatives abroad as well as with senior government officials in other ministries at home and to command the respect of members of the diplomatic corps accredited to Nigeria [12].

The Iyalla-Arikpo restructuring followed the division of the ministry along geographical and functional lines. However it upgraded divisions into larger units called departments. Besides, some old divisions were split into more realistic units. For example, the former Euro-American Division which handled Nigeria's relations with the whole of Europe and America was split into American and European departments. The Economic Division was reorganised and strengthened into a fairly big department.

Furthermore the 1972 structure was based on the concept of decentralisation in authority. Each of the new departments was headed by a very senior officer of ambassadorial rank designated director, who would have sufficient authority to meet and discuss with principal envoys in Lagos and thus relieve the Permanent Secretary of some burdens. The director was empowered to act and take decisions on matters within the departmental jurisdiction in accordance with laid-down policy and procedure. The director was accountable to the Permanent Secretary who, as chief executive, was to be concerned mainly with broad policy and operational matters. Directors could report either through the Permanent Secretary to the Commissioner/Minister or to the Minister of State dealing with the relevant matter. Finally, five new special units were created. These were Policy Planning and Coordination, Pilgrimage Commission, Overseas Communication Service Inspectorate Service, and Internal Liaison. The sixth unit — the Passport and Travel Control Unit — pre-dated the Iyalla-Arikpo reorganisation. Each of the departments was subdivided into divisions and each division further subdivided into sections (see Figure 4.2).

Each of the four geographical departments collect and collate information and interpret developments in their receptive countries. The functional departments are assigned responsibilities which are similar to their titles. The International Organisation Department deals with the UN and its agencies as well as with the nonaligned movement. The OAU, the Commonwealth, and the Economic Community of West African States (ECOWAS) do not, however, come under the jurisdiction of this department. Rather, these are looked after by other departments because of the close relationship between the work of these bodies and other departments. For instance, the OAU is under the Africa Department and the Commonwealth under the European Department while ECOWAS matters are treated by the Economic Department. The Research Department has, however, remained notoriously ineffective as it is not equipped with the right type of personnel to perform research. As noted below, they do not have the appropriate training or skills for research. Besides, the ministry's library is poorly stocked: even the ministry's own publications cannot be found there!

The special units, like the geographical and functional departments, also perform tasks that bear relevance to their titles. For instance, the Pilgrimage Commission is entrusted with matters relating to the ever-increasing number of Nigerian pilgrims, while the Overseas Communication

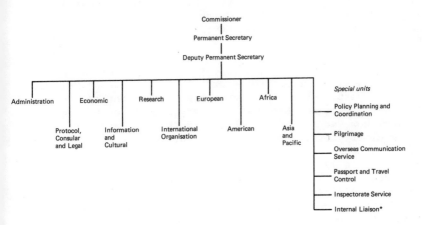

Figure 4.2   The Ministry of External Affairs after the
               Iyalla-Arikpo reorganisation

Services Unit is in charge of communication between the
ministry and its overseas missions. The Policy Planning and
Coordinating Unit, which is supposed to be concerned with
long-term policy thinking and planning, could not survive
pressures from the directors of the political departments as
the unit itself was never staffed with the right type of
officers [13].
     Since 1972 the structure of the ministry has largely re-
mained unchanged with only minor modifications — for
example, the Economic Department has been renamed the International Economic Department — and this despite recommendations for substantial structural changes in the ministry in
1976 from the Adedeji Committee on Foreign Policy [14].
Although government accepted these recommendations, very few
of them have so far been implemented. The Committee sought
the abolition of the post of Deputy Permanent Secretary. It
also wanted the whole ministry to be restructured into three
big 'super' departments headed by officers with the same

rank as the Permanent Secretary. All political departments
would come under the supervision of one 'super director';
the other two directors would supervise economic and functional departments and policy planning and coordination
units respectively. In all there would be three geographical
and six functional departments which would be headed by
directors whose ranks were lower than that of the Permanent
Secretary. The Committee also proposed the creation of a
Secretariat for the National Advisory Council on Foreign
Policy.

The only changes that occurred as a result of the Adedeji
Committee's recommendations were the abolition of the post
of the Deputy Permanent Secretary, the upgrading of Protocol
into a separate department and the establishment of the
Secretariat for the National Advisory Council on Foreign
Policy. However the establishment of this Secretariat within
the ministry never got off the ground. And the National
Advisory Council itself only functioned for a short time,
between late 1976 and sometime in 1978; even then it was
serviced largely by a unit within the Cabinet Office although an officer from the MEA did act as its secretary. It
used to meet under the chairmanship of the then Chief of
Staff, Supreme Headquarters with the Commissioner for
External Affairs as his deputy.

The non-implementation of major aspects of the Adedeji
Report was due mainly to the unworkability of some of its
proposals. The creation of three 'superdirectors' with the
same status as the Permanent Secretary would have meant
having four permanent secretaries in the ministry at once.
This would no doubt have created a lot of complex administrative problems which would have certainly had a negative
effect on the efficient performance of the ministry's tasks.
Furthermore the abolition of the Asian and Pacific Department would have been unreasonable given the importance of
the region to Nigeria.

Although the ministry's structure has largely remained
what emerged from the Iyalla-Arikpo reorganisation, the
principles and purposes underlying it seem to have been
jettisoned in recent times. By the end of the 1970s there
was a high degree of centralisation and decisions on very
trivial matters such as annual leave, allocation of quarters
and subscriptions to newspapers were said to be the exclusive prerogative of the Office of the Permanent Secretary.
This is a very sad development indeed. This coupled with
the prevalence of what an informed Daily Times correspondent
described as 'bare-faced favouritism and sectionalism' [15]
polarised the ministry into mutually suspicious and antagonistic groups. It suffices to say that an organisation

which is internally divided against itself is not likely to operate efficiently. Coordination of the work of the ministry is inevitably affected. Although there was a weekly meeting of directors with the Permanent Secretary, the meeting hardly coordinated anything. Since the Permanent Secretary appears to be either not sufficiently interested in political and other policy issues or not willing to share his ideas with his colleagues, the meetings concentrated on routine administrative matters — such as use of vehicles — rather than on policy issues.

This has resulted in directors reporting directly to the Commissioner/Minister on major policy matters without the knowledge of other directors, and in some cases of even some members of the same department. This situation was frowned on by the Adedeji Committee in 1976 as being very unsatisfactory. The Committee recommended greater coordination within departments, between departments and with the home ministries. However nothing significantly important has happened along this line, except that in more recent times there appears to be more coordination with the other home ministries whose duties impinge upon foreign policy. Sending copies of advice, opinions and policy recommendation given the Commissioner/Minister to other departments in the form of flimsies, as it is currently done, is obviously not the proper way to coordinate activities and prevent wasteful duplication of effort. It also does not contribute anything to the much needed *esprit de corps* within the ministry or to its organisational cohesiveness and efficient performance.

ORGANISATION OF DIPLOMATIC MISSIONS

The organisation of Nigeria's diplomatic missions depends on the size of each mission. This itself is dependent on the extent of Nigeria's interests in the host country. For example, in most African countries, where Nigeria's interests are minor, the size of the missions is small whereas in capitals like London and Washington where the country's interests are multifarious and complex our missions are quite large.

The organisation of a small mission is relatively simple. At the head of the mission is an Ambassador or a High Commissioner who has overall responsibility for its management. The rest of the mission is divided usually into three sections: the chancery, the accounts section and the administration. The chancery is usually headed by a First Secretary who may be assisted by one or two home-based staff (depending on the size of the mission). The head of chancery is charged with the supervision of the day-to-day work of the embassy. Although the head of chancery may have an administrative officer immediately below to deal with details, responsibility for intricate personnel and welfare issues falls on the chancery head. The accounts section is usually headed by an executive officer while the administrative section may be headed by a First or Second Secretary. The administration usually includes a unit that handles consular matters. It is not unusual in the very small missions to find one officer combining the functions of information and consular attaché.

In larger missions the structure is more complex (see Figure 4.3). Apart from the chancery, there may be other units such as information, commercial, consular, administration, recruitment, defence, communications and security. Some of these units are staffed by external affairs officers while others are headed by officers of home ministries with responsibilities for particular subject matters. For example, the recruitment section in the London High Commission is headed by staff from the Federal Republic Service Commission while the defence section is staffed by military personnel from the Ministry of Defence.

The coordination of the work of the smaller missions is relatively easy because much of it is done on an informal day-to-day basis as the staff involved is not usually larger than three in most cases. There is usually no problem where personal relationships are good. In some other missions, however, heads of various sections meet once a week under the chairmanship of the head of the mission. Olajide Aluko in a recent study of the ministry, however, claims that poor relations between head of mission and the minister or deputy have adversely affected the work of some missions [16]. In other cases, the deputy high commissioner/ambassador or some other heads of sections may not even know what is going on in the mission. There are even instances in which attachés do not keep the ambassador informed about their dispatches to Lagos.

This situation is most unsatisfactory and all efforts should be expended to ensure a team spirit among the staff of each mission. All heads of sections should attend regular meetings meant to coordinate the activities of the mission. It is even inadequate to limit meetings to once a week. In those larger missions where it is not possible for all officers to meet informally because of their large number there should be at least three formal meetings weekly. There seems to be nothing wrong if heads of sections get together first thing every morning to review their own

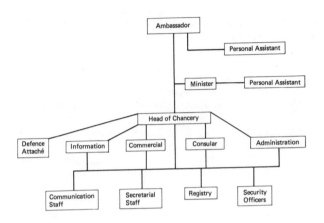

Figure 4.3 Typical Structure of a Large Nigerian Mission

activities and any developments in their host country. Apart
from fostering a sense of belonging among staff, such a
daily meeting will also be advantageous in three important
ways. First, it will keep officers informed of developments
both within the mission and in their host country; it is a
fact that many of our officers are quite ignorant of developments going on around them. Second, it will reduce or
possibly eliminate the habit of late-coming, notoriously
evident in some of the large missions. And third, it will
provide a forum for thorough discussions of ways and means
of improving both the performance and public image of each
mission in particular and of the foreign service in general.
For instance, while it is true that some of the criticisms
levied against the foreign service or particular missions
have been malicious and unjustified, it is also true that
most of our missions need to address themselves to improving their consular functions. A lot of our diplomats also
misconstrue diplomatic privileges and immunities as licence
for misbehaviour.

RECRUITMENT

The mode of recruitment into the foreign service depends upon the type of officer that is to be recruited. Basically, Nigerian foreign service officers are hierarchically divided into four categories or branches, namely:

Branch A: corresponds to the administrative class of home ministries — officers in this class are appointed for diplomatic and administrative duties;
Branch B: corresponds to the executive class and officers in this branch are appointed for executive duties;
Branch C: appointed for secretarial and clerical duties;
Branch D: other junior grades like drivers and messengers.

Appointment into branches A and B is done through the Federal Civil Service Commission while others are usually recruited directly by the MEA, although such appointments have to be made formally by the Commission. The criteria for recruitment into the foreign service are broadly similar to those for home ministries. Until very recently a university honours degree in any discipline was the only academic qualification required to be recruited into branch A. However, with the growing complexity of the country's involvement in international economic and other specialised fields, more and more emphasis is being placed on graduates with specialisation in economics, law, international relations, political science, modern European languages such as French, German and Portuguese, and those with a good knowledge of Arabic.
    Foreign service officers are either recruited through lateral transfer of serving officers from state civil service or through appointment by the Federal Civil Service Commission. The bulk of the personnel recruited in the early years of independence was through lateral transfer from the regional civil services; nowadays direct recruitment via the Commission is more common.
    Recruitment is based on interviews conducted by the Federal Civil Service Commission with one or two senior foreign service officers present. The obsession with the idea of ensuring ethnic balancing or in current parlance 'reflecting the federal character' in federal ministries has, at least for the time being, ruled out the possibility of emulating the practice adopted by some state civil services of combining interviews with competitive examinations. This principle of ethnic balance explains why recruitment through lateral transfer from regional/state civil services has remained one of the major ways of recruiting personnel into

the foreign service. This has also been one of the major sources of frustration within MEA as relatively junior and less competent officers were transferred from regional/state civil services to supersede or 'boss' officers already serving in the ministry. It is however said that the number of people coming into the MEA through lateral transfers has significantly decreased in recent times, although the principle of ethnic balance is being emphasised more than ever before. It is said that 'federal character' is the most important criteria for appointment, promotion and even posting of officers to departments or missions abroad [17].

Another method of recruiting people into the foreign service between 1960 and 1966 was by political appointment, usually at the ambassador and high commissioner level. The Constitution vested the right to appoint ambassadors in the President on the advice of the Prime Minister. During the early 1960s a number of appointments were made of people whose credentials were no more than their ethnic or party affiliation; out of thirteen Ambassadors in 1962, ten were non-career diplomats [18]. This had a demoralising effect on the officials of the ministry as some of the political appointees were put above more knowledgeable, experienced and competent career diplomats. This practice was rightly stopped by the military. With the second coming of the politicians, however, it is being resuscitated.

The 1979 Constitution vested the power of appointment of ambassadors in the President subject only to the approval of the Senate. It should be said that there is nothing inherently wrong with this idea. However it should also be said that in the more advanced countries of Europe and North America, there is less and less resort to it. Besides political appointees abroad are usually brilliant, knowledgeable, experienced and well-respected people; they are usually people of high probity and of unquestionable character. Moreover foreign posts are not left without heads for ridiculously long periods as is now the case with many key posts abroad just so that political appointees could be sent to fill them.

TRAINING

The need for proper training of foreign service officers was recognised even before the formal establishment of the service. Before independence, British embassies in Bonn, Rio de Janeiro, the Hague and Ottawa were used as training grounds for those who were later to form the nucleus of the foreign service. Similarly, the Nigerian Offices in London,

Washington, Khartoum and Fernado Po were used for training.
A section was created within the Department of Administration, as a result of the reorganisation in 1972, charged
with the training of foreign service officers [19].

Two kinds of formal training are provided for officers.
The first is a three-month induction course given to newly
recruited foreign service officers; this consists of a
series of lectures on the service, the organisation of the
MEA, and the functions of its various departments, given by
very senior officers of the ministry. Occasionally, some
lecturers from the University of Lagos and the staff of the
NIIA are invited to talk on aspects of international politics, diplomacy, international economic relations and international law. At the end of the course, the new officers
then embark on a familiarisation tour of the country. The
second type of formal training involves a year or so in
disciplines relevant to the work of the service in institutions of higher learning at home or abroad. University
graduate officers who have served for about four years or
non-graduates who have spent a longer time in the service
are given the opportunity for this type of training. However very few officers were sent for this type of training
and then usually in foreign institutions, despite the existence of comparable institutions at home. In recent years
training has not received adequate attention at the ministry, although officials have blamed this on lack of funds
[20]. While it is true that the ministry felt the financial squeeze of the last years of the military administration like other governmental agencies, the fact that for
over two years the ministry could not send a single officer
for training only reflected the low priority given to
training and staff development by MEA.

Moreover no attention is given to training of senior
foreign service officers, a situation the Adedeji Committee
viewed with dismay. The need for continuous training of
officers of all ranks cannot be overemphasised. The complexity of international relations increases from day to
day and there is thus an obvious need for continuous acquisition of specialised knowledge and skills to be able to
grapple with the changes. Furthermore, the acquisition of
specialised knowledge and skill would enable officers to
deal on a more equal basis with other civil servants and
professionals outside the civil service whose expertise is
an accumulation of specialised knowledge. This would increase the stature of the foreign service and stop the
erosion of some of its functions by the other technical and
specialised ministries.

Little attention has been given to language training.

Although the Foreign Service Regulation stipulates that for a branch A officer to advance beyond grade 8 — i.e. the point of entry for university graduates — the officer must pass a 'higher standard' course in French, this is rarely observed. Again, although government provided a language gratuity to encourage officers to learn the language of their host countries little has been done beyond that. In the 1977-8 fiscal year, only ₦398 was spent as language gratuity [21]. The provision of such a gratuity is not enough: government should make it obligatory for officers to learn the language of their host countries. A lot more would be known about the socio-political development of hosts if officers spoke and understood local languages. Apart from French, officers should be encouraged to learn at least one other international language such as Portuguese, German, Russian or Arabic. The need for Nigerian officers to learn French has been duly recognised. Such recognition should be extended to Arabic in view of the fact that it is one of the three official languages of the OAU.

DEPLOYMENT OF STAFF

Foreign service officers are deployed to duties either at headquarters in Lagos or in any of the missions abroad. The criteria which govern such deployment are as follows:

(1) principle of ethnic or state balancing;
(2) even spread of senior and junior grade officers;
(3) specialist training; and
(4) length of stay at posts [22].

In theory all categories of officers are eligible to be posted to missions abroad. In practice, however, most of those sent overseas usually belong to branches A and B. This is because of the enormous cost involved in maintaining diplomats abroad. The functions performed by branches C and D at headquarters are usually done by locally recruited personnel overseas. It is only in cases where tasks performed by junior grade officers impinge on national security or require high confidentiality that branch C and particularly branch D officers are posted abroad.

When serving abroad, officers receive representational, child and clothing allowances; the rate of these varies with rank and marital status. The clothing allowance, for instance, ranges from a maximum of ₦600 to a married branch A officer to a minimum of ₦200 to an unmarried branch B officer. It is paid on first posting and then after every three years.

In order to be able to discharge their functions efficiently, officers enjoy certain diplomatic privileges and
immunities which are usually based on the principle of
reciprocity. However the practice of issuing 'diplomatic
passports' to branch A officers and 'official passports' to
branch B officers is unjustifiable. Both categories of
officers often work under similar conditions and in many
missions their functions are not neatly compartmentalised
into 'administrative' and 'executive' duties.

CONCLUSIONS AND RECOMMENDATIONS

The Nigerian foreign service has grown tremendously over the
past two decades. During this period there has been continuous soul-searching on how best to organise the service to
discharge its duties efficiently. This produced two major,
internal, structural reorganisations in 1962 and 1972, as
well as other 'minor' reforms. However the experiences of
the service particularly since 1972 have underlined the need
to review and reform it again. An inter-ministerial committee is said to be doing this. Whatever structural reforms
the internal committee may recommend, it is pertinent to
remark that there are some other issues which need to be
looked into. Some of these have been highlighted in this
chapter.

There are hints that Nigeria plans to open new missions in
Europe, Asia and South America that will bring the number of
such missions to eighty-nine. The rationale behind such an
increase needs to be closely examined. Many of our present
missions are not properly financed or equipped. For example,
many do not have enough vehicles to meet the day-to-day
operations of embassy work. The conditions in some of the
missions are so bad that they do not give Nigeria a good
image. In some African countries, for example, the standard
of Nigerian missions does not compare favourably with those
of poorer African countries. A Daily Times correspondent
reported in September 1977 that almost every other country
in Africa spent a larger percentage of its annual budget on
its foreign ministry than did Nigeria [23]. On the one hand,
many of our missions abroad are also grossly understaffed.
On the other hand, there are quite a large number of officers at headquarters who either have no desks and chairs or
who share these with colleagues in overcrowded rooms. The
reason given for this situation is that apart from the
'normal' shortage of office space, officers have had to be
recalled home to save money.

There is, therefore, a need for a comprehensive review of the establishment of missions abroad. Some of the existing posts could conveniently be closed without affecting the country's interests. It is better to have a few well-staffed and well-equipped missions that can perform efficiently than a proliferation of missions which only give the country a bad image abroad and cause unnecessary hardship and frustration for our diplomats. More serious attention needs also be given to the conditions of officers at the headquarters. The ministry is chock-full. It is, however, hoped that the completion of the new office block being built along Broad Street in Lagos will solve the office accommodation problems, at least until MEA moves to the new federal capital at Abuja.

The plight of officers returning home should also be given greater priority. The MEA should consider as a matter of urgency building its own transit guest houses in Lagos where officers can be accommodated conveniently until they either are provided with permanent quarters or are able to find their own accommodation. The ministry will thereby save on the huge amount of money spent on hotel rooms and some of the agonies experienced by returning officers and their families will be eliminated.

The need for formal and informal coordination at the headquarters in Lagos and the mission abroad cannot be over-stressed. This is an important area which any review committee cannot afford to ignore. Coordination at all levels should be made compulsory. And there should be proper coordination between the MEA and other home ministries. The ministry should also experiment on interchanging officers with other government departments as is practised in some of the developed countries [24] with very good results. Under such a scheme, some senior diplomats would be posted on attachment to other ministries and vice versa.

The undue emphasis placed on everything in the ministry reflecting 'federal character' should be stopped. While every effort should be made to ensure that every section of the country is 'represented' in MEA, criteria such as merit and good education should be the main yardsticks in recruiting and promoting staff.

The intellectual base of the ministry should be improved by encouraging people with specialised skills and post-graduate degrees to join the service. There is also a need to encourage officers to specialise in certain fields. While it is good for officers to have a broad knowledge about every geographical area of the world, it is also necessary for the ministry to have a crop of officers who are very knowledgeable and experienced in the affairs of particular

regions. This can be developed by concentrating the posting
of certain officers in particular regions. An officer on
the Middle East desk, for instance, should be moved from
one Middle Eastern country to another rather than to North
America and later to Europe.

Finally, there is need to reorganise the Research Department to enable it to provide 'systemic analysis and background research' as well as to assist in the formulation and
determination of policy. The staff of this department could
be recruited by processes different from those applied to
other diplomats. They should be people with postgraduate
degrees and should be distinctly academic and reflective men
and women who are devoid of customary diplomatic ambitions.
They should be left essentially in this particular department although a few of them may be posted to missions abroad
for limited periods where such postings would assist them in
their research. In short, although Nigeria's foreign office
has grown and matured over the last twenty years it still
has some way to go in acting as an efficient and presentable
branch of the federal government in its multiple external
relations [25].

NOTES AND REFERENCES

1. Hans J. Morgenthau, <u>Politics Among Nations</u> (New York:
   Alfred Knopf, 1968), p. 522.
2. The name of the ministry was changed to the Ministry of
   External Affairs in 1963.
3. See Olajide Aluko, 'The Foreign Service', <u>Quarterly
   Journal of Administration</u>, 5 (1), October 1970, p. 34,
   and Mazi Ray Ofoegbu, <u>The Nigerian Foreign Office - Its
   Structures and Functions</u> (unpublished manuscript, n.d.).
4. See <u>Federal Republic of Nigeria Official Gazette</u>, 52
   (33), April 1965.
5. See <u>Federal Republic of Nigeria Official Gazette Extra-
   ordinary</u>, 62 (34), July 1975.
6. <u>Federal Government Estimates 1979-80</u>.
7. On the structures of other African foreign offices see,
   <u>inter alia</u>, Timothy M. Shaw, 'The Foreign Policy System
   of Zambia', <u>African Studies Review</u>, 19 (1), April 1976,
   pp. 31-66; I. William Zartman, 'Decision-making Among
   African Governments on Inter-African Affairs', <u>Journal
   of Development Studies</u>, 2 (2), January 1966, pp. 98-119;
   Okwudiba Nnoli, <u>Self-Reliance and Foreign Policy in
   Tanzania</u> (New York: NOK, 1978), pp. 33-40; Peter J.

Boyce, 'Foreign Offices and New States', <u>International Journal</u>, 30 (1), Winter 1974-5, pp. 141-61; and Maurice A. East, 'Foreign Policy-making in Small States: Some Theoretic Observations Based on a Study of the Uganda Ministry of Foreign Affairs', <u>Policy Sciences</u>, 4, December 1973, pp. 491-508.

8. <u>New Nigerian</u> (Kaduna), 24 February 1976.
9. For a more detailed exposition of these inter-ministerial rivalries, see H. A. Asobie, 'Bureaucratic Politics and Foreign Policy: the Nigerian Experience, 1960-1975', <u>Nigerian Political Science Association</u>, Port Harcourt, March 1980, and Chapter five.
10. Aluko, 'The Foreign Service', p. 48.
11. Ministry of External Affairs, Circular no. 4/1972 of 24 July 1972.
12. See Olajide Aluko, 'The Iyalla Reorganisation of the Foreign Service' in C. Baker and M. J. Balogun (eds.), <u>Ife Essays on Administration</u> (University of Ife Press, 1975), p. 137.
13. See Olajide Aluko, 'The Organisation and the Administration of the Nigerian Foreign Service', <u>Seminar on Nigerian Foreign Policy in the Eighties</u>, Institute of Policy and Strategic Studies, Jos, September 1980, p. 15.
14. <u>Report on the Review of Nigeria's Foreign Policy Including Economic and Technical Cooperation Under the Chairmanship of Dr Adebayo Adedeji</u> (Lagos, 1976).
15. <u>Daily Times</u> (Lagos), 10 December 1979.
16. Aluko, 'The Organisation and the Administration of the Nigerian Foreign Service', p. 21.
17. Interview, Lagos, July 1980.
18. Aluko, 'The Foreign Service', p. 42.
19. On the training and education of African foreign service officers see Anthony H. M. Kirk-Greene, 'Diplomacy and Diplomats: the Formation of Foreign Service Cadres in Black Africa' in Kenneth Ingham (ed.), <u>Foreign Relations of African States</u> (London: Butterworths, 1974), pp. 279-319, and Benedict V. Mtshali, 'The Zambian Foreign Service, 1964-1972', <u>African Review</u>, 5 (3), 1975, pp. 306-14.
20. Interview, Lagos, July 1980.
21. Aluko, 'The Organisation and the Administration of the Nigerian Foreign Service', p. 31.
22. <u>Guidelines for Staff Recruitment and Development in the Ministry of External Affairs</u>. Mimeograph prepared for newly recruited External Affairs Officers by the Deputy Director (Staff and Establishments), Ministry of External Affairs, Lagos (n.d.), p. 2.

23. <u>Daily Times</u>, 10 September 1979. For comparative data see
Douglas G. Anglin and Timothy M. Shaw, <u>Zambia's Foreign
Policy: Studies in Diplomacy and Dependence</u> (Boulder:
Westview, 1979) pp. 72–110. See also entries on 'African
States Foreign Policies' in Mark W. DeLancey, <u>African
International Relations: an Annotated Bibliography</u>
(Boulder: Westview, 1981), pp. 15–57.
24. See Geoffrey Morehouse, <u>The Diplomats: the Foreign
Office Today</u> (London: Jonathan Cape, 1977), p. 134.
25. See Chapter five.

5 Bureaucratic Politics and Foreign Policy Decision-making in Nigeria

OLAJIDE ALUKO

The original proponents of the bureaucratic politics model, Graham Allison and Morton Halperin, thought that while their model was the most satisfactoy way of explaining foreign policy outcomes for industrialised countries, it was inapplicable to the study of non-industrial countries [1]. In a recent study of foreign policy decision-making in Africa, Christopher Clapham has endorsed their view, adding that 'bureaucratic approaches to decision-making derived from more institutionalised political systems clearly fail to apply' [2]. He added that what matters in the foreign policy decision-making of African countries is the personalities of individual leaders rather than the character of bureaucratic institutions [3]. I disagree with such arguments, given the contemporary situation in Africa in general and Nigeria in particular.

For not only are these views culture-bound, they are also based on inadequate facts about decision-making processes in many developing countries. As Christopher Hill has ably argued, there is hardly any modern state in which the bureaucrats play no part in either formulating or implementing foreign policy decisions [4]. So it is the main thesis of this chapter to assert that in foreign policy decision-making in Nigeria the bureaucrats have played a more critical role than any other individual or organisation in the country since independence. While not going to the extreme of Allison Ayida, the former Secretary to the then federal military government and Head of the Federal Civil Service, who said in 1973 that the civil servants had been 'the initiator and originators' of all policies both under the First Republic and under the military [5], there is no doubt that the bureaucrats have been crucial to the making of policies in Nigeria especially under the military. By February 1967 the Nigerian Tribune lamented that the country had come under civil service rule [6]. Indeed the Lagos correspondent of the San Francisco

<u>Chronicle</u>, John Parker, referred to the civil service top-notchers late in 1967 as 'the new Nigerian ruling class' [7].

The Murtala Mohammed/Obasanjo regime that replaced the Gowon government in the 1975 coup first took a negative attitude to the civil servants who were seen to be reactionary. In actual fact, in the middle of 1976 General Obasanjo as Head of State told a meeting of all Nigerian ambassadors in Africa that his government was unhappy with their performance and that they should be more imaginative and positive rather than spending their time in their posts 'wining and dining' [8]. No sooner was this said than the Obasanjo regime became increasingly dependent on the same foreign service. Indeed his government came so to respect the advice, views and judgement of the Ministry of External Affairs and its overseas missions that some responsibilities hitherto performed by home ministries — for example, external publicity, and international economic and financial matters and institutions, and the implementation abroad of decided policy on behalf of such home ministries, both federal and state — were given to External Affairs [9]. Since the coming to office of the civilian administration in 1979, the heavy reliance on the civil service has continued [10]. For example, the initiative to provide a sum of ₦10 million as an independence gift to Zimbabwe came from the Ministry of External Affairs [11].

As the Adedeji Committee recognised in 1976, the Nigerian foreign service has been the linchpin of foreign policy decision-making in the country [12]. In this chapter, I will examine three decisions to illustrate this thesis of bureaucratic pre-eminence and shall then try to offer some explanation for this. However before dealing with the role of the bureaucrats in Nigerian foreign policy decision-making, I intend to examine briefly the essence of this model of bureaucratic politics in a very critical way.

BUREAUCRATIC POLITICS MODEL

Unlike Model I of Allison — rational policy model — Model III, which is the bureaucratic politics model, does not perceive there to be a unitary actor; rather it considers many actors to be players: players who focus not on a single strategic issue but on many diverse intra- as well as international problems as well. These players are seen to choose in terms of no consistent set of strategic objectives, but rather in accordance with various conceptions of national security and of organisational, domestic and personal

interests. So players are assumed to make governmental decisions not through a single rational choice, but by 'pulling
and hauling'.

Plausible as the essence of this model seemed to be, no
sooner was it widely published than it came under severe
criticisms, some of which were justified. In a detailed
critique, Stephen Krasner argued, in an article entitled
'Are Bureaucracies Important or Allison Wonderland' [13],
that Allison had overstressed the importance of the bureaucrats even in the Cuban missile decision. First, Krasner
argued that some people without any standing in the bureaucracy participated in the Cuban decision. Second, he argued
that the model was a pernicious one, for it could result in
the undermining of the democratic philosophy of the United
States in which the political heads of the various departments, including the White House, are held responsible for
the actions of the units over which they preside; for
example, in the case of the President if the electorate
finds the administration unacceptable the President could
be 'punished' at the next presidential elections and it
would be wrong or unnecessary for the electorate to do this
if the President were not effectively in charge of decision-
making in the administration. And third, Krasner argued that
the best and most effective way to influence US foreign
policy is to have easy access to and enjoy the confidence of
the President, rather than to engage in bureaucratic
battles.

Lawrence Freedman has also criticised the bureaucratic
politics model on a number of grounds, only a few of which
will be mentioned here. First, Freedman argued that both
Allison and Halperin take a very narrow view of politics —
'bargaining and the trade-off' among the bureaucrats —
which he regards as being at the periphery of power; instead, politics should properly be seen as being integral to
the structure of power at the centre of the state apparatus.
Freedman agreed with Krasner that the focus of power lies
with the President of the US. Second, Freedman criticised
the model for taking the context for granted and for not
dealing with the important questions of value consensus,
shared images and assumptions of the bureaucrats. And third,
Freedman went further to argue that politics in any case
does not consist of 'pulling and hauling' alone; it also
involves alliances, coalitions and log-rolling [14].

Apart from all these now-established perspectives, the
model can be criticised further on other grounds. First, it
exaggerates the importance of the bureaucrats in a political
system where the executive has to submit itself to election
or re-election once every four years. And second, the model

is quite unsatisfactory in explaining non-crisis decisions
which involve a longer period of time and a series of incremental decisions before choices are actually made. What is
clear from the above is that the bureaucratic politics
model is rather inadequate to explain foreign policy decisions in any industrialised state and, of course, is of even
less value in developing states.

Perhaps Allison has recognised some of these problems himself. Hence he said in the *Essence of Decision* that the
three models — i.e. the rational policy model, the organisational process model and the bureaucratic politics model
— can complement each other [15]. I shall try to do this
myself in this chapter on Nigeria. Nevertheless the psychological environment of the bureaucrats will also be considered. But in order to put this analysis in a proper perspective it is pertinent to say something first about the
machinery for formulating foreign policy in Nigeria [16].

THE MACHINERY FOR POLICY FORMULATION

In the Nigerian administrative system, as in most modern
states, the administrative field is carved up. However constant inter-departmental consultation is necessary to offset
the difficulties that arise, because in practice given
issues can rarely be broken down into purely military, economic, political or other component parts. While in theory
the Nigerian Head of State/Government and thus the Office
have ultimate responsibility for external relations, in
practice different aspects of Nigerian external relations
are parcelled out into different federal ministries. Until
the 1970s the Ministry of External Affairs was concerned
largely with 'political' aspects of foreign relations [17].
As earlier indicated, it has since been given additional
responsibilities for some functional matters such as external publicity, international economic and financial institutions, etc.

Given the nature of external affairs, an executive that
meets once a week hardly plays an important role in foreign
policy decision-making. In most cases decisions are made by
the Head of State/Government and the Ministry of External
Affairs, but are later referred to the executive council for
formal ratification, which is automatic in most cases. In
view of the crucial position of the ministry in the making
of the country's foreign policy, I will say something about
its structure.

Like most ministries of external affairs in contemporary
states, the Nigerian Ministry of External Affairs is run by

a Minister or Commissioner for External Affairs as its
political head; immediately below is the administrative
head, the Permanent Secretary. Below the Permanent Secretary, the ministry is split into ten departments — four
geographical departments and six functional departments.
There are also six special units. Each department is headed
by a very senior external affairs officer, in most cases
people who have served as heads of missions abroad. Each
geographical department is divided into divisions, and in
turn these are subdivided into sections and then into countries (see Figures 4.1 and 4.2 in previous chapter).

I am not concerned here with the work of each department,
division or unit [18]. In general, the process of decision-
making takes the form of drafts prepared by desk officers
after considering all vital and relevant information, especially diplomatic dispatches; then these are forwarded to
the heads of divisions who, in turn, modify or support the
policy proposals. From there the files are taken to the
directors of the relevant departments from where they are
sent with firm policy recommendations to the Permanent
Secretary or to the Minister or Commissioner for External
Affairs. Indeed, in many cases, government action is essentially authorised at that point.

None the less, it has to be recognised that much of the
work of the ministry centres on the collection and interpretation of information on developments in foreign countries. This is the main source of advice and policy proposals tendered to the Minister/Commissioner for External
Affairs, and to the Head of the State/Government.
Such information is used for briefing other ministries; for
ministries preparing for visits abroad; for discussions with
foreign visitors; for drafts of questions in the National
Assembly; and for preparing speeches. This represents the
core expertise of the Ministry of External Affairs and its
most distinctive function.

In examining the role of the foreign service and other
bureaucrats in the making of Nigerian foreign policy the
bureaucratic politics model is inappropriate. This is not
only because of the several reasons given earlier but also
because the Nigerian service does not operate by 'pulling or
hauling'. Neither does it engage in bureaucratic battles
apart from skirmishes with some home ministries in the 1960s
and early 1970s over the external control of such matters as
information, and international economic and financial cooperation. Indeed the foreign service has tended to act as a
single actor in Nigerian decision-making. Therefore the
rational policy model will be more suitable. In fact, both
the former Head of the Federal Civil Service, Allison Ayida,

and Ambassador E. O. Kolade, presently Director of the
Department of Information and Cultural Affairs in the ministry, have said that their policy proposals were made after
a rational calculation of costs and benefits of the options
available to them [19].

RATIONAL POLICY MODEL

This model is based on the assumption that the state is
actor in a foreign policy situation and that each of its
actions arises out of a well-formulated intention to meet
some strategic problem. If a state carries out an action, it
must have an end for which this action provides the best
means of attainment; out of a range of alternatives, the one
chosen is expected to achieve the most desirable consequences at minimum cost; a 'cost-effectiveness' calculation.
In short, a state is assumed to select an action from a number of alternatives in a conscious decision to maximise its
goals after a careful weighing of available means and of
possible consequences.
  Rational policy is an ideal; a government or an administrator can only approximate to it in practice [20]. There
are two main reasons for this. First, the costing of alternatives and consequences for administrators and diplomats
is far more difficult than for economists; and even they
cannot be wholly correct in their predictions. And second,
elements of irrationality such as values, sentiments, likes
and dislikes often influence the views and judgements of
decision-makers. Therefore I will say something about the
image values or the psychological environments of bureaucrats in the three case studies to be examined here.
  These cases of Nigerian foreign policy acts are (1) the
decision not to break diplomatic relations with Britain in
December 1965 over UDI in Rhodesia (now Zimbabwe); (2) the
decision to join other African, Caribbean and Pacific (ACP)
countries in negotiating Lomé I; and (3) the decision to
close the High Commission in Kampala following the overthrow
of the Amin government with the involvement of Tanzanian
troops in April 1979.

THE DECISION NOT TO BREAK DIPLOMATIC TIES WITH BRITAIN
OVER RHODESIA IN DECEMBER 1965

Within forty-eight hours of the unanimous decision of the
OAU special Ministerial Council meeting in Addis Ababa on
5 December 1965, that all member states should sever

diplomatic ties with the UK if by 15 December the British government did not crush and suppress the Smith rebellion in Salisbury, the Nigerian government took a decision that it would not comply with the resolution. Apart from the then Prime Minister (who was also his own Minister for External Affairs), Sir Abubakar Tafawa Balewa, only a very few officials in the ministry participated in this decision. The most important were the then Minister of State in the Ministry, Alhaja Nuhu Bamali, the then Permanent Secretary, Mr C. Nwokedi, and the then Head of the Commonwealth Division of the ministry, Mr I. C. Olisemeka.

Images of Decision-Makers

Both Sir Abubakar Balewa and Nuhu Bamali were pro-British and displayed a sentimental attachment to Britain. Indeed Balewa said that Britain required compassion rather than condemnation over the handling of the events that immediately followed UDI [21]. Balewa added that 'the Rhodesian question was a delicate one, and no government would like to rush over a delicate matter' [22].

Decision Process

While Messrs Nwokedi and Olisemeka were not as pro-British as Balewa, they none the less had some attachment to British institutions. Both had their first 'on-the-job training' in British diplomatic missions shortly before independence. Despite this, however, they produced a policy proposal which could be said to have been based on cost-benefit analysis, however crudely calculated.

Nwokedi and Olisemeka argued that breaking diplomatic ties with Britain would cost too much (1) in terms of trade and financial resources lost to Nigeria, and (2) in terms of the opportunity lost to influence the British government over the Smith rebellion without any commensurate compensation. Moreover in December 1965 Britain was the largest single source of aid to Nigeria and the largest market for her exports and source for her imports. They also argued that Nigeria's break of diplomatic ties with France in 1961 over atomic tests in the Sahara had been more costly than beneficial; they suggested that this had created problems for Nigeria in her first effort to negotiate an associate agreement with the EEC during the 1963-5 period (see below). Further, they said that the resolution of the OAU Council of Ministers was not binding. Finally, Nwokedi and Olisemeka argued that a break in diplomatic ties with Britain over UDI would not improve the lot of the African majority in that territory. So they recommended that the Nigerian government should not sever diplomatic ties with Britain.

Implementation

The Balewa government accepted this policy proposal. And the decision was implemented through a formal communication to the British High Commission in Lagos almost immediately. Later in a press statement on 12 December 1965 Sir Abubakar said that breaking off relations with the UK was too serious to be accepted easily by his government.

NEGOTIATION OF LOMÉ CONVENTION I

By the middle of 1973 the Nigerian government decided firmly to join, and to lead the other African countries in negotiations with, the EEC in what later became the first Lomé Convention which was signed in February 1975. Essentially this issue falls within the responsibilities of the federal Ministry of Trade. Although the then Commissioner for this federal ministry, Mr Wenike Briggs, showed some lively interest in the negotiation, his permanent officials seemed less interested. So the Ministry of External Affairs, largely because of the negotiations' wide-ranging implications for Nigeria's policy in Africa, the Caribbean and the Pacific, took over the initiative. Nevertheless a series of inter-ministerial meetings was held among the federal ministries of Trade, Economic Development and Finance with the Ministry of External Affairs.

However only a few people were crucial to the decision to join in the negotiations later. For from early 1971, when the UK opened full negotiations with the EEC, until early 1973 all the conclusions reached at the inter-ministerial meetings mentioned above came out in opposition to any such arrangement with the EEC. Their reasons were largely sound. First, by 1972 crude oil formed nearly 80 per cent of Nigerian export earnings and this product did not come under EEC tariff barriers. Second, the percentages of any Nigerian agricultural exports to the EEC were lower than 10 per cent of the country's total export earnings and so they did not come under STABEX (i.e. the fund designed to ensure stable export earnings for any such agricultural products when they accounted for not less than 10 per cent of an associate country's total export earnings in any one year). This situation had worsened after 1970 because there had been a marked decline in the output of these agricultural products in Nigeria. Third, even during the civil war (July 1967 to

January 1970) when crude oil exports were virtually brought
to a standstill, the country was able to survive well without having any operational pact with the EEC. Fourth, joining other ACP countries in the negotiations was seen by
these top officials as bringing Nigeria within the 'neo-
colonialist' orbit of the EEC, along the lines of the
Yaounde Conventions of the 1960s. And fifth, Nigeria did not
require capital aid from the European Development Fund [23].
Despite all these cogent arguments, in the middle of 1973
the Nigerian government decided not only to be a party to
the negotiations but also to lead them.

The decision to reverse the position early in 1973 was the
work of a few government officials, namely: top officials in
the ministries of External Affairs and Economic Development;
the Federal Commissioner for Trade, Wenike Briggs; and, more
importantly, the inclination of General Gowon especially
after being elected the Chairman of the OAU at the summit of
June 1973. Those critical to the decision in the Ministry of
External Affairs were the then Commissioner for that ministry, Dr Okoi Arikpo; Ambassador E. Olu Sanu, who was appointed Nigeria's Ambassador to the EEC and then leader of
the negotiating team with the EEC on behalf of all ACP
states; then Director of the International Economic Department of the ministry, A. Adeduoye; and, later, Ambassador
Peter Afolabi. In the federal Ministry of Economic Development the most important figure was its Commissioner who was
then Dr Adebayo Adedeji. And, as indicated above, Wenike
Briggs, the then Federal Commissioner for Trade, was the
most important figure in that Ministry. Finally, there was
General Gowon who was then Head of State, and who became
the Chairman of the OAU in July 1973 until the 1974 summit.

Images of Decision-Makers

While Dr Okoi Arikpo was sceptical about the utility of such
negotiations with the EEC, he was realistic enough to understand that only a united Africa could win better terms from
Europe for the less fortunate African countries. Furthermore, basic to his philosophy was that whatever could be
done to reduce the dependence of the West African francophone states on France should be done in the interest of
Nigeria's own security. Sanu, Adekuoye and Afolabi, all with
the Ministry of External Affairs, broadly shared Arikpo's
views. As far as Adedeji was concerned he knew very well
that only Nigerian participation in the negotiations with
the EEC would pave the way for the ECOWAS, a cause which his
ministry had been championing since April 1972. Briggs would
support any move that might improve the country's trading

prospects. And Gowon was emotionally committed to bringing
the ECOWAS to life, a cause he was convinced would be frus-
trated if his government refused to have anything to do with
the EEC. Also Gowon's election as OAU Chairman for 1972-4
left him with few options but to champion the African position in the negotiations. For the 1973 summit that elected
him Chairman in Addis Ababa also adopted a 'Charter of Economic Independence'. This same summit formally adopted the
recommendations of the Abidjan meetings of African Ministers
of Trade and Development in May 1973. The main essence of
those meetings was that all the OAU member states should
unite in their negotiations with the EEC.

Decision Process

Faced with pressures from outside, as well as recognising
the implications of non-participation in the negotiations,
top Nigerian officials finally decided to participate in
them on the basis of some rough calculations. First, it was
argued that given the economic and financial weight of
Nigeria, her participation would help to win better terms
for all African states. Second, it was widely believed in
Lagos that Nigerian leadership of the negotiations would
eliminate vestiges of neo-colonialism typical of the Yaounde
Convention, such as the Consultative Assembly. Third, it was
calculated that the successful completion of the negotiations with the EEC would certainly clear the road for the
formation of the ECOWAS. This it really did; for Sanu, who
headed the ACP negotiating team with the EEC from late 1973
until early 1975, has confirmed that without Lomé I in February 1975 there would not have been an ECOWAS in May 1975
[24].

In terms of direct monetary benefits, Nigerian officials
did not expect much. On the contrary the Nigerian government
saw its decision to participate in the negotiations as a way
to promote African unity and reduce economic and political
Balkanisation. Indeed, dismissing the possibility of any
major economic or financial returns from the decision, Sanu
said: 'history might also record that our (Nigerian) act of
solidarity with African states was a major contribution towards the goal of African unity and inter-African economic
cooperation' [25]. Given these interests and calculations,
the Nigerian government endorsed the policy proposals to
join and to lead the negotiations with the EEC in the middle
of 1973.

Implementation

The Nigerian government informed both the OAU Secretariat
and the EEC Commission, as well as the Commonwealth Secretariat in London, of its readiness to participate actively
in the negotiations in mid-1973. It was this that led to
the successful agreement embodied in Lomé I in February
1975.

CLOSURE OF THE MISSION IN KAMPALA IN APRIL 1979

The Nigerian government, after a series of incremental decisions involving the gradual reduction of staff in the High
Commission from late 1978, decided to close down its mission
in Kampala in April 1979. This was done partly to save the
lives of the Nigerian diplomats in Uganda and partly to pro-
test Tanzanian military involvement in the overthrow of Idi
Amin.
   The key decision-makers involved in this decision were the
then Head of State, General Olusegun Obasanjo, the then
Nigerian Commissioner for External Affairs, Major-General
Henry Adefope, the Director of Africa Department in the
Ministry of External Affairs, Ambassador L. S. Osobase, and
the then Nigerian High Commissioner to Tanzania, Ambassador
S. U. Yolah.

Images of Decision-Makers

All the key decision-makers involved were committed to the
OAU principles of non-interference in the internal affairs
of member states, as well as respect for the territorial
integrity, sovereignty and independence of member states.
Much as they disliked Amin's excesses, all the Nigerian
decision-makers including the then Head of State, General
Obasanjo, believed that President Nyerere was an adventurer
who was bent on establishing his hegemony over Uganda and
much of East and Central Africa. This view dates back to
Nyerere's recognition of 'Biafra' in 1968. Recently, the
involvement of his troops in the Seychelles, in the Comoro
Islands, in Rwanda and in Uganda confirmed these fears about
Nyerere's goals in East Africa [26]. As far as the Nigerian
government was concerned, Nyerere's apparent designs against
other African countries were unacceptable; and his breach of
the inviolability of territory boundaries was intolerable.
It was these values and principles that went a long way to
shape Nigeria's position on the Tanzanian-Uganda war of
1978-9.

Decision Process

The dispatches that were sent by Ambassador Yolah from Dar
es Salaam in late 1978 and during the first half of 1979
were critical to the decision process. In one of his dispatches in January 1979 Yolah argued eloquently that if the
situation were to deteriorate in Uganda the Nigerian government (1) should put an end to its mediatory role between
Amin and Nyerere which the latter had openly criticised; and
(2) should take urgent action to evacuate Nigerian diplomats
in Kampala and close down the mission there. This position
reflected a rough calculation that it was better to save the
lives of diplomats rather than leave them to face attack and
perhaps death at the hands of the 'invading' Ugandan Liberation Front troops and Tanzanian military forces. This position was backed by the Director of Africa Department, by the
then Commissioner for External Affairs, and by the then Head
of State.

Implementation

The Ministry of External Affairs put out a press statement
late in April 1979 that, given prevailing circumstances in
Uganda, it was unsafe to keep Nigerian diplomats there.
Therefore the government has decided to close down its mission in Kampala until such a time as the situation in that
country returned to normal.

As can be seen from the three case studies above, the input of the foreign service has been critical to all the
decisions taken. Why has this been so?

EXPLANATIONS FOR THE 'POWER' OF THE FOREIGN SERVICE

Several 'explanations' can be offered for the apparent importance of the foreign service in the making of Nigerian
foreign policy decisions. Only the most salient of these
will be dealt with here. These are (1) shared values and
images among bureaucrats and political leaders; (2) the command of information and expertise by the service; (3) the
permanent nature of officers' careers; (4) the apparent
ability of the service to frustrate policy decisions it does
not like; (5) the dire consequences of ignoring the opinions
of the foreign service in the past; and (6) the lack of experience in foreign affairs of both the Minister of External
Affairs and members of the Senate Committee on Foreign Relations. I will discuss each of these variables very briefly.

First, because of the shared values, sentiments and images
among the top foreign service officers and political leaders
it has been easy for them to get their policy proposals
adopted by the government. Apparently this was the case over
the decisions not to break diplomatic relations with the UK
in December 1965 and to close down the Nigerian mission in
Kampala early in 1979.

Second, despite occasional apparent lapses among some top
officials of the foreign service, there can be no doubt that
a substantial number of them surely command information and
expertise acquired partly out of formal training and partly
on the job after years of service. Some of them have skills
in different modern European languages and some are good
economic and financial experts in their own right.

Third, the 'permanent' nature of their careers has helped
to ensure their security of tenure as well as afford continuity of service. Foreign service officers do not change
with the political or military leadership of the country.
The purge of the public service of late 1975 hardly touched
the foreign service. Many of the most senior Nigerian federal civil servants — many with over twenty years of continuous service — can be found in the foreign service. For
instance, while there are now nine officers on level seven-
teen in the foreign service, there is only one on that level
in each of the home ministries. In many respects, the permanent officials of the foreign service have tended to see
themselves as 'the guardians' of the national interest
rather than serving the sectional interests of the governments of the day that can be changed by ballot or by bullet.
Much of the confidence and pride they have can be traced to
their effective performance under the military. They put
emphasis on consistency, coherence and national interest
rather than on partisan perspectives.

Fourth, in a negative way, the collective indifference of
the foreign service to any policy decision it did not like
could reduce the impact of political leaders to something
less than marginal. For instance, the indifference of the
service to the sudden recognition of the MPLA government by
the Mohammed government on 25 November 1975 went a long way
towards frustrating that initiative. In this instance, the
negative attitude arose because the decision on Angola was
taken over and above senior members of the foreign service.

Fifth, despite its failings, the views and judgements of
the service have on the whole been sound. Conversely, in
cases where these had been ignored, such as the break of
diplomatic relations with France in 1961 and the rather sudden and 'opportunistic' recognition of the late Neto government in November 1975, the government made serious errors in

judgement [27].

Sixth, the top leaders of both the executive and the legislature lack experience in foreign affairs. The members of the Senate Committee on Foreign Relations have been too busy with personal emoluments and other perquisites of office including diplomatic passports to find time to understand the complex problems of international life that daily confront the country. The same is true of the Foreign Relations Committee of the House of Representatives. Consequently both the legislature and the executive are heavily dependent on the foreign service for advice, policy proposals and briefings on developments in foreign countries.

CONCLUSION

From the above it seems that for the foreseeable future the Nigerian foreign service will continue to remain the linchpin of the country's foreign policy. However, with time, the Minister of External Affairs and other Ministers of State in that ministry can gain experience and insight into foreign policy matters. If members of the Foreign Relations Committees of both Houses could wake up and be alive to their duties, then they can have some influence on the country's foreign policy. Finally, if President Shagari could come to grips with foreign policy and provide effective direction, leading the foreign service from the front rather than from behind, he could have considerable impact on the decision-making process. Despite all these 'ifs', it is safe to say that given present and past performances, the foreign service will for some time to come continue to be central to the making of Nigerian foreign policy.

NOTES AND REFERENCES

This chapter was presented originally at a conference of the African Studies Association in Philadelphia in October 1980.

1. On this model see Graham T. Allison and Morton H. Halperin, 'Bureaucratic Politics: a Paradigm and Some Policy Implications', in Raymond Tanter and Richard H. Ullman (eds.), Theory and Policy in International Relations (Princeton University Press, 1972) pp. 40-79, and Graham T. Allison, Essence of Decision: Explaining the Cuban Missile Crisis (Boston: Little, Brown, 1971) passim.

2. Christopher Clapham, 'Sub-Saharan Africa', in Christopher Clapham (ed.), Foreign Policy-Making in Developing States (Farnborough: Gower, 1977), p. 88.
3. Ibid., p. 89.
4. See Christopher Hill, 'Theories of Foreign Policy Making for the Developing Countries', in Clapham (ed.), Foreign Policy-Making in Developing States, pp. 4–6.
5. Allison Ayida, 'Presidential Address to the Nigerian Economics Society', 1973.
6. Nigerian Tribune (Ibadan), 4 February 1967.
7. San Francisco Chronicle, 3 December 1967.
8. See Nigerian Herald (Ilorin), 6 August 1976.
9. For details, see Chapter 4.
10. See Federal Government Estimates 1979/80 (Lagos: Government Printer, 1979).
11. See Report of the Observer Team to Zimbabwe (Lagos, March 1980, mimeo).
12. For details see Report on the Review of Nigeria's Foreign Policy Including Economic and Technical Cooperation Under the Chairmanship of Dr Adebayo Adedeji (Lagos, 1976).
13. See Stephen D. Krasner, 'Are Bureaucracies Important or Allison Wonderland?', Foreign Policy, 7, Summer 1972, pp. 159–79.
14. See Lawrence Freedman, 'Logic, Politics and Foreign Policy Processes: a Critique of the Bureaucratic Politics Model', International Affairs, 52 (3), July 1976, pp. 434–49.
15. See Allison, Essence of Decision, p. 275.
16. Also see Chapter 4.
17. See Federal Republic of Nigeria Official Gazette, 34 (62), 16 July 1975.
18. This has been done elsewhere; see Olajide Aluko, 'The Organisation and Administration of the Nigerian Foreign Service', Seminar on Nigerian Foreign Policy in the Eighties, Institute of Policy and Strategic Studies, Jos, September 1980.
19. See Federal Republic of Nigeria Official Gazette, 34 (62), 16 July 1975.
20. For details see Peter Self, Administrative Theories and Politics: an Enquiry into the Structure and Processes of Modern Government (London: Allen & Unwin, 1972) pp. 33–5.
21. Africa Research Bulletin, 2 (11), November 1965, p. 395A.
22. Ibid.
23. For further details see Ambassador E. Olu Sanu, The Lomé Convention and the New International Economic Order (Lagos: Nigerian Institute for International Affairs, 1975).

24. See ibid.
25. Ibid.
26. See <u>Daily News</u> (Dar es Salaam), 21 January 1979.
27. Brigadier Joe Garba, then the Commissioner for External
    Affairs, had to warn the students of Ahmadu Bello
    University in Zaria in mid-1978 that the federal
    government would not be pushed into making the same
    types of mistakes it made over Angola or Zimbabwe. See
    <u>New Nigerian</u> (Kaduna), 16 May 1978.

6 Nigerian Foreign Policy: a Case of Dominance or Dependence?

STEPHEN WRIGHT

Nigeria has increasingly come to demand the attention of other actors in the international system. The principal reasons for this are that Nigeria is the continent's largest oil producer, has the biggest Gross National Product in black or white Africa and possesses the largest population. Before the mid-1970s the country's leaders were generally content to follow a quiet path in foreign affairs, but since that date foreign policy has taken on a more dynamic shape.

The aim of this chapter is to consider the pattern of Nigerian foreign policy today and to analyse the factors which determine it (see preceding chapters). On the one hand, Nigeria appears to be using its oil power to stand as the champion of Africa, to be outspoken over the burning issues of Southern Africa, and to be the major initiator of moves towards integration within the Economic Community of West African States (ECOWAS). On the other hand, the country's economy continues to display the major features of a dependent one, with exports of primary products and imports of industrial and manufactured goods, with a dependence upon expatriate expertise and a pattern of trade almost exclusively with the developed economies of the Western world. It is along this continuum, this tightrope, between the poles of aggressive dominance and passive dependence that I shall travel in this assessment of Nigerian foreign policy.

FOREIGN POLICY OBJECTIVES

The 1979 Constitution contains only one section relating to the country's foreign policy objectives:

The State shall promote African Unity, as well as total political, economic, social and cultural liberation of

93

Africa and all other forms of international co-operation
conducive to the consolidation of universal peace and
mutual respect and friendship among all peoples and
states, and shall combat racial discrimination in all
its manifestations [1].

This general statement is common to most of the constitutions of African states, as well as to the OAU Charter, but
Nigeria's relative strength within Africa combined with the
importance given to the country by Western nations, has
provided the Nigerian government with greater potential to
pursue these objectives than most other African states.
    The level of involvement in the international system has
not been constant with successive governments since independence. Much has been written about the achievements of
the previous civilian and military regimes, and so it is
not necessary to go into detail here [2]. However, some
pertinent comments can be made to help in our assessment of
the present commitment to foreign policy goals. Most analysts have agreed that until around the mid-1970s, Nigerian
policies were basically quiet and conservative, with political leaders content to remain within the evolving neo-
colonial framework. This period was also one dominated by
domestic upheaval, with the breakdown of the Westminster
system prior to 1966, the coups and civil war in the latter
half of that decade, and the period of reconciliation and
readjustment in the early 1970s. It is hardly surprising
that the major domestic problems forced foreign policy
issues into the background.
    The change in the level of commitment to foreign policy
initiatives became more obvious and accentuated in 1975
following the removal of Yakubu Gowon from power by Murtala
Mohammed. The buoyant economy and the increasing desire to
play a role in international affairs commensurate with the
country's perceived strength provided the impetus for a
radical shift in both the content of policy and its implementation. The Angolan crisis, and Nigeria's rebuff of US
advice in recognising the MPLA government (see Chapter 3),
marked a watershed by showing a new aggressiveness in
foreign policy [3].
    Apart from the universal goals of security and welfare
(which of course require interpretation), four broad areas
of interest emerged which today remain the principal bases
of foreign policy [4]. The first area concerns Southern
Africa. The intervention in the Angolan crisis and the
explicit pressure exerted on Britain over the fate of
Zimbabwe in the months prior to the Lancaster House conference, highlighted the willingness to force the pace of

change in Southern Africa. Nigeria has, through the threat
of economic retaliation, now turned to the West and asked
it to reconsider its relations with the Republic of South
Africa, but in the absence of any military initiative by
black Africa, this appears to be a long-term process.

The second objective of foreign policy concerns the
social and cultural renaissance of the African personality.
The colonial period had witnessed, and had been a major
cause of, the undermining of traditional values and societies, and so the Nigerian government considers it necessary
to counter and reverse this trend. A major effort was made
with the FESTAC celebrations in Nigeria in 1977 [5], which
attempted to rejuvenate interest in traditional culture,
but to wipe out the memory of a century of colonial rule is
not an easy task.

The third major aim of foreign policy is to integrate the
region into a viable unit through the Economic Community of
West African States. The formation of ECOWAS in 1975 came
largely as a result of Nigerian initiatives and its continuing progress is something to which the present government
is committed. The goal of total regional integration is
obviously a long-term one, but this will be pursued because
Nigeria stands to benefit greatly from the increased trade
between partner states.

The fourth area of foreign policy overlaps with the goal
of regional integration in that the aim is to have complete
economic — and thus political — independence throughout
the African continent. The signing in 1980 by OAU Heads of
State of the Lagos 'Plan of Action' [6] as the blueprint
for an Economic Community of Africa was considered very
significant by the Nigerian government, and this desire to
correct imbalances in the world economic order is evident
in the tone and temper of relations with countries of the
developed world.

Although these objectives are self-explanatory, there are
several factors to note which prevent a wholly consistent
and uniform approach to foreign policy. In terms of the
implementation of policy, problems exist concerning the
types of policy to be pursued as well as the levels of
commitment attached to them. Such problems are common to
all states, but in Nigeria they are accentuated by the
conflict between decision-makers' perceptions of the power
status of the country and the desire not to pursue policies
likely to alienate fellow African states. There have been
doubts, for example, over how best to achieve the goal of
integration in ECOWAS, because direct pressure from Nigeria
could easily bring the opposite result. Similarly, there
has not been a fully coherent stand over South Africa

because of an inability to agree upon, and implement, particular economic or military strategies.

These problems of implementation are worsened by the disagreement within Nigeria over how active an 'active' foreign policy should be, and who should be its major benefactor. There has been debate as to whether Nigeria should be more aggressive and stand as the continent's champion, so taking into consideration continental aspirations as much as, if not more than, national ones. The crusading element is a strong influence on policy-making, but the general preoccupation is with 'national' interests (cf. Chapter 10). Of course there is no clear demarcation line between these categories as many so-called national issues have great relevance to the rest of the continent, but the emphasis, understandably, is on Nigeria.

If one turns to the formulation of Nigerian foreign policy, there are also serious difficulties. The problem of 'what constitutes a "nation"?' is universal to all countries and is of special importance in this analysis. Despite attempts to weld Nigeria into a single nation, there are major divisions within society. First, there remains an important ethnic element to the polity and so policy, rather than reflecting the federal nature of the country, is at times bogged down by other considerations. Second, it is possible to see a division within the ruling élite between those with apparently the nation's interest at heart and those of a comprador persuasion willing to trade off national for personal gain [7]. The combination of these two factors — comprador policies backed by the manipulation of ethnic support — undermines the maximum potential of Nigeria in the external environment.

END

RESOURCES, POWER AND DEPENDENCE

The aim of this section is to consider the extent to which the resources of the country allow for a strong and influential foreign policy. Of course it must be remembered that there has to be the political willingness and ability to maximise the resource potential of the country in the implementation of active policies. This discussion, then, hinges not only upon resources and power, but also upon internal and external constraints, both economic and political, which limit the maximisation of power.

It is the resources of Nigeria which have given rise to the view that the country is the most dominant in Africa. Here the term 'resources' is used to encompass natural, industrial, human and infrastructural resources in their

widest senses. A crucial factor, however, is not only the
development of the resource potential, but also the issue
of who controls the resources and how they are used. As
will become evident, the control of the resources in
present-day Nigeria rests largely in external hands, and so
the forces of 'neo-colonialism' have an important role to
play in shaping Nigerian society.

The total area of the country is 923,773 sq. km (about
four times the size of Great Britain) of which approximately three-quarters could be said to be arable or potentially arable land. Agriculture provides an occupation for
two-thirds of the population and was until recently the
mainstay of the economy. Its contribution to Gross Domestic
Product (GDP) fell from 63 per cent in 1960 to 23 per cent
in 1975, while exports of commodities accounted for 80 per
cent of the total value of exports in 1960 but fell to a
mere 6 per cent by 1974 [8]. This decline can be explained
by several factors, notably a gradual fall in production of
the main commodities — cocoa, groundnuts, palm oil, rubber
and cotton — combined with an increase in domestic demand,
a dramatic increase in the production and importance of
petroleum, and the relative lack of concern shown by the
government. In 1976 the government introduced 'Operation
Feed the Nation' (OFN) — renamed in 1980 the 'National
Council on the Green Revolution' — in an attempt to boost
production and strengthen the country's economic base, and
since then has injected large sums of money into the agricultural sector. It will take time, however, for any significant results to show.

The most important minerals found in the country are tin,
coal, columbite and petroleum. Apart from petroleum, none
of the minerals are of particularly good quality or are
easily accessible and so have had a marginal role to play
in the economy. Iron ore is present, but has only recently
been mined in anticipation of the opening of the iron and
steel mill in Kwara State. At the beginning of 1980 the
National Uranium Mining Company (NUMCO) was established
and began exploratory work in Bauchi with the French corporation, Minatone, but it remains to be seen what successes will be scored in this field [9]. Natural gas is found
in abundance, but owing to the lack of storage and processing facilities only around 2 per cent of production has
in the past been actually tapped. It has been estimated
that 10 per cent of the country's total reserves have
already been flared and wasted, but a recent agreement with
several West European countries should allow for the export
of a larger percentage of the gas produced [10]. The United
States promises to be the best export market for Nigerian

gas, but negotiations were still taking place in 1981.

By far the greatest resource at the disposal of the Nigerian government is petroleum. By 1978 Nigeria was the seventh largest oil producer in the world and the largest in Africa [11]. In 1979 there were record figures for production at a total of 840.94 million barrels, an average of 2.3 million bpd, and revenue was estimated to be 89 per cent of the country's total export revenue [12]. Earnings from the sale of the high-quality, low-sulphur oil largely contributed to the steady growth of GDP in the late 1970s at around 8.5 per cent a year.

Overall control of the oil industry is in the hands of the Nigerian National Petroleum Corporation (NNPC) although, as Table 6.1 shows, responsibility for production rests with the large multinational corporations. In 1973 the government took one-third interest in all of these corporations and in May 1974 further increased its share to 55 per cent [13]. The nationalisation of British Petroleum in mid-1979 in retaliation for BP's sales to South Africa and as a means to pressurise the UK government over the Zimbabwe issue, showed Nigeria's ability to use its oil strength in dealings with more-developed countries. Whether Nigerian actions forced the hand of the British government cannot be accurately gauged and will be discussed later, but an oil scandal in 1980 showed the tenuous grip that Nigeria had on its oil industry.

The 'oil-gate' scandal broke early in the year when it was discovered during a routine auditors' check that some ₦2.8 billion (£2.2 billion) of oil revenue was missing. It was alleged by some that the money had been paid 'by mistake' into a private London bank account, and subsequent allegations and counter-allegations forced a government enquiry. While it is difficult to extract the truth from the speculation, there are several undeniable facts which emerged that are significant to this chapter. The scandal highlighted the fact that no accurate accounts of oil deals had been kept by the NNPC and that many fringe contracts had been arranged, especially in the final days of the military government, which appeared to be unnecessarily and hastily signed. Such revelations made many fear that contracts had been signed more in the interests of the compradors than of the nation. Allied to this disturbing news was the finding that the NNPC had no figures of its own regarding oil output, but that it was totally reliant upon the multinationals for information. This discovery led to public fears that millions of barrels had probably been 'stolen' from the country in previous years [14]. It also showed the extent to which Nigeria relied upon external

Table 6.1   Oil: production and destination of exports in
           November 1977

	Month total	57,518,295 barrels	
	Daily average	1,917,277 barrels	
	Total exports	55,976,802 barrels	

Producer	(%)	Destination	(%)
Shell-BP	55.8	USA	35.9
Gulf	15.8	Netherlands	12.0
Agip	12.0	Curacao	8.7
Mobil	9.0	Dutch Antilles	8.1
Elf	4.0	France	7.5
Texaco	2.5	West Germany	5.5
Pan Ocean	0.5	UK	5.4
NNPC	0.4	Brazil	2.2
	100.0	Ivory Coast	1.8
		Others	12.9
			100.0

Source: Nigerian National Petroleum Corporation: Monthly
        Petroleum Information, November 1977 (Lagos:
        NNPC, 1977).

interests in the economic sector and so pointed to possible
limitations in the country's ability to pursue independent
policies.

It is significant to add, given the importance of oil in
Nigerian economic and political development, that as recent
as 1977 the country was forced to import half of its total
requirement of petrol, diesel and kerosine because of its
lack of sufficient refineries. Since then, refining capacity
has been increased by the opening of a second refinery at
Warri to help the overworked Port Harcourt plant, while a
third refinery at Kaduna began operations in 1980. The increased capacity has eased, though not totally solved, the
distribution problems within the country caused largely by
domestic demand increasing at 25 per cent a year [15]. It
has also helped to offset the country's dependence upon

imported oil and given more room for control of its own supplies, though still within the framework of the multinationals.

The heavy reliance of the economy on the export of primary
products — albeit mainly oil — highlights the underdeveloped nature of the economy. Oil reserves are estimated at
between twenty to thirty years during which time the hope is
to develop the economy into an industrialised and largely
self-sufficient one. This would certainly be a prerequisite
for giving Nigeria the strength to pursue a powerful and independent foreign policy, but there is a long way to travel
before this position is reached. At present, manufacturing
accounts for less than 10 per cent of the GDP and manufactured and semi-finished goods form approximately three-
quarters of the country's total imports [16], which, as
Table 6.2 shows, originate in countries of the developed
world.

The country's plans for an iron and steel complex have
only slowly materialised despite efforts over two decades.
Original surveys by Western countries found that a plant
would be uneconomic and so the governments backed away from
giving any assistance. A majority of Nigerians believed that
this was a deliberate decision by the West to maintain
Nigeria's underdeveloped status [17], and they were pleased
to accept assistance from the USSR which realised the political dimension to the issue. Unfortunately Soviet help has
also been criticised within the country. In May 1980 the
then Minister of Steel Development, Mr Paul Unongo, attacked
the USSR for its inaction over the Ajaokuta Steel Works and
expressed fears over the influx of 15,000-20,000 Soviet
'experts' [18]. However, following the commissioning of the
plant in 1981 by President Shagari there were increased
hopes for the success of the scheme.

The human resources of the country have a large measure of
influence over the domestic and foreign policies pursued.
The size of the population provides a major stimulus to
foreign countries to trade and invest in Nigeria because of
the potential of the consumer market. Population size is a
highly political factor in the country because federal revenue is partly apportioned on such grounds, and attempts by
both civilian and military administrators to get accurate
figures have failed in the past. Consequently the country
still works from projections of the 1963 census and it is
accepted that the population numbers at least eighty million [19]. The significance of this is further underlined by
the fact that around 25 per cent of all Africans are
Nigerian. The size of the population, then, serves as a huge
magnet attracting foreign companies with the lure of large

Table 6.2 Main trading partners (%)

EXPORTS	1976	1977
USA	36	40
Netherland Antilles	15	15
Netherlands	11	11
UK	11	8
France	9	7
West Germany	7	6
Commonwealth West Indies	7	6
Others	4	7
	100	100

IMPORTS	1976	1977
UK	23	22
West Germany	16	16
USA	11	11
Japan	9	11
Italy	6	7
France	7	7
Netherlands	5	4
Others	23	22
	100	100

Source: <u>Quarterly Economic Review of Nigeria: Annual
Supplement 1979</u> (London: Economist Intelligence Unit,
1979), p. 25.

profits and foreign governments with the hope of political
influence, through the medium of Nigeria, in the continent.
It also provides a large labour force which has helped push
the country's GNP to the highest in Africa.

Although there is reason for optimism when considering
human resources, there are also grounds for concern. The
rapid growth of the economy has laid bare the inadequate
level of skilled labour in Nigeria. The inability of indige-

nous labour to control the economy has allowed expatriate personnel to maintain a prominent, possibly dominant, position in the economic system, thus helping to maintain a dependent relationship with the developed world. Even some nationalised corporations have been handed back to foreign organisations for supervision and reorganisation. In 1978 the railways were placed under the care of Rail India [20], while in 1979 Nigeria Airways, ironically the symbol of independence yet the favourite focus of popular disenchantment, was taken over by KLM Royal Dutch Airlines [21]. The lack of skilled labour, then, has placed constraints on the development of infrastructural resources, not just with the railways and airways, but also with roads, water and electricity.

Another equally serious dimension to the human resources question is the polarisation of society between the rich and poor. In 1978 the per capita annual income figure stood at $560 [22], an average figure by African standards, but one which masked the disparity in wealth between the 'masses' (to be rhetorical) of labouring poor and peasantry on the one hand and the privileged minority or bourgeoisie on the other. The disparity between the groups has been caused partly by the unfair salary structure [23] which appears to provide greater rewards — seemingly at an exponential rate — as a person moves upwards, as well as by the ability to run the system to one's advantage when in charge. The control of the political offices by this bourgeoisie led to the squandering of large amounts of foreign currency on questionable imports to the extent that in 1978 there was a large balance of payments deficit [24]. This forced stricter import controls on certain items and so helped to alleviate the immediate financial problems.

This privileged minority has also prospered from the gradual indigenisation programme, which has allowed more opportunities for Nigerians to move into better-paid employment. Of course, contrary to government pronouncements, indigenisation and neo-colonialism are not mutually exclusive. The aim of neo-colonialism is to continue to control the economic system which evolved in the pre-independence period, irrespective of the political structure. In Nigeria, indigenisation has not prevented economic exploitation but has provided opportunities for the compradors to benefit as much as the foreign concerns, so maintaining the underdeveloped nature of the economy [25]. The Lockheed [26] and oil-gate scandals are examples of a general trait of corruption in Nigerian business practice that can only serve to undermine the economic potential of the country.

Although it is possible to over-blacken Nigerian business

practice when corruption appears widespread in other, more-
developed countries, there is a further disquietening feature to mention about current Nigerian politics which illu-
minates the divergence between the 'national' and 'local'
interests. The transfer of power from a military to a civilian government in October 1979 ushered in a new era of
political rivalry and intrigue. Few observers of the political scene could deny that the political pattern of 1980 and
1981 is comparable with that of the early 1960s, despite a
change to the Presidential system of government. The political parties which fought the elections seemed to be rein-
carnations of the old parties and, despite efforts made by
the military government to prevent it, all depended for a
majority of their support on a single ethnic region.

In a nation so fragile as Nigeria, the boundary between
healthy and acceptable opposition on the one hand and out-
right subversion on the other is a thin one. In just over
two years of civilian government, the reappearance of the
familiar political problems of the 1960s has given many
cause for concern. The internal splits in the two smallest
parties, the Great Nigeria People's Party (GNPP) and
People's Redemption Party (PRP), have left the other three
dominating the political scene. A loose coalition between
the dominant National Party of Nigeria (NPN) and the Nigerian People's Party (NPP) has left Chief Awolowo's Unity
Party of Nigeria (UPN) as a *de facto* opposition. Though the
regions have been weakened by the evolution of nineteen
states in the federation, there is still more than a resi-
due of ethnic bias in the parties.

There is a distinct possibility that increasing domestic
problems will limit further the federal government's ability
to pursue an active and aggressive foreign policy. Some of
the more serious domestic issues can be outlined to illuminate the problems facing the country. Early in January 1980,
President Shehu Shagari commented that 'since the inception
of the new Presidential system of government, I have been
inundated with reports of denials of the rights of political opponents from all parts of the country' [27]. The major
form of intimidation came in business, where companies which
had supported the losing parties have been hounded out of
the states. But problems have also occurred at governmental
level. The federal government in January 1980 deported to
Chad the GNPP majority leader of Borno State Assembly,
Alhaji Shugaba Abdurrahman, on the grounds that he was not a
Nigerian [28]. This was a dangerous move, both because
Shugaba had already fought an election and won, and also
because it set a precedent for possibly millions of Nigerians whose ancestors cross borders frequently and cared

little for nationality. In a major court case the government's decision was reversed and Shugaba awarded ₦350,000
in compensation [29].

The inter-party hostility in Kaduna State came to a head
in June 1981 when the NPN-dominated State Assembly successfully impeached the PRP Governor, Alhaji Balarebe Musa. The
continuation of the old parliamentary party system of operations under the new Presidential system made Musa's impeachment inevitable (with hindsight), because he lacked the
support of the majority of the Assembly as well as his own
party. However the manner in which he was finally brushed
aside by the NPN majority caused concern to many observers
[30]. The only remaining PRP Governor, Alhaji Mohammed
Abubakar Rimi, was also under heavy fire from his own party
and others. The Maitatsine fanatics' riots of December 1980
left thousands dead and questioned his control and credibility in Kano State. His challenge to the Emir of Kano — and
through him traditional authority in the state — in July
1981 led to a second series of riots which destroyed most
government property in Kano. The fact that the PRP accused
the NPN of having a hand in the riots was representative of
the political rivalry between the parties [31] and highlighted how delicate many political issues remain within
Nigeria.

President Shagari has made repeated efforts to stay above
party conflicts and bring all the parties together, but with
little success. The UPN leader, Chief Awolowo, never a great
admirer of northern leaders, decided not to become involved.
Other actions by 'Awo' left no doubt as to his vehement opposition to the Shagari government. Awolowo displayed his
art of brinkmanship in August 1979 by challenging Shagari's
victory on the constitutional question of what was two-
thirds of nineteen states. During the last two years, UPN
states have adopted an educational policy discordant with
that of the federal government and have even refused to display the President's picture on official premises. Awolowo
has criticised the government on many occasions, but chose
an embarrassing time during the OAU economic summit in Lagos
in 1980 to attack Shagari's foreign policy, his economic
policies and the poor record of the OAU [32]. Of course, as
has already been noted, this is within his rights, but does
not augur well for national unity. However the federal government continues to hold the upper hand by controlling the
allocation of oil revenue to the states, as well as by
acting as the legal watchdog on all transactions between the
states and other countries abroad [33].

To turn away from the domestic political environment, I
will look at the final area of resources, namely the mili-

tary. The armed forces of Nigeria, at a total strength of 146,000 men [34], are the second largest in black Africa. The military has been prominent in the country, having ruled from 1966 to 1979, and yet military strength has rarely been used as a resource of foreign policy. The army's strength has undoubtedly deterred other neighbouring states from becoming involved in Nigeria's domestic politics, though this is based upon the assumption that those states had a desire to meddle in Nigeria's affairs. The recognition of Biafra by several African countries presented the best opportunity for external interference, but the federal government faced no real threat then of external military attack.

The military has been used to positive effect by successive governments as major peacekeeping forces abroad, either offered directly or else through the good offices of the Organisation of African Unity. In recent years the government has also threatened to send Nigerian troops to fight alongside the liberation forces in Southern Africa, but nothing came of these offers. The unfavourable response from those fighting in the region deflected Nigerian foreign policy towards economic methods of liberating the continent. That the military government responded to domestic pressures for demobilisation, bringing the army size down from 250,000 to 160,000 men between 1977 and 1979, was a further indicator that armed force was not considered to be the central tenet of Nigeria's policy towards the South.

During the last year, however, there appears to have been a slight change in this stance. In a major speech at the end of June 1980, President Shagari announced that there was to be a renewed effort to forge the military into a strong fighting force in order to back up the country's foreign policy posture [35]. In November 1980 in Lagos, Shagari stated that Nigeria would be willing to match South Africa in an arms race if it was necessary to bring down the apartheid regime, while in July 1981 a decision was taken to start initial research for Nigeria to go nuclear, again with the aim of matching South Africa's alleged nuclear military capability [36].

The moves towards nuclear power by Nigeria present many issues for discussion, but these are beyond my scope here (see Chapter 10). What is important to note is that Nigeria needs to strengthen generally its armed forces for any political threats to be credible, given all the reports circulating of Pretoria's political intentions and military preparations [37]. This is difficult, however, given Nigeria's dependence upon foreign powers for imported weaponry and ammunition. As was found out to Nigeria's cost during the civil war, withdrawal of supplies at a vital moment can pre-

vent positive action and such an event could reoccur if the
West decided to support South Africa, openly or tacitly, in
a confrontation with black Africa. Nigeria does get assistance from the Soviet Union, especially in the air force,
but this diversification itself causes problems at times in
terms of servicing, spare parts and training. An interesting
point to mention is that the International Institute for
Strategic Studies alleged that in 1978 Nigeria bought weaponry from South Africa itself. If this is true, then it is
a rather ironic and curious breach of the country's foreign
policy stance [38].

In concluding this section, then, it is clear that the resources and power potential of Nigeria are quite substantial, though not unlimited. However resources *per se* do not
give power, as there must be both the political willingness
to follow a systematic plan of action [39] as well as the
ability to bring influence to bear on other actors. In order
to be able to judge the relative strength of Nigeria in the
international system, I go on to discuss foreign policy
towards African states and then within the global arena.

RELATIONS WITH AFRICAN STATES

During the 1960s Nigeria made little impact upon African
affairs. This was, as observed earlier, because of the quiet
and conservative policies of the Prime Minister, Sir
Abubakar Tafawa Balewa, and then the country's factional
strife in the civil war. The 1970s witnessed a rapid increase in economic strength and gave Nigeria a firm base for
its emergence as a leading force on the African political
scene. This leadership role was not an automatic consequence
of economic power but derived from a change of attitude towards foreign policy.

Since the beginning of the 1970s, and especially after the
coup which brought into power the Mohammed/Obasanjo administration, it has been evident that the Nigerian leaders have
wanted to take a prominent position in African politics and
be the 'guardian' or 'champion' of the continent in its relations with external powers. The first sign of this changed
attitude in foreign policy came in 1973 when a Nigerian initiative in the OAU led to the African Declaration of Cooperation, Development and Economic Independence, which forged
a united African approach for the negotiation of the Lomé
Convention [40]. Nigeria also started to play a major part
in peacekeeping activities throughout the continent, especially between Ethiopia and Somalia, Tanzania and Uganda,
and, nearer to home, in Western Sahara and Chad. Although

mediation is not the sole prerogative of a strong nation,
clearly Nigeria's military and financial resources gave
the opportunity to play an important mediatory role in the
continent.

Diplomatic initiatives, especially in ECOWAS and over the
question of Southern Africa, have provided evidence of
Nigeria's influence in black Africa, but it is necessary to
consider on what basis this influence rests. Two fairly distinct areas can be isolated for study, namely the West African region and the rest of the continent.

Within West Africa the country clearly stands *primus inter
pares*. By means of successful diplomacy Nigeria was able to
get the other countries of the region in 1975 to form
ECOWAS, an organisation which is attempting to cut across
linguistic and cultural barriers left by colonialism. As a
sign of its strength and size relative to its partners,
Nigeria houses the headquarters in Lagos, provides 30 per
cent of the budget and has a GNP roughly equivalent to all
the other members combined. Given such potential power, the
regional environment is one in which Nigeria could be assumed to be playing a dominant role, but there are some
limiting factors. The majority of ECOWAS members are francophone countries which, as a heritage of colonialism, still
maintain suspicions (occasionally fuelled by France) of
Nigeria's intentions [41]. In any case, it is a basic fact
of international politics that the weaker members of any
organisation will be wary of the influence of the stronger.
A precedent has already been set in East Africa, where the
collapse of the Community can be largely explained by the
dominance, real or perceived, of Kenya over the weaker members. In order not to cause a similar breakdown in West
Africa and bring the Community to a premature end, Nigeria
has to move cautiously in its foreign policy towards its
neighbours. Caution itself causes problems, however. As Dr
Joseph Wayas, President of the Senate, commented, Nigeria
'has been so sensitive and careful of her image ... that, at
least in her foreign policy, she has often appeared timid
and impotent' [42]. Perhaps one feasible way of minimising
conflict could be through the common defence force agreed
upon in 1981, but given the problems faced by other organisations in pooling military resources, this appears to be
a long way off from successful implementation [43].

The policies pursued by Nigeria within the region are
motivated both by self-interest and by a genuine willingness
to assist. In terms of aid, for example, Nigeria built a
bridge at Birni Nkonni free of charge for the Niger government and also offered to assist with roads in the Sahara,
because this helped to complete a section of the trans-

Sahara road from Algiers to Lagos. The government also provided a road from Lagos to Cotonou, again to promote trade
links. In Guinea, Nigeria is providing funds to help with an
iron ore project; much of the ore will be used in the
Ajaokuta iron and steel works when they are opened. In 1980
Nigeria sent relief supplies to Ghana to help with the food
crisis, as well as helping Benin, Guinea and Congo in the
airlift of supplies to Chad [44].

Although the aid element is an important feature of
Nigeria's regional policy, it is clear that economic advantages, and thus political influence, are also factors
brought into consideration. Trade with neighbouring countries has been increasing, especially with the export of
oil, and plans to remove gradually the trade barriers between ECOWAS members will allow Nigeria to expand its trade
and influence further. But, as two scholars have pointed
out, Western 'neo-colonial' interests will also benefit
greatly by using Nigeria as a springboard to expand their
own regional operations and so the results of any such expansion are complex [45].

Two recent events in West Africa have led to speculation
that the country is now beginning to use its power openly in
the implementation of its foreign policy. A first example of
the use of its 'oil weapon' was seen in the military government's opposition to the 1979 coup in Ghana led by Flt. Lt.
Jerry Rawlings. The then Nigerian Head of State, Olusegun
Obasanjo, appealed to the Ghanaian government for an end to
the bloodbath [46], which eventually saw the execution of
three former Ghanaian leaders among others. When Rawlings
ignored these requests, while publicly accepting them, the
Nigerian government cut off all its oil supplies to the
country with the aim of forcing Rawlings to modify his policies. This action backfired to some extent because it made
Ghanaians more resolute to continue their 'clean-up' operation and not be bullied into submission by their stronger
neighbour [47].

A second example of Nigeria's use of economic power was
witnessed in the ability of President Shagari to have Master-
Sergeant Samuel Doe of Liberia excluded from ECOWAS and OAU
meetings in 1980 [48]. The strong decision made by Nigeria
proved sufficient to bring other ECOWAS members into line.
The main grounds for this move were to play a moderating
role in Liberia's domestic politics as well as to prevent
similar occurrences in other parts of the region, because
the maintenance of the status quo in West Africa is important for Nigeria's economic policies. It is important to
stress, though, that neither in Ghana nor Liberia did Nigerian pressure appear to have any significant effect upon the

domestic politics. Furthermore Nigerian problems in 1981 in
dealing with border clashes with Benin and Cameroon, as well
as Colonel Gaddafi's incursion into Chad, also underlined
the difficulty in converting potential power into direct influence over its neighbours.

If I can now turn to consider the continent as a whole,
Nigeria's apparent influence — and its willingness to try
to exert this influence — in Africa has become more notice-
able in recent years. This can be seen, for example, in the
country's lead in negotiations for the Lomé Convention, the
recognition of the MPLA government in Angola in 1976 thus
helping to break the deadlock in the OAU, and also by the
role played in discussions on the Anglo-American plan for
Zimbabwe culminating in the economic threats made towards
Britain at the time of the 1979 Commonwealth Conference in
Lusaka. These examples illuminate the status and influence
which the country appeared to have within the continent.

It is pertinent to ask again on what basis this apparent
influence rested. The simple answers are the country's economic power and resource potential, but the question is more
complex than that. In 1973 as much as 73 per cent of imports
from African states came from five countries only, while 75
per cent of exports went to just four countries. Only
Angola, Zaire and Morocco of countries outside of the region
had any meaningful trade with Nigeria. Although this position has improved in recent years, it is still true to say
that the vast majority of African states have little or no
direct contact with Nigeria at all. To take this point further, it is only in 1981 that ECOWAS capitals will have
direct communication links and so links with other parts of
the continent are, for the time being, of a problematic
nature [49]. The question arises that if Nigeria has little
contact with the majority of African countries, what real
medium can Nigeria use to bring direct pressure upon them?
Why black Africa responds, or should respond, to Nigerian
initiatives could perhaps be explained by the hope that in
the future trade links, aid and technological assistance
will be forthcoming; but for the present few such links
exist.

Another possible explanation for the status accredited
Nigeria derives more from the country's relationship with
the developed world than with Africa. For the first time
there is a black African country with an economy and potential worthy of note by the developed world. Furthermore the
'oil weapon' and the promise of large returns from the expanding economy make sure that Nigeria is listened to in the
world arena. It is perhaps on these grounds — for economic
and political gains from the developed world — that Africa

supports Nigerian initiatives and not because of any dependence upon that country. At present the US and Britain see Nigeria often as the 'key' to continental support, but this is a slight misperception. It will be some time before Nigeria can directly influence its fellow African states.

If one reflects upon which African states have been most influential *within* the continent over the last two decades, then the conclusion is reached that 'weak' states can be as influential as 'strong' ones. Broadly speaking, during the 1960s Ghana, under Kwame Nkrumah, was perhaps the most influential, while the 1970s saw Tanzania as the home of the OAU Liberation Committee and, through Julius Nyerere, one of the most outspoken and persuasive countries in Africa. Neither Ghana nor Tanzania could be said to have had economic power or infinite resources, but both in their way had some influence. By the same token, Nigeria's apparent strength could not by itself guarantee the country support in Africa. For example, late in 1977 most African states refused to withdraw their support for Niger's candidature to the United Nations Security Council after Nigeria had announced its decision to stand [50]. The fact that Nigeria chose to stand against the OAU candidate was significant both as a pointer to the country's own self-esteem as well as a snub to the continental body.

Government leaders in Nigeria often explain their country's dynamic role in the continent by pointing to the general apathy and inactivity of other African states. They contend that it is not that the country is positively trying to be the continent's leader, but that it fills the vacuum left by the negation of responsibility by the majority. Once the Mohammed/Obasanjo administration projected Nigeria into the international limelight, then the rest of the continent was content to give its backing. The presence in Lagos of twenty-seven African embassies [51], even more than in Addis Ababa, the home of the OAU, testifies to the status given Nigeria by the continent. But this is perhaps too negative an interpretation. It is becoming evident that so long as Nigeria continues to expand its economic penetration of the continent and does not alienate its neighbours with too aggressive a foreign policy, then the country's economic strength will allow it to play an increasingly dominant role in the continent.

FOREIGN POLICY IN THE GLOBAL ARENA

The aim of this final section is to look in detail at Nigerian foreign policy towards non-African countries and to see

whether policy reflects a dominant or dependent nature. The
formal political philosophy is one of nonalignment with the
major power blocs. Despite this, the vast majority of Nigeria's economic links are with Western countries, and in particular Britain and the US. Indeed some of the more important policy goals, such as the liberation of Southern Africa
and a change in the world's economic relations, necessitate
a continuing dialogue with these Western countries.

Some attempts have been made to diversify trade, notably
with Brazil and several East European countries, but these
relations are very limited. The Soviet Union won the favour
of the federal government during the civil war when it supplied Nigeria with arms and supplies after Western countries
were hamstrung by domestic Biafran lobbies. The continuance
of Soviet links is witnessed by the possession of Mig 21
fighters in the air force and the purchase in 1979 of T-55
combat tanks [52], as well as the assistance given for the
Ajaokuta plant. But despite the federal government's apparent attempts to maintain a non-committed posture in foreign
policy, it could not — and did not want to — prevent a
close association with Western countries. For example, in
1975 imports from the USSR were only 1 per cent of imports
from the UK [53]. In 1977 the government turned to the US
for $45.5 million worth of military helicopters [54], while
in 1979 the major construction contracts for the iron and
steel works went to West German companies rather than Soviet
ones. At the end of the 1970s exports to all countries with
centrally planned economies stood at less than 1 per cent of
total exports [55].

Throughout the two decades since independence, Nigeria's
ambivalent relations with the Western powers have been influenced by domestic considerations as well as events in the
external environment. The relative strength of the Nigerian
economy and the benefits to be gained from investments there
have led to competition between Western countries and companies for contracts, and so has allowed the federal government some freedom of manoeuvre between them. However the
vast majority of business remains with a limited number of
countries, of which the most important are the US and
Britain.

During the mid-1970s links with these two countries were
at a nadir. The Nixon-Ford years had displayed an American
disinterest in Africa, while Henry Kissinger's forays in
international diplomacy did nothing to alter the unfavourable image of the US. Britain, for its part, was denigrated
for being the power behind the Head of State, Yakubu Gowon,
before he was overthrown in 1975, and for being heavily im-
plicated in the assassination of Murtala Mohammed early in

1976, especially as Britain refused to allow extradition of
the refugee Gowon.

In the latter part of the 1970s a gradual thaw in relations took place. All three countries had reason to seek
better relations. For Nigeria, the country's development and
growth was largely dependent upon external assistance, particularly in construction and labour needs, and so there had
to be a continuing relationship with the West. The US and
the UK, for their part, had important economic reasons for
maintaining good links with Nigeria. In 1977 the US had
$1500 million invested in Nigeria, mostly in oil [56]. Im-
ports of oil stood at around one-eighth of total American
imported oil and with doubts always hanging over the Middle
East supplies Nigeria was a very important supplier. Nigeria
was also the country with which the largest trade debt existed and so the US hoped to push for greater exports there,
particularly in agricultural machinery [57]. For Britain,
Nigeria stood as the largest export market outside of the
developed world — the ninth largest in all — and the country with which the biggest trading surplus was recorded.
Furthermore there were over one hundred British companies
operating inside Nigeria [58].

Both Britain and the US realised the political importance
of Nigeria within Africa and so made moves to get back on
good terms with the country. In 1977 the new American President, Jimmy Carter, gave positive signs of the *rapprochement*
through his selection of Andrew Young, a black American, as
US Ambassador to the United Nations. Young's visit to
Nigeria early in 1977 laid the basis of an understanding
which allowed Carter to visit Nigeria early the following
year, the first visit to Africa by any American President
[59]. In between, Obasanjo's meeting with Carter in the US
in late 1977 helped to cement this friendship (see Chapter
3). The flying visit to Kano in September 1978 by British
Premier, James Callaghan, to discuss the Zimbabwe situation
with President Kaunda of Zambia and Nigerian officials left
little doubt that Nigeria was considered to be most influential within the continent [60].

The Zimbabwe issue during 1978 and 1979 proved to be a
major test both for the level of relations between Nigeria
and the West, as well as the country's ability to use its
economic strength as a means to bring a successful outcome
to the dispute. The Anglo-American initiatives on Zimbabwe
floated during 1978 were generally accepted by the federal
government which, although supporting the war waged by the
Patriotic Front, hoped for a constitutional conference to
bring all the nationalists together. The demise of the
Labour government in Britain early in 1979 and the appear-

ance of a hard-line Tory government under Mrs Margaret
Thatcher worried Nigerians who felt that there would be a
'sell-out' over Zimbabwe by the new British government.

In order to avert this possibility, the Nigerian government decided to use its economic strength to pressurise
Britain into not recognising the 'illegal' regime formed by
the internal settlement. As Britain was about the only state
heavily involved in Zimbabwe, it was possible to threaten
action against Britain without jeopardising relations with
other Western countries and without appearing too selective
in its policy which would have undermined the political rationale of the exercise.

The pressure put on Britain by the government increased
during 1979. Early in that year a consortium of three
British construction companies had its tender for a port
development project at Onne disallowed by the government.
The British government had tied £31 million in aid to this
project and so the rejection gave a warning to the British
[61]. In March and May, two South African oil tankers were
arrested in Nigerian waters and their cargoes confiscated.
The Nigerian government appeared serious in its attempts to
prevent ships coming from, or going to, South Africa and
British Petroleum, the company responsible, was punished by
the loss of 1.6 million barrels of oil and by the threat to
cut deliveries by up to 100,000 bpd from 1 August 1979 [62].

The full implications of the Bingham Report [63], showing
how BP in particular had managed to get around the sanctions on trade with Zimbabwe and supplied the rebels with
oil, were not lost on Nigeria. At the end of July, immediately prior to the Commonwealth Conference in Lusaka, the
government acted and nationalised BP's operations in Nigeria. This gave the maximum political gain for the lowest
economic dislocation, because BP was largely a sleeping
partner in Shell-BP operations and so production was not
impaired. The decision also allowed Nigeria to sell the oil
at world market prices which were higher than those agreed
with BP, although the government denied that this was the
intention [64]. The political effect was a stunning one in
that a major broadside was fired at Britain before the
Conference, so leaving nobody in doubt as to Nigeria's determination to stand beside the Patriotic Front and not
allow a 'sell-out' in Zimbabwe through the recognition of
Bishop Muzorewa's government.

It would be difficult to say with confidence that the
country's economic threats and actions caused a reversal of
British foreign policy, because Mrs Thatcher may well have
been contemplating a softening of Britain's approach to the
problem. Behind the scenes pressure from other Commonwealth

countries could also have influenced the British decision
[65]. What could be said is that Britain recognised that it
could not afford to lose its economic position in Nigeria to
other Western countries which were ready to step in [66].
The federal government showed that, even within a 'neo-
colonial' setting, it had some power to carry out its
threats and gave notice that it would be prepared at any
time in the future to use its economic resources to gain
leverage over Britain and the West in general concerning
South Africa.

News of the Nigerian success was well received within the
country and the continent at large. The government-owned New
Nigerian wrote in an editorial that 'the use of the oil weapon' had to be continued to ensure future successes in the
struggle for an independent Africa [67]. In September 1980,
prior to his first official visit to the US, President
Shagari reiterated Nigeria's willingness to use its oil weapon [68]. It would be wrong, however, to see Nigeria's influence as unlimited as this is clearly not the case. Despite the success of 1979, the last two years have not seen
corresponding gains for Nigerian diplomacy. The federal
government has been unable to bring any change in the Namibian question, for instance, nor has it been able to prevent
the continued subversion of the Angolan government by US-
supported groups.

There are several reasons which help to explain these
quiet two years. The US government, firstly under Carter and
then Ronald Reagan, has switched back to a global, rather
than regional, strategy concerning Africa and so the continent is merely seen as a bloc in terms of the renewed Cold
War with the USSR [69]. Such a perception heightens the need
for friendship with South Africa because of its strategic
importance, therefore relations with Nigeria are made more
difficult. The Nigerian government itself has not been
willing to force the pace of change in the continent. The
transfer of power from military to civilian rule has been a
delicate process and has absorbed the time of decision-
makers. Also there has been a desire to promote national
development, rather than worry too much about continental
aspirations. This has been especially so in 1981 with a depressed world market for oil and, consequently, potential
cash problems for Nigerian development programmes.

Nigerian decision-makers have generally been aware of the
country's limitations and necessities. So, for example, in
1978 the West German Chancellor, Helmut Schmidt, had bluntly
stated in Lagos that his country would not support the liberation movements in Southern Africa nor cut trade with the
Republic [70]. Despite this rebuff, Nigeria increased trade

with West Germany, as it did also with France [71]. Similarly, in 1978 Nigeria opened diplomatic relations with the
Shah's Iran, the major oil supplier to South Africa [72].
Since President Shagari took office the government has gone
out of its way to improve relations with Britain. In 1980
there was a flurry of official visits [73], while Shagari's
visit to London in March 1981 cemented this friendship [74].
Despite difficulties in getting the UK government to bend to
his wishes, Shagari threw open the door to increased trade
with Britain. Such a move showed the desire to promote
Nigeria's national development before other considerations,
as well as pointed to the continuation of the dependent
relationship with Britain.

CONCLUSION

This chapter has attempted to stimulate debate regarding the
nature and dynamism of Nigerian foreign policy. Both military and civilian governments have shown awareness of the
country's capability and, at times, have attempted to use
this strength to bring change in the international system.
The successes for Nigerian diplomacy have highlighted the
country's potential to play a dominant role in international
politics, but the fact that the economy remains a largely
dependent one has brought limitations to this role. The
government has been able to use its power directly to bring
positive results in some areas of foreign policy but in its
relations with the West, its greatest strength lies in the
denial of trade — oil to the US and imports from the UK.
  The effect of the dependent economy has been to prevent a
more dynamic foreign policy and this has often led to a
failure to achieve a specific goal pursued. This divergence
between the espoused and achieved goals has brought frustration and criticism. A New Nigerian editorial summing up the
1970s said: 'On the international scene, apart from our support for the MPLA and Angolan independence, there is nothing
to write home about. Foreign policy for about half of the
decade was characterised by flowery language, flamboyance
and much inaction' [75]. Another source summed up foreign
policy succinctly by saying that 'while Nigeria is clearly
becoming very influential, its diplomacy has yet to produce
any dramatic results' [76]. In July 1981 another editorial
in the New Nigerian spoke of 'the need to shake up our
foreign policy' to make it more effective [77]. One Nigerian
scholar has even criticised foreign policy for being too
reactionary and pro-Western, with its attempts at peace-
keeping in Chad, Western Sahara and the Ogaden, by trying to

hold back change in Liberia and Ghana, and by seeking a negotiated rather than revolutionary settlement in Zimbabwe
[78].

While all states allow pragmatic considerations to influence foreign policy, Nigeria could perhaps have a clearer
definition of its foreign policy goals and a more accurate
account of its strengths and weaknesses. In this way it
could set out to achieve the goals which were within its
capabilities. But perhaps the crucial test for Nigeria will
be in its continuing conflict with South Africa; the outcome
of this will best determine the relative strength of Nigeria
in the international system.

NOTES AND REFERENCES

1. The Constitution of the Federal Republic of Nigeria
   (Lagos: Government Printer, 1979), section 19.
2. See, for example, Olajide Aluko, 'Nigerian Foreign
   Policy' in Olajide Aluko (ed.), The Foreign Policies of
   African States (London: Hodder & Stoughton, 1977) pp.
   163–95; Gavin Williams and Terisa Turner, 'Nigeria' in
   John Dunn (ed.), West African States: Failure and Pro-
   mise: a Study in Comparative Politics (Cambridge Univer-
   sity Press, 1978) pp. 132–72; A. B. Akinyemi (ed.),
   Nigeria and the World: Readings in Nigerian Foreign
   Policy (Ibadan: Nigerian Institute of International
   Affairs/Oxford University Press, 1978); James O. Ojiako,
   13 Years of Military Rule (Lagos: Daily Times, 1979);
   Oyeleye Oyediran (ed.), Nigerian Government and Politics
   under Military Rule (London: Macmillan, 1979); David
   Williams, 'Nigeria: Political Developments' in Graham
   Hancock (ed.), Africa Guide 1980 (Saffron Walden: World
   of Information, 1979) pp. 283–94; I. A. Gambari, Party
   Politics and Foreign Policy: Nigeria Under the First
   Republic (Zaria: Ahmadu Bello University Press, 1980).
3. A. Bolaji Akinyemi, 'Mohammed/Obasanjo Foreign Policy'
   in Oyediran, Nigerian Government and Politics Under
   Military Rule, pp. 150–68.
4. In 1976, the then Head of State, Lt.-Gen. Olusegun
   Obasanjo, outlined his goals in a major speech; see
   Joseph Wayas, Nigeria's Leadership Role in Africa
   (London: Macmillan, 1979) p. 20.
5. FESTAC, the Second World Black and African Festival of
   Arts and Culture, cost the country ₦141 million and
   was criticised by some for the expense.

6. *Africa*, 106, June 1980, pp. 13-19.
7. Terisa Turner, 'Commercial Capitalism and the 1975 Coup' in Keith Panter-Brick (ed.), *Soldiers and Oil: the Political Transformation of Nigeria* (London: Frank Cass, 1978) pp. 166-97; Gavin Williams (ed.), *Nigeria: Economy and Society* (London: Rex Collings, 1976).
8. S. O. Olayide (ed.), *Economic Survey of Nigeria (1960-1975)* (Ibadan: Aromolaran, 1976) pp. 24-5.
9. *Quarterly Economic Review of Nigeria: 2nd Quarter 1980* (London: Economist Intelligence Unit, 1980) p. 17.
10. Ibid. Also *New Nigerian* (Kaduna), 22 November 1979.
11. Colin Legum (ed.), *Africa Contemporary Record 1977-78* (New York: Africana, 1979) B753.
12. *Quarterly Economic Review of Nigeria: 2nd Quarter 1980*, p. 15.
13. Alan Rake (ed.), *New African Yearbook 1978* (London: International Communications, 1978) p. 199.
14. For the President's full statement upon setting up the official enquiry see *New Nigerian*, 17 April 1980; also, Eddie Iroh, 'The "Oil-gate" Scandal', *Africa*, 107, July 1980, pp. 39-41. As a result of the findings, Nigeria challenged oil corporations to pay for the 'lost' oil: 'Nigeria vs the Oil Majors', *Newsweek*, 25 August 1980, p. 37. For a general discussion of the Nigerian oil business see Turner, 'Commercial Capitalism and the 1975 Coup'.
15. *Quarterly Economic Review of Nigeria: Annual Supplement 1979* (London: Economist Intelligence Unit, 1979) p. 12.
16. Legum, *Africa Contemporary Record*, B759; Rake, *New African Yearbook*, p. 199.
17. '... the exploitation of iron is yet to be started as some outside interests appear to be delaying the start of an iron and steel industry.' This laconic statement is made in Olayide (ed.), *Economic Survey of Nigeria*, p. 74.
18. *New Nigerian*, 24 May 1980. The Minister resigned from the government shortly after on a separate issue, *New Nigerian*, 2 September 1980. The original agreement with the USSR was signed back in 1968; for a discussion see Guy Arnold, *Modern Nigeria* (London: Longman, 1977) pp. 156-60.
19. *Quarterly Economic Review of Nigeria: Annual Supplement 1979*, p. 6.
20. *New Nigerian*, 6 October 1978.
21. KLM's contract is for two years, which is one year less than that of Rail India.

22. <u>World Development Report</u> 1980 (New York: International Bank for Reconstruction and Development/Oxford University Press, 1980) p. 110. See also Christopher Stevens, 'Nigeria: Economic Survey' in Hancock (ed.), <u>Africa Guide</u>, pp. 295–320.

23. In June 1981 the minimum monthly wage was fixed at ₦125. The union leaders were accused of leading the country to fascism by forcing these demands; see an editorial in the <u>New Nigerian</u>, 22 June 1981.

24. The deficit in 1978 was $2.4 billion; see <u>Quarterly Economic Review of Nigeria: 1st Quarter 1980</u> (London: Economist Intelligence Unit, 1980) p. 19. In the 1970s Nigeria's average annual growth rate for imports stood at 25 per cent, a figure only beaten by two countries in the world; see <u>World Development Report 1980</u>, pp. 124–5.

25. E. O. Akeredolu-Ale, 'Private Foreign Investment and the Underdevelopment of Indigenous Entrepreneurship in Nigeria', in Williams (ed.), <u>Nigeria: Economy and Society</u>, pp. 106–22. For some comparative work on Kenya see Colin Leys, <u>Underdevelopment in Kenya: the Political Economy of Neo-Colonialism 1964–1971</u> (London: Heinemann, 1975).

26. Turner, 'Commercial Capitalism and the 1975 Coup'.

27. <u>New Nigerian</u>, 9 January 1980.

28. Ibid., 26 January 1980.

29. Ibid., 26 July 1980.

30. For useful summaries of the Musa impeachment see <u>West Africa</u>, 6 July 1981 and <u>Times International</u> (Lagos), 6 July 1981.

31. New Nigerian, 13 July 1981.

32. Ibid., 30 April 1980. Also, 'Focus on Nigeria', <u>New African</u>, 152, April 1980, pp. 55–79. Awolowo was himself highly embarrassed by the exposure of his ownership of large areas of prime land on Victoria Island, Lagos; 'The Awo Land Uproar', <u>Africa</u>, 107, July 1980, pp. 33–5.

33. <u>New Nigerian</u>, 19 April 1980.

34. <u>The Military Balance 1980–1981</u> (London: International Institute for Strategic Studies, 1980) pp. 53–4.

35. <u>New Nigerian</u>, 28 June 1980.

36. <u>The Punch</u> (Lagos), 2 July 1981.

37. 'South Africa's Military Buildup', <u>Newsweek</u>, 29 September 1980, pp. 12–19; on South Africa's potential nuclear capability see Martin Walker, 'What Went Bump in the Night?', <u>Guardian</u>, 2 October 1980. Also, Robert S. Jaster, <u>South Africa's Narrowing Security Options</u>, Adelphi Paper no. 159 (London: International Institute for Strategic Studies, 1980).

　　In September 1980, South Africa's total mobilisable force was put at 404,500 with 204 combat aircraft,

compared with 146,000 men and 21 combat aircraft for Nigeria; The Military Balance 1980-1981, pp. 53-5.
For an in-depth analysis of Nigeria's military pre-paredness see New Times (Lagos), special edition, end-January/mid-February 1981.

38. The Military Balance 1979-1980 (London: International Institute for Strategic Studies, 1979) p. 106.

39. This is discussed in I. William Zartman, 'Africa' in J. Rosenau, K. W. Thompson and G. Boyd (eds), World Politics (New York: Free Press, 1976) p. 571.

40. Ibid., p. 573. See also Dennis Austin, Politics in Africa (Manchester University Press, 1978) pp. 48-9.

41. For example, Leopold Senghor had always called for the inclusion of Zaire in ECOWAS to offset Nigeria's domi-nance; see Okon Udokang, 'Nigeria and ECOWAS: Economic and Political Implications of Regional Integration' in Akinyemi (ed.), Nigeria and the World, pp. 57-81. Also see Bolaji Akinyemi, 'French Policy in Africa and the Cameroun Issue', New Nigerian, 16 June 1981.

42. Wayas, Nigeria's Leadership Role in Africa, p. 46.

43. 'Defence Pact Fears', Africa, 107, July 1980, pp. 35-6. For views within Nigeria following the agreement to establish the force in 1981 see West Africa, 6 July 1981, p. 1555.

44. New Nigerian, 11 January 1980. The country also sent ₦10 million to Zimbabwe in April 1980 to help personnel training, New Nigerian, 21 April 1980. For details of other aid given see Arnold, Modern Nigeria, p. 139; and Austin, Politics in Africa, p. 49.

45. Williams and Turner, 'Nigeria'.

46. Daily Times (Lagos), 22 June 1979.

47. Afrique (London), 26, August 1979, p. 10.

48. New Nigerian, 29 May 1980. Also, 'OAU: House Politics and Issues Beyond', Africa, 107, July 1980, pp. 18-22.

49. Olufemi Fajana, 'Nigeria's Inter-African Economic Relations: Trends, Problems and Prospects' in Akinyemi (ed.), Nigeria and the World, pp. 17-31.

50. New Nigerian, 31 October 1977 and 6 December 1977.

51. The Europa Yearbook 1978: a World Survey (London: Europa, 1978), vol. 2, pp. 1091-2.

52. West Africa, 22 October 1979, p. 1963. The order was allegedly for 100 tanks, but only 64 were delivered.

53. The Europa Yearbook 1978.

54. Olajide Aluko, 'Nigeria, the United States and Southern Africa', African Affairs, 78 (310), January 1979, p. 97.

55. World Development Report 1980, pp. 130-3.

56. Aluko, 'Nigeria, the United States and Southern Africa', p. 96.

57. An agricultural agreement was signed in July 1980; New Nigerian, 24 July 1980.

58. Quarterly Economic Review of Nigeria: 3rd Quarter 1979 (London: Economist Intelligence Unit, 1979) p. 3.

59. Aluko, 'Nigeria, the United States and Southern Africa', pp. 91-102; Oye Ogunbadejo, 'A New Turn in US-Nigerian Relations', World Today, 35 (3), March 1979, pp. 117-26; Richard H. Ullman, 'Salvaging America's Rhodesian Policy', Foreign Affairs, 57 (5), Summer 1979, pp. 1111-22.

60. New Nigerian, 22 September 1978.

61. Quarterly Economic Review of Nigeria: 3rd Quarter 1979, p. 6.

62. Ibid., p. 17.

63. T. H. Bingham and S. M. Gray, Report on the Supply of Petroleum and Petroleum Products to Rhodesia (London: HMSO, 1978).

64. New Nigerian, 9 August 1979; Observer, 5 August 1979.

65. Derek Ingram, 'Behind the Scenes at Lusaka', Commonwealth, October-November 1979, pp. 3-5.

66. For example, Japan was quickly in to buy the oil but Nigeria said it was for the Third World.

67. New Nigerian, 13 August 1979. The 'oil weapon' had been used in similar circumstances in Angola in 1976 when Gulf Oil defended its payments to the MPLA government on the grounds that if it did not pay then Nigeria would retaliate by blocking its access to Nigerian markets; see Terisa Turner, 'Energy in Africa' in Richard Synge (ed.), Africa Guide 1978 (Saffron Walden: Africa Guide, 1977) p. 32.

68. 'Wielding Africa's Oil Weapon', Time, 6 October 1980.

69. David Ottoway, 'Africa: US Policy Eclipse' in William P. Bundy (ed.), Foreign Affairs: America and the World 1979 (New York: Pergamon, 1980) pp. 637-58. For an earlier discussion of America's need to seek better relations with Nigeria see Jean Herskovits, 'Nigeria: Africa's New Power', Foreign Affairs, 53 (2), January 1975, pp. 314-33.

70. New Nigerian, 29 June 1978.

71. Ibid., 6 March 1978.

72. Legum, Africa Contemporary Record, B752.

73. In January 1980 Britain's exports to Nigeria were 43 per cent up on January 1979. For the year of 1979 Britain's exports to Nigeria totalled £636 million, but were expected to top £1 billion in 1980, equivalent to 20 per cent of UK's total exports; see Quarterly Economic Review of Nigeria: 2nd Quarter 1980, p. 18; also Enukora Joe Okoli, 'Mending Anglo-Nigerian Fences', West Africa, 28 July 1980, pp. 1373-5.

74. West Africa, 30 March 1981; New Times, March 1981;
    Shagari in UK (Lagos: Times Press, 1981).
75. New Nigerian, 1 January 1980.
76. Quarterly Economic Review of Nigeria: Annual Supplement
    1979, p. 6.
77. New Nigerian, 2 July 1981.
78. Yusufu Bala Usman, For the Liberation of Nigeria
    (London: New Beacon, 1979) pp. 135-98.

Part II
Alternative Projections for Nigerian Foreign Policy

7 Indigenisation in Nigeria: Renationalisation or Denationalisation?

THOMAS J. BIERSTEKER

During the 1970s there has been a growth in the role of the state and an assertion of economic nationalism throughout Africa. As in the rest of the developing world, most national states have increasingly taken on regulative, welfare and planning functions, and the state has become a major (if not *the* major) economic actor in many countries [1]. At the same time, policies of economic nationalism (nationalisation and indigenisation) have become widespread in Africa and most host-countries have levied increasingly stringent regulations on the operations of foreign firms [2].

Both the growing role of the state and the assertion of economic nationalism have taken place in an international environment characterised by the breakdown of the post-Second World War hegemonial dominance of the United States [3]. The convergence of these interrelated trends has created both new policy opportunities and the appearance of a real change in the position of many poor countries in the world economy. This is especially true with regard to the relationship between transnational corporations and the state in the Third World. The growth of state involvement in the national economy and the increase in the frequency and extent of regulations affecting foreign firms have created the impression that it is the transnational corporation, rather than the nation-state, that is increasingly 'at bay' in the contemporary world economy.

Nigeria appears to be no exception to these global trends. As a member of OPEC, it has been at the forefront of the confrontation with the transnational corporation. It has relied on this experience in its expansion of state involvement in the economy, notably in the petroleum and related petro-chemical sectors. Direct state involvement has also increased in other areas of the economy as well (notably in mining, utilities, banking, insurance, vehicle assembly and agriculture). Although Nigeria has historically offered potential investors a number of investment incentives, a basic objective of its foreign investment policy since the end of the civil war in 1970 has been to increase indigenous control over economic activities (see Chapter eight). There have been recurring pressures for the indigenisation of personnel, and later, of share capital in virtually every foreign company operating in the country [4]. There have also been intermittent, but significant, limitations placed on the repatriation of profits and dividends from Nigeria.

A closer examination of the sources of and responses to Nigeria's indigenisation programme provides an illustration of the extent to which its growth of state power and assertion of economic nationalism may prove illusory however. Rather than increasing national control over its economy, Nigeria's indigenisation exercise may actually have reduced it.

SOURCES AND OBJECTIVES OF INDIGENISATION

Although Nigeria's most far-reaching and controversial indigenisation decrees were promulgated during the 1970s, there is a long history of indigenisation pressures in the country. Proposals for increasing Nigerianisation of the economy were first incorporated in official policy statements describing investment opportunities for potential investors during the late 1950s. A national committee to promote the Nigerianisation of business enterprises was created by the colonial government in 1956 [5]. The 1958 Tax Relief Act required transnational corporations seeking 'pioneer' company status both to increase Nigerian ownership and personnel, and to use Nigerian materials in production. However it was not until after independence that significant legislation was passed. After being supported in principle in both the first national development plan and in a 1961 House of Representatives resolution, provisions for increasing Nigerianisation were codified into law in the 1963 Immigration Laws. The rather stringent set of controls and regulations established quotas for expatriates working for newly established transnational corporations and were designed to increase Nigerian participation in the highest levels of management.

There has been a broad base of popular support for any assertion of economic nationalism in Nigeria since independence was attained in 1960. Indigenisation has been justified as a response to popular pressures and public support has consistently been mobilised in defence of the exercise. However it would be misleading and inaccurate to suggest that indigenisation has been pursued as a response to broad-based public pressures. Such a response would imply a commitment to an egalitarianism that was neither a central motive nor objective of the indigenisation exercise [6].

On the contrary, from the time of its inception during the 1950s the indigenisation process in Nigeria has stemmed from two primary sources, with different and occasionally contradictory objectives. Indigenisation has been instituted by an amenable military élite in response to intermittent but recurring pressures from an indigenous economic élite. Nigerian businessmen had been agitating for protection against competition from foreigners in the distributive trade since the late 1950s [7]. This agitation became more insistent during the six years of civilian rule after independence in 1960 [8]. It was not until after the Nigerian civil war, however, that indigenous businessmen found a Nigerian government with the willingness and ability to carry out a more comprehensive indigenisation programme.

The federal military government had experienced the consequences of excessive reliance on foreign governments and transnational corporations during the Nigerian civil war. The indecision of transnational oil companies about whether to make payments to the federal government or the Biafran government had a significant impact on the military rulers and created serious doubts about whether transnationals could be trusted [9]. The civil war also encouraged the growth of state involvement in the economy to manage the war effort. The general strengthening of the state increased its confidence against foreign involvement in the Nigerian economy.

The civil war also fostered the rise of a new bourgeoisie who accumulated 'easy wealth' by supplying equipment and war material to both the Biafran and federal governments. Since this bourgeoisie did not owe its wealth to foreigners, it could afford to fan the flames of popular nationalism and put pressure on the state to Nigerianise the economy after the war [10]. There is a great deal of evidence that indigenous businessmen applied increasing pressure on the federal military government for an indigenisation programme during this period. Alhaji Aminu Dantata, Kano State Commissioner for Trade and Industry in 1972, commented that 'by promulgating the decree the Federal Government has done what businessmen themselves wanted so badly for several years past'. P. C. Asiodu, former Minister of Mines and Power, suggested that 'it was in the period between 1968 and 1971 that the widest consultations were undertaken leading to the promulgation of the Enterprise Promotion Decree of 1972'.

The influence of these pressures on a military élite

increasingly distrustful of foreign capital led to the announcement of the Nigerian Enterprises Promotion Decree in
1972. The central objectives of the 1972 decree reflected
the dual sources of support for indigenisation from the
government and local business community. The central objective of the federal military government was to obtain
Nigerian control over the economy in general, and over
strategic enterprises in particular. Former Head of State,
Yakubu Gowon, described the objective of the decree as
'consolidating our political independence' and many observers have viewed it as an assertion of economic nationalism
or an anti-dependency measure in response to the civil war
experience. Paul Collins maintains that the decree was meant
to give Nigerians greater involvement in economic and commercial affairs [11]. In mid-1972 the Federal Commissioner
for Trade said the goal of indigenisation was to 'make the
country's economy truly Nigerian' [12], and E. O. Akeredolu-
Alu has suggested that indigenisation was inspired by a desire to reduce Nigeria's external dependence [13].

At the same time, local businessmen wanted a protected
niche in the economy free from foreign competition and a
share of the proceeds of the most successful (foreign-domi-
nated) sectors of the economy. Both of these objectives were
consistent with the federal military government's objectives
of increased national control over the Nigerian economy.
Sule Kolo, Nigeria's High Commissioner to the United Kingdom
in 1972, commented that the indigenisation decree was aimed
at small expatriate concerns in trade and services which
'excite resentment among rival indigenous enterprises' [14].
Accordingly, much of the pressure from Nigerian businessmen
in 1972 was directed mainly against the Lebanese-controlled
commerce and retail sector [15]. This explains why these
commercial activities were reserved for 100 per cent local
participation, while many of the largest European and North
American-based transnationals were not at all affected by
the different schedules established in the 1972 decree.

The 1972 Nigerian Enterprise Promotion Decree stipulated
that, by March 1974, no person other than a Nigerian citizen
could be the owner or part-owner of enterprises in twenty-
two selected industries in Nigeria (called Schedule I industries). The industries affected included small, labour-
intensive manufacturing and local service-related enterprises, many of which were already predominantly Nigerian in
1972. The 1972 decree also stipulated that aliens could not
participate in thirty-three other industries (called Schedule II industries), where the paid-up share capital of the
enterprises was less than ₦200,000 or the turnover of the
enterprise was less than ₦500,000, whichever the Nigerian

Enterprises Promotion Board (NEPB) deemed appropriate. The NEPB was granted sweeping discretionary powers to administer the decree's provisions.

Enterprises exempted on the basis of their size were required to make available to the Nigerian public up to 40 per cent of their total equity. The businesses in this second schedule included construction firms, some large import substitution industries, and wholesale and retail distributors. Because of the 1972 decree's exemption of large-scale enterprises in its Schedule II list of industries, most transnational corporations were not required to make available more than 40 per cent of their total equity to the Nigerian public. A great number of Nigeria's largest and most important manufacturing industries (tobacco and textiles, for example) were completely unaffected by the 1972 decree.

The release of a government White Paper on the implementation of the decree in 1975 revealed that only one-third of the affected enterprises had complied fully with the decree's provisions. Thereafter, pressures for increased indigenisation came to a head. The new Obasanjo government responded in less than a year with an extension of the 1972 decree, first announced in June 1976 and formally promulgated in January 1977. The Nigerian Enterprises Promotion Decree of 1977 reorganised the Board responsible for implementing the decree and increased its discretionary powers to inspect enterprises, conduct prosecutions and seal up the premises of offending enterprises. In addition, twenty new industries were added to the list of Schedule I industries to be completely indigenised in ownership. Among those industries added were the wholesale distributors of local manufactures and other locally produced goods, major retail stores with an annual turnover of less than ₦2,000,000 ($3.3 million), commercial agents such as manufacturers' representatives and most commercial transportation companies. Thirty-three new industries were added to the second schedule, and the mandatory sale of shares raised from 40 to 60 per cent. Among the most significant of the new activities added were banking (commercial, merchant and development banks), insurance, shipping agencies, food manufacture, basic iron and steel manufacture, and petro-chemical industries. A third schedule was added to the revised decree which listed all remaining industries and required that they make available 40 per cent of their equity to Nigerian subscribers. The Schedule III enterprises include the largest transnationals in tobacco concerns and textile firms, previously exempted from indigenisation, as well as high-technology enterprises. Thus at present, only enterprises engaged in single, non-renewable projects are exempt from indigenisation. All other enterprises are required to make at least part of their equity (a minimum of 40 per cent) available to Nigerian subscribers. Thus the 1977 decree clearly contains more far-reaching and stringent regulations than the 1972 version of the decree which exempted most of the largest and most important transnational corporations.

The extension of the indigenisation decree in 1977 once again reflects the dual sources and changing objectives of the military and business élites in Nigeria. The Obasanjo government of the late 1970s was more strongly committed to an ideology of economic nationalism than their predecessors in the Gowon government [16]. Accordingly, the revised de- cree was quite explicit about the desire to obtain control over important aspects of production. Included among the basic objectives of the 1977 decree are 'to advance and promote enterprises in which citizens of Nigeria *shall participate fully* (italics added) and play a dominant role' and 'ensur- ing the assumption of the control of the Nigerian economy by Nigerians in the shortest possible time' [17].

In addition to being explicit about its objectives, the Nigerian government appears to be serious about its inten- tion to obtain control over important aspects of production. Indigenisation is the most prominent component of Nigeria's foreign investment policy and there is no evidence of either internal bureaucratic opposition to the decree or a tendency to trade off compliance with indigenisation for other ('more important') concessions from transnational corporations.

Having already reserved a protected niche for commercial and low-technology activities in the 1972 decree, indigenous business modified its objectives and pressed for a larger share of the proceeds of foreign enterprises located throughout the economy with the extension of the decree in 1977. Since most of the share capital offered by transna- tional corporations in 1972 was heavily oversubscribed, the 1977 extension of the indigenisation programme offered in- vestment opportunities for businessmen left out of the original exercise. It also provided investment opportunities for Nigeria's newest economic élite developing around the oil boom during the mid- and late-1970s.

These objectives were broadly consistent with, but more limited than, those of the federal military government in 1977. While the central objective of the governmental decree was control of the economy and full participation by Nige- rians, some of the strongest backers of indigenisation among Nigeria's economic élite were more interested in a share in the proceeds of the economy than control of the economy. Some indigenous businessmen have expressed concern about the growth of public sector (state) acquisitions during indige-

nisation, reflecting an uneasiness in the alliance between
the state and local capital in Nigeria [18]. When this divergence of objectives is accompanied by a sophisticated
array of transnational corporate responses to indigenisation, the programme can be effectively neutralised.

RESPONSES TO INDIGENISATION

Nigeria appears to be a model case of the growth of the
state and an assertion of economic nationalism. It is frequently cited as an illustration of these phenomena [19].
The state is gradually assuming a greater role in economic
activities, the number of state corporations is growing,
more stringent regulations affecting the transnational corporation have been enacted over time, and a majority of
the equity of new operations is being acquired by the state
and indigenous local investors. Not only has there been a
marked increase in the frequency of state actions designed
to control the operations of transnational corporations
since 1970, but these actions give the appearance of being
increasingly effective. According to official government
reports, 1858 firms have complied with indigenisation requirements since 1972, selling over 500 million shares
valued at more than 472 million naira (more than $800 mil-
lion). There have been very few instances of overt conflict
between transnationals and the Nigerian government [20],
and virtually every transnational operating in Nigeria has
complied with the equity sharing requirements of the recent
decrees. In addition, Nigeria appears to fit the model of a
gradual and incremental shift in the balance of bargaining
power in the direction of a host country. Its successive
indigenisation decrees have required a gradual increase in
the number of economic activities affected, as well as in
the amount of equity that must be shared with local capital.
  Despite this apparent growth of state power, transnational
corporations are still quite eager to invest in Nigeria.
The 'gold rush' of the mid-1970s, when foreign investors
could recover their entire investment in one or two years,
is over. However most foreign executives currently working
in the country maintain that there is ample room for new
firms not interested in a quick return, but in a longer-term
profitable investment in one of the fastest growing markets
in the world. Only two of the hundreds of large, transnational corporations operating in the country have chosen an
'exit' option, and pulled out of Nigeria as a result of its
increasing demands on foreign operations. And a number of
the largest transnational corporations in the world not

already operating in Nigeria are contemplating direct investments there. New foreign capital has continued to flow into Nigeria at an annual average of $331 million during the 1970s. It increased from $305 million to $377 million after the 1972 indigenisation decree, but declined to around $200 million immediately after the 1977 decree. It has risen even further in the wake of the return to civilian rule in October 1979, to a total of $595 million in 1980 [21].

Why should transnational corporations be so eager to invest in a country in which the state is imposing increasingly stringent controls on their operations? The explanation of this apparent paradox is that transnational corporations are not yielding managerial control. The sharing of equity directed in Nigeria's indigenisation effort is not equivalent to the sharing of control in the newly established joint ventures. Virtually every transnational corporation involved in Nigeria has found ways to neutralise the indigenisation requirements. The specific strategy or combination of strategies varies from firm to firm. However they are all designed to ensure a minimal loss of control over the operations. Transnational corporations either (1) fight to retain a majority of the equity, or (2) find ways to retain control with a minority share of the equity.

This conclusion is based on detailed interviews conducted during July and August of 1979 with senior executives of twenty-three of the largest transnational corporations operating in Nigeria [22]. When asked to characterise the outcome of the indigenisation process, not a single one of the executives of the thirteen firms in the sample which were reduced to a minority equity shareholding position was concerned about having lost managerial control over their Nigerian operations. A few minor changes had taken place since indigenisation (more expenditure on housing schemes and other employee benefits, for example). However there was virtually no concern expressed when asked specifically about loss of control over day-to-day operations. Several company executives said they would not stay in Nigeria if they were to lose control over their investments. At least eight of the remaining ten firms in the sample should have yielded a majority of their equity to Nigerian subscribers according to the 1977 decree, yet have managed to obtain exemptions (or find other ways) to avoid becoming minority shareholders.

There are as many different strategies to avoid losing control as there are transnational corporations investing in Nigeria. Only a handful of the major transnational corporations have chosen 'exit' or 'voice' options as responses to

Nigerian indigenisation, often with deleterious consequences, as Citibank and American International Insurance have discovered. Most have chosen a variety of other options, ranging from benignly legal strategies to blatantly illegal ones. Most of the transnational corporations choosing to remain in Nigeria have employed one or a combination of several of the following strategies to ensure that Nigeria's indigenisation programme will not alter control of their operations.

Public Sale of Shares

Several executives explained how they encouraged the public sale of their share capital to ensure that there would be no single indigenous subscriber with a bloc of shares comparable to the 40 per cent retained by the transnational corporation. As one executive advised: 'Once you've made the decision to go public, spread your shares as widely as possible.' Another added, 'the broader the distribution, the easier it is to control the operation'. In part, this strategy was unintentionally encouraged by the 1977 Indigenisation Decree which attempted to prevent the huge concentrations of shareholding among a small number of Nigerians that had accompanied the 1972 decree. The transnationals most likely to favour this strategy include the most visible and best-known manufacturing firms with a long-term presence in Nigeria. Manufacturers of well-known consumer products are most likely to attract a broad range of shareholders necessary for the effectiveness of this strategy.

Technical Services Agreements

A second way for minority partners to retain control over their Nigerian operations is to negotiate a technical services agreement with their Nigerian partners which provides the transnational with responsibility for technology choice, maintenance and innovation. Agreements for the training of personnel can also ensure that the structure and standard operating procedures of the former transnational remain unchanged. As one executive confidently responded to a question about his parent firm's ability to control its Nigerian operation with only 40 per cent of the equity: 'It's because of our technical expertise ... We still train all the managers.' The negotiation of technical service arrangements is becoming an increasingly important aspect of the changing bargaining relationship between states and transnational corporations. This strategy is particularly prevalent among large, transnational banks and manufacturers engaged in high-technology activities.

Negotiate Exemptions

A number of transnational corporations have simply tried to negotiate themselves into exemptions from certain of the requirements of the indigenisation decrees. Many have negotiated extensions for compliance with the provisions of the 1972 and 1977 decrees. Others have negotiated themselves into different schedules (requiring less of a commitment of capital to local subscribers, 40 per cent as opposed to 60 per cent). Some have negotiated complete exemptions from the indigenisation decrees altogether. One executive commented: 'This is a beautiful place for business, because everyone keeps talking ... everything is in flux, everything is negotiable. That's why you need a hustler, an expeditor.'

Transnationals in the oil industry, and those operating in industries with very little international competition, have found it easiest to negotiate exemptions. Companies involved in one-time contractual arrangements with the government also rely on negotiating exemptions. As one executive described his negotiation with government officials: 'I told them, you either want the product or you don't. Don't force the issue.' He complained that indigenisation would disrupt the tight schedule the government had imposed on the project and was granted an exemption from indigenisation in his firm's contract. Although this strategy has worked for transnationals in oil, for those with few competitors or for those receiving government contracts, it has not been as successful when attempted by large, diversified manufacturing firms or by insurance companies.

Two-Company Strategy

Many of the larger, diversified manufacturing transnationals in Nigeria have responded to indigenisation with a two-company formula. Since the Nigerian government has classified economic activities into categories (or schedules) requiring 40, 60 and 100 per cent local equity participation, diversified manufacturers have similarly divided their own operations. They have completely sold any subsidiaries requiring 100 per cent local participation and have formed two subsidiaries for their remaining product lines or economic activities. In one subsidiary, the transnational retains 60 per cent of the equity and organises the production for the products assigned to this category (or schedule) by the indigenisation decree. The economic activities in which transnational capital is restricted to 40 per cent are

organised in a second subsidiary in which local capital has
60 per cent of the shares.

In this way the transnational corporation retains uninhib-
ited control over all of its product lines assigned to the
subsidiary in which it holds 60 per cent of the shares.
Control is exercised over the other subsidiary in several
ways. The two subsidiaries are usually established with
identical organisational structures — and often have overlapping memberships on their boards of directors. In most
instances the same indigenous partners hold the local equity
in each of the subsidiary companies. It is not unusual for
the subsidiary in which the transnational holds the minority
equity to negotiate a technical services agreement with the
subsidiary in which it holds majority equity. Often the two
companies exist almost exclusively on paper. Only one factory is constructed, with one administrative building containing two incorporated companies. The physical proximity
of the two companies (usually across the hall) also facilitates control over the subsidiary in which the transnational
holds only 40 per cent of the equity.

In most 'two-company' arrangements, the subsidiary in
which the transnational has a minority equity position man-
ages the distribution, sales, and servicing for the products
produced by the other subsidiary. The two-company strategy
can also provide other benefits in addition to retaining
control for transnationals. According to one executive: 'It
also facilitates splitting government contracts between the
two companies, thus minimising our Nigerian tax liability in
respect of such contracts.'

Fronting

'Fronting' generally refers to the placing of Nigerians in
positions of apparent ownership or responsibility, when in
fact they are only operating as cosmetic 'fronts' to provide
legitimacy for the continued presence and dominance of
foreign capital. Such overt instances of 'fronting' are
specifically prohibited by the 1977 indigenisation decree
and are relatively rare. Less overt forms of fronting are,
however, much more common.

In their efforts to retain control over their operations
in Nigeria, most transnational corporations search for local
partners and managers who conform to their business interests and standard procedures. This makes good business sense
for the transnational corporations, because it minimises
local conflicts. Critics of the transnationals describe this
phenomenon as the grooming of a 'comprador élite', whose
primary allegiance is to the interests of international

capital. With either interpretation, it is a modified form
of fronting whenever it is deliberately employed by transnationals to retain control over the operations in which
they have been reduced to a minority equity position.

Most foreign executives advise potential investors in
Nigeria to take care to choose the 'right' local partners.
One emphasised the importance of 'making the right selection', while another recommended that new ventures should
look for 'sensible' directors. One pragmatic American executive summed up his company's policy as one 'looking for non-
controversial people with money'. An oil company executive
provided a more detailed recommendation: 'Make investments
with the most powerful people (not so that they control
operations ... so that they can provide access). It's important to spread your risk. This [Nigeria] is the most corrupt
country in the world ... therefore, it's necessary to buy
protection.'

Several foreign executives commented that they deliberately have 'no management role by their board of directors'.
One company memorandum assigned specific weights to the
contributions it expected from its local partners. The financial resources and the political clout and connections
of the local partners were valued most highly and each
assigned a weight of 40 per cent. Within the remaining 20
per cent, the management ability and knowledge about manufacturing were least valued and each assigned a weighting
value of only 2 per cent.

Similar procedures are employed in the selection of local
managers by transnational corporations. Choosing the 'right'
local managers for the firm often involves grooming them in
the training programmes offered by transnational companies
and 'bringing them up through the ranks'. Unlike their local
partners, local managers often have to be trained to be sure
they share the transnational's business objectives and conform to their standard operating procedures. To ensure that
the Nigerian managers exert very little influence over company policy, they are often given virtually no management
responsibilities.

Another way to ensure that local managers or partners
serve as no serious threat to the control of indigenised
firms is to make them personally dependent on their foreign
partners. Transnational corporations can accomplish this by
guaranteeing the bank loans required by their local partners
to buy into the company. Some firms even go as far as making
contractual agreements with their Nigerian partners guaranteeing that commercial, financial and technical management
is the responsibility of the transnational corporation, that
the managing director is appointed by the foreign partner,

that the use of the transnational's trademark can be dis-
continued at any time at its request and even that the company can be liquidated, if the transnational loses control
of the management.

Change Voting Rules

A much less subtle, but still legal, way to maintain control
over a subsidiary is to change its voting rules. Several
transnational firms have made changes in their company char-
ters prior to indigenisation which ensure that no important
policy changes can be made without their support after they
have sold a majority of the equity to local subscribers. The
usual formula is to raise the number of votes required for
passage of any major motions from a simple majority to two-
thirds or three-fourths. As one executive described his company's policy: 'We don't want to give the control of the
company to Nigeria at the present time. The company can
write voting rules any way it wants.' An internal memorandum
from another transnational corporation was equally explicit.
It identified a number of measures to ensure that it would
retain 'a suitable measure of control over its investment'.
Among them were proposals to amend the Articles of Association (i.e. charter) of its Nigerian subsidiary 'so that no
decision can be taken without (our) consent, i.e. two-thirds
or three-quarters majority required' in the company's general meeting. The Articles were to be similarly amended for
board meetings 'so that all decisions require the affirmative vote of at least one of the non-resident ... appointed
directors, i.e. affirmative vote of six directors'.
   A variant of this strategy is to change company standard
operating procedures in ways that minimise the prospects for
Nigerian influence in management. For example, one company
simply began to hold fewer board meetings after indigenisation and shifted many of its important decisions to other
branches of the firm.

Divide the Board

A somewhat more malicious, but still legal, strategy for
maintaining control is to select board members from different ethnic groups with the hope that disputes between them
will distract them from trying to manage the company. This
is not a very widely employed strategy. Only one of the
twenty-three firms interviewed suggested that it was able to
retain control by neutralising its indigenous board members,
'playing Hausas and Yorubas against each other'. Most transnational corporations select board members from all regions

of Nigeria, but they do so in self-defence, to ensure that
they are not closely identified with a single ethnic group
in the country.

Add Extra Expatriates

Among the illegal strategies occasionally employed by transnationals in their efforts to retain control is the addition
of expatriate employees without official work permits to key
positions of the firm. The Nigerian government specifies
strict expatriate quotas for each foreign investment, and
most transnationals do not exceed them by bringing in expatriate employees on tourist or other visas that explicitly
prohibit accepting employment in the country. However there
are ways around the expatriate quotas for large, diversified
investors. One transnational corporation obtained permission
to sponsor what it claimed were 'necessary', but were in
fact 'redundant', expatriate employees for one of its subsidiaries in Nigeria where it has majority control of the
equity. Once these expatriates were in the country, they
were simply transferred to another subsidiary of the same
transnational where it held only a minority of the equity.

Bribing

When asked about the extensiveness of bribery in Nigeria,
one senior executive replied: 'Any successful business is a
dirty operation.' Bribery certainly is widespread in
Nigeria, particularly in the granting of large, multi-
million dollar contracts. Although none of the executives
interviewed admitted paying any bribes themselves, one was
able to quote the going rates for certain permanent secretaries and another commented: 'Personally, I don't know how
we got our contracts (pause) I haven't asked (pause) I
don't want to know.'

The senior expatriate executives of a transnational corporation are rarely directly involved in the handling of
bribes. They usually provide their Nigerian managers with
vague directives to 'get the job done', expecting them to
make use of their local connections, and do not bother to
ask them how they managed to do it.

The bribing of government officials can be used to retain
control in the face of indigenisation pressures. Special
exemptions from certain aspects of the indigenisation decrees can be 'negotiated', and a number of firms are keenly
interested in ensuring that their new product lines are
classified in the schedule of the decree that requires that
they make available only 40 per cent of their total equity

to local subscribers. However bribery is probably more common in the awarding of contracts than it is in the granting of exemptions from the indigenisation decrees. There are simply too many other means available to maintain control.

Unilateral Violation of Law

A handful of transnational corporations have retained control over their Nigerian subsidiaries by only partially complying with or by totally ignoring Nigeria's indigenisation requirements. The construction industry is classified as a Schedule II activity, an area where foreign capital cannot exceed 40 per cent. However at least one large transnational construction company has retained a majority of the equity, selling only 40 per cent to local subscribers. Its senior executives know they are in violation of the decree, but are not concerned about the consequences: 'There have been no objections raised yet with distribution requirements. We expect some in the future, but nothing much will change for a few years.' The company is fully willing to comply with the decree when confronted by the government. In the meantime, however, it is not going out of its way to raise the issue and is operating in Nigeria with a clear majority of the equity.

Another form of unilateral violation of the law is much more widespread. A number of international banking agents, shipping agents and representatives for international airlines contend that the indigenisation efforts should not apply to their activities. Since most of them have no equity in the country, there is some basis for their position. Nevertheless several have been informed that they are in violation of Nigerian law and have chosen to ignore requests that they file papers with the Nigerian Enterprises Promotion Decree Board. As one executive confidently put it: 'We have never properly registered with the NEPB, never produced a balance sheet for them. If they pursue it, we'll pay the penalties for not filing. Or we could type up the documents later, say the NEPB lost the copy we sent them, and produce an "original".' It should be emphasised that this type of strategy (and arrogance) is restricted to transnational corporations with very little at stake in Nigeria.

In conclusion, the range of strategies available to transnational corporations is impressive. By employing benignly legal methods (such as encouraging a wide distribution of shares) or blatantly illegal ones (such as bribery) transnational corporations have had little difficulty retaining effective managerial control over their Nigerian operations

in the face of Nigeria's 'assertion of economic nationalism'. As well as Nigeria may appear to fit the model of a
growth in the role of the state and economic nationalism,
transnational corporations show no signs of being held 'at
bay' in the country.

CONCLUSIONS: RENATIONALISATION OR DENATIONALISATION?

The responsive (and defensive) capacities of transnational
corporations have quite effectively neutralised the state's
objectives in Nigeria [23]. The indigenisation exercise has
failed to ensure that Nigerians 'participate fully' or 'play
a dominant role' in the enterprises that have been Nigerianised. Indigenisation has also done very little to increase
Nigerian control over the economy in general. More than
majority equity participation is required to ensure 'the
assumption of the control of the Nigerian economy by Nigerians'. Indigenisation has essentially shifted the financial
risk burden of new and existing investments on to Nigerian
investors without any appreciable increase in their control
over the enterprises. Rather than import capital or obtain
it from local sources on their own, transnational corporations have been provided with capital from Nigerian shareholders or partners.

The opportunity costs of indigenisation are also very
high, especially in light of the state's objective of increasing Nigerian control over the economy. Indigenisation
makes possible the purchase of shares from transnational
corporations, enterprises with the best reputation for a
safe, profitable return. Since Nigerian society is pervaded
by the idea that 'foreign is better', indigenisation inevitably encourages investments in transnational corporations.
There are no counter-incentives for investments in indige-
nously controlled enterprises, hence the programme undermines the basis of accumulation by a national, capitalist
class. Although some pockets of local accumulation exist, a
risk-averse, profit-maximising Nigerian investor will buy
shares in foreign-owned and dominated concerns. Indigenisation thus encourages a comprador role for local business in
a society already plagued by strong comprador tendencies
[24]. Accordingly, indigenisation may have contributed to a
decrease, rather than an increase, in Nigerian control of
the economy.

Although the state's objectives of increased Nigerian control of the economy have been effectively neutralised, the
objectives of local capital have fared much better. Local
businessmen have obtained state sponsorship in their bid to

create a protected niche reserved for their enterprises in the distribution and commercial sectors of the economy. They have also succeeded in obtaining state sponsorship in their efforts to secure access to a share of the proceeds of the enterprises in the dynamic sectors of the economy under the control of transnational corporations. Since they are largely satisfied with a comprador role and function (and never really wanted to control foreign enterprises in the first place), most indigenous businessmen have attained their essential objectives through the indigenisation exercise.

Local capital has thus been engaged in a dual alliance with the state, on one hand, and with foreign capital, on the other. At one level, local capital has been allied with the federal military government in support of a policy of indigenisation. Both local capital and the state have employed the rhetoric of economic nationalism to mobilise support for the exercise, but only the state has pursued that objective with any conviction. Local capital has been able to attain its more limited objectives without going as far as assuming control over the indigenised enterprises. At another level, local capital has been allied with foreign capital in the latter's efforts to neutralise the state's objectives. The modified form of 'fronting' taking place in Nigeria requires the cooperation of a transnational corporation interested in maintaining control and a local partner satisfied with a largely intermediary function (providing information about local markets or important political connections). Similarly, a change in the voting rules or unilateral violation of the law require cooperation between local businessmen unwilling to report violations and transnational corporations willing to commit them. It is not just their 'cleverness' that enables transnationals to neutralise the Nigerian indigenisation programme. They also require the assistance of their local allies from the Nigerian private sector.

Although Nigerian indigenisation is broadly supported as an assertion of economic nationalism, the divergent objectives of the state and local capital, combined with the responsive capacities of transnational corporations, have contributed to a decrease, rather than an increase, in Nigerian control of the Nigerian economy. Indigenisation may appear to reflect a growth of state power and an assertion of economic nationalism in the Third World. Under closer examination, however, these global trends appear illusory in the Nigerian case.

A POLICY POSTSCRIPT: WHAT COULD BE DONE?

Nigeria's present approach to indigenisation is seriously
flawed. However that should certainly not lead one to conclude that the programme should be scrapped altogether. The
broad outlines of an alternative approach can be sketched
which offer the promise of an indigenisation programme that
does not necessarily result in a decrease in Nigerian control of the economy. Assuming that the Nigerian state wants
to increase indigenous control of the economy and has no
intention of departing from a capitalist or market approach
to its national development, there are several measures that
could be considered.

According to the analysis summarised in the preceding
pages, one of the central flaws of the existing indigenisation programme is the extent to which it provides an incen-
tive for the misallocation of local capital. Purchasing
shares from transnational corporations is less risky and
more likely to be profitable than investing in the productive enterprises of local entrepreneurs. The dividends received from such activities are most likely to be used for
immediate consumption, the purchase of land, or re-invest-
ment in other transnational corporations. A revised indigenisation programme could attempt to reallocate local capital toward investment in sectors of the economy which could
lead to accumulation by a national capitalist class.

To accomplish this, the government could begin by taxing
the dividends and other payments of the transnational corporations to their local partners and shareholders. Transnationals could be asked to withhold a certain percentage of
their dividends and payments and provide them to the government. Perhaps the NEPB could be upgraded to perform the task
of monitoring and recording the amounts withheld. The NEPB
(or another entity created for this purpose) could then
identify sectors, projects or enterprises where it appears
local capital investment will lead to accumulation. If local
businessmen chose to invest in these 'approved' areas, an
income tax credit could be granted up to the amount withheld
from their dividend payments from transnational corporations. Thus by taxing the dividend income of local businessmen, the state could encourage reallocation of private sector investment away from comprador, intermediary activities
toward productive investments with a potential for indigenous accumulation. The state could encourage the emergence
of effective local competitors to foreign capital in a number of strategic areas.

If an indigenisation policy could be developed incorpora-
ting some of these ideas, the holding of shares of trans-

national corporations could become less profitable relative
to investment in activities that lead to local accumulation.
Some state protection or subsidies might be required to
assist the establishment of local investments in certain
areas (especially in those areas presently dominated by
foreign capital). This proposal has advantages over a programme of direct state subsidies or investment in such
areas, however. State subsidies could be derived directly
from revenues obtained from the dividend tax which are not
redistributed as tax credits. Such a programme would avoid
reliance on state oil revenues for financing local capitalists, who have already received a disproportionate share of
support from the state as a result of the indigenisation
process of the 1970s.

Although a great many details would have to be worked out,
this proposal has the potential to construct an indigenisation programme in Nigeria that does not facilitate a denationalisation of the economy. It will not solve all of the
problems identified with the present approach to indigenisation. Comprador tendencies among the local business élite
would undoubtedly remain, and transnational corporations
would continue to control the most important aspects of
their enterprises. This proposal would, however, offer an
improvement to the existing approach to indigenisation by
providing a basis (within the confines of a capitalist
approach to development) for increasing local control of the
national economy.

A proposal of this sort would most certainly encounter
strong opposition from Nigeria's current comprador business
class. There is little likelihood that the current civilian
regime would embark on an indigenisation programme of this
kind. The state is now less autonomous than it was under
military rule, more penetrated by representatives of local
capital, less nationalistic, and accordingly less concerned
with increasing local control of the economy. However the
longer the present approach to indigenisation remains unchanged, the further the denationalisation of the Nigerian
economy is likely to proceed.

NOTES AND REFERENCES

1. Alfred Stepan, The State and Society: Peru in Compra-
   tive Perspective (Princeton University Press, 1978).
2. C. Fred Bergsten, Thomas Horst and Theodore H. Moran,
   American Multinationals and American Interests
   (Washington: Brookings Institution, 1978).

3. Robert Gilpin, U.S. Power and the Multinational Corporation (New York: Basic Books, 1975).
4. The term 'indigenisation' is used to distinguish this general policy from its more specific form, 'nationalisation'. Indigenisation of share capital refers to the requirement that shares be sold to indigenous subscribers in the local private *or* public sector. 'Nationalisation' requires that the shares be sold to the public sector only.
5. Ankie Hoogvelt, 'Indigenisation and Foreign Capital: Industrialisation in Nigeria', Review of African Political Economy, 14, January–April 1979, pp. 56–68.
6. O. Aboyade, 'Closing Remarks' in Nigeria's Indigenisation Policy, proceedings of the Symposium organised by the Nigerian Economic Society (University of Ibadan, 1974); P. C. Asiodu, 'Closing Remarks' in Nigeria's Indigenisation Policy.
7. Hoogvelt, 'Indigenisation and Foreign Capital'.
8. Asiodu, 'Closing Remarks'.
9. Paul Collins, 'The Policy of Indigenisation: an Overall View', Quarterly Journal of Administration, January 1975.
10. Omafume F. Onoge, 'The Indigenisation Decree and Economic Independence: Another Case of Bourgeois Utopianism' in Nigeria's Indigenisation Policy.
11. Collins, 'The Policy of Indigenisation'.
12. Briggs, quoted in West Africa, 23 June 1972.
13. E. O. Akeredolu-Ale, 'Private Foreign Investment and the Underdevelopment of Indigenous Entrepreneurship in Nigeria' in Gavin Williams (ed.), Nigeria: Economy and Society (London: Rex Collings, 1976).
14. Sule Kolo, quoted in West Africa, 23 June 1972.
15. Terisa Turner, 'MNCs and the Instability of the Nigerian State', Review of African Political Economy, 5, January–April 1976, pp. 63–79; Gavin Williams, 'A Political Economy' in Gavin Williams (ed.), Nigeria: Economy and Society (London: Rex Collings, 1976) pp. 11–54.
16. The ideology of economic nationalism was also useful for providing legitimacy and broad-based support for a regime in power less than two years and already shaken by the assassination of its Head of State, General Murtala Mohammed, in February 1976.
17. Federal Government of Nigeria, 'Nigerian Enterprises Promotion Decree, 1977', Supplement to Official Gazette, 64 (2), part A (Lagos: Ministry of Information, Printing Division, 1977) p. A19.
18. Some observers of Nigerian indigenisation have suggested that indigenisation has been a deliberate attempt by the state to create a national capitalist class in Nigeria.

The successive federal military governments had no objections to capitalism or capitalist development. However, a capitalist bourgeoisie was already present lobbying for its protection and assistance, not for its creation. Indigenisation has thus far been only an inadvertent or unintentional effort on the part of the state to create a capitalist class in Nigeria.

19. For example, Bergsten cites Nigeria's indigenisation programme as an illustration of growing economic nationalism in the Third World; C. Fred Bergsten, 'Coming Investment Wars?', <u>Foreign Affairs</u>, 53 (1), October 1973, pp. 135–52. Evans devotes a section of his concluding chapter to apply his triple alliance ideas to Nigeria; Peter Evans, <u>Dependent Development: the Alliance of Multinational, State and Local Capital in Brazil</u> (Princeton University Press, 1979) pp. 309–14. See also Chapter 1 in this book.

20. The well-publicised experience of the American-International Insurance Group appears to be an exception.

21. These data are obtained from the IMF's monthly <u>International Financial Statistics</u> (Washington: IMF, various years).

22. The interviews were conducted with the most senior foreign executives in twenty-three of the largest transnational corporations in Nigeria. Eighteen of the firms interviewed are included in the UN Centre for Transnational Corporations' list of the 200 largest enterprises in the world. Seven of the firms were engaged in banking activities, seven in manufacturing, four in petroleum or petro-chemical activities, three in consulting firms, two in services, two in construction and one in insurance. The total number of activities in this itemised breakdown exceeds twenty-three because a number of transnational corporations have established diversified investments in Nigeria and therefore operate in more than one sector.

23. The 'state' is not defined here solely in terms of its relationship to a dominant class. Rather, it is considered an analytically separable entity, composed of the principal institutions of the governmental apparatus (the military, police, civil service and administrative bureaucracies). The state has a monopoly on the legitimate use of force within a given territory and also has a financial basis of support through taxation.

24. Although Nigerians have historically played an intermediary role in West African trade and commerce, it would be a mistake to suggest that their present approaches to

transnational corporations simply reflect an inability or an unwillingness to play any other role today. See especially E. O. Akeredolu-Ale, <u>The Underdevelopment of Indigenous Entrepreneurship in Nigeria</u> (Ibadan University Press, 1975), and Thomas J. Biersteker, <u>Distortion or Development? Contending Perspectives on the Multinational Corporation</u> (Cambridge, Mass.: MIT Press, 1978) for examples of Nigerian capabilities in the performance of productive and non-intermediary functions in economic activities.

*The assistance of Marc R. Cohen with the research and conduct of interviews in Nigeria was indispensable and is gratefully acknowledged. An expanded version of this paper (with a more extensive theoretical and less policy-oriented discussion) will appear in Paul M. Lubeck (ed.), <u>The African Bourgeoisie: The Development of Capitalism in Nigeria, Kenya and the Ivory Coast</u> (forthcoming).

8 Nigeria's Development Strategy in Global Perspective

SONNI TYODEN

Since the 1860s when Nigeria became part of the world capitalist economy — initially as a result of the commercial
activities of British trading companies on the coast of
present-day Nigeria and of the later imposition of British
imperial control — she has over the years witnessed a qual-
itative and progressive process of integration into the
world system. This notwithstanding, subsequent structural
developments particularly in the Nigerian political economy
have over the years made the Nigerian state relatively autonomous of external capitalist agents; a development that
has put the Nigerian state at a relatively advantageous
position in its bargaining with agents of international monopoly capital and in its moulding of a domestic capitalist
socio-economy.

The cumulative result of these developments has been not
only the increased participation by the state and indigenous
capitalist forces in the process of capital accumulation in
the country but also the furtherance of bourgeois rule and
control. This I think is the current state of affairs. Before this contemporary 'developmentalist' phase in Nigeria's
development strategy, however, Nigeria had since independence been pursuing what I term a 'clientist' development
strategy [1].

THE CLIENTIST PHASE

From this perspective a clientist peripheral state is not
only peripheral as far as the global division of labour is
concerned but its articulation with the world capitalist
system is as much as possible mediated through its former
colonial overlord. In other words, irrespective of formal
independence, the patron-client relationship of the colonial
period is retained. The peripheral state (now controlled by
the indigenous bureaucratic bourgeoisie) simply joins

imperial capitalist forces in 'intensifying surplus extraction from the labour-force through a variety of post-colonial working relationships outlined under the rubric of "dependent neo-colonialism" ' [2]. Put differently, this means that no structural changes are envisaged and development strategy is basically a continuation along lines already laid down by the erstwhile imperial power during the colonial era. The metropolitan power continues to be the major actor in the process of capital accumulation, continues to be the main source of investment capital for and imports to the client state, and continues to be the main market for the export goods for the peripheral state.

This means that independence for this kind of state is a mere substitution of implements of control by the metropolitan power; the indigenous bourgeoisie now serves as an avenue for heightening imperial exploitation in order to extract a share of the surplus for themselves. Open access to raw materials, liberal tax laws and a horde of incentives to foreign investors characterise such a clientalist development policy [3].

It is my suggestion that Nigeria before the civil war was basically this type of peripheral state. As the Private Secretary to Nigeria's first Prime Minister stated, independence in Nigeria 'had not led to a search for new beliefs and new systems' [4]. This is not surprising considering that the new governing élite shared the same ideological outlook as their former colonial counterparts.

Be that as it may, in his first speech as Prime Minister, Sir Abubakar Tafawa Balewa stated that though the Nigerian economy had been closely linked to that of Britain it was the intention of his government to strengthen further such links.

> After independence, we shall continue to look *first* to Britain to supply those Technical Officers whose services we so much need. We are grateful to the UK for many things and it is our desire that our association shall continue even closer than now [5].

Put another way, this meant that Nigeria would not only continue her participation in the global capitalist economy, but such participation would continue to be mediated through Britain; or at least Britain would be the main actor on the other side (core) of the system. It is thus not surprising that at the time of the fall of the First Republic in 1966, Britain was the dominant actor in the Nigerian economy. By this time she owned 53.3 per cent of cumulative foreign investment in the country, controlled about 40 per cent of the

Nigerian market, and was the major source of Nigerian imports and loans [6] while serving as Nigeria's main export market [7].

Although the emphasis at this stage was on the continuation of extant economic links with the former colonial power, the capital demands of the independent government particularly after the launching of the 1962-8 Development Plan necessitated a deliberate attempt at attracting capitalist interests in other countries at the core of the world system. As early as 1956 the government had described its policy towards private investment (from whatever source) as one of encouragement not competition [8]. In the first independent budget speech, the Minister for Finance reasserted this policy when he stated: 'It will be the cardinal aim of this government's policy to maintain in Nigeria a climate conducive to the attraction of foreign capital whether in the public or private sector' [9]. With this policy preference, therefore, private investors were not only encouraged and urged to invest in Nigeria, but it became conscious government policy to create a favourable climate for private capital accumulation through the provision of a series of incentives.

Starting with the Aid to Pioneer Industries Ordinance of 1952 which gave a three to five-year income tax holiday to firms in 'pioneer industries', other fiscal measures were enacted in subsequent years. In 1957 the Industrial Development (Import Duty Relief) Act was passed. Under these measures, a firm could be granted concessionary rates of duty on raw materials imported for its manufacturing activities. That the government was quite liberal in the implementation of these policies can be seen from the fact that cases of 100 per cent duty relief were a common occurrence [10]. In 1958 the Industrial Development (Income Tax Relief) Act was passed. This Act provided for the declaration of a firm as a 'pioneer industry' on its acquisition of a pioneer certificate from the government. It was basically an extension and a formalisation of the 1952 Ordinance with the tax holiday depending on the firm's capital outlay [11].

Tariff rates were also very liberal. Most capital goods carried no import duties at all. Intermediate goods carried import duties varying from 10 to 15 per cent while finished consumer goods had rates ranging from 25 to 30 per cent. Allowances such as the Accelerated Depreciation Allowance and attractive tax provisions were part of the incentives package as already noted. In his 'People's Budget' of 1958 the Finance Minister, Chief Festus Okotie-Eboh, stated that in order to attract foreign investment company tax was to be reduced from nine to eight shillings in the pound while

losses could be carried forward indefinitely instead of the
ten-year period initially in force [12].

Other fiscal measures included the provision of industrial
sites in all parts of the country: the Yaba Industrial
Estate in Lagos, Mushim-Ikeja in the then Western Region,
Wapa in Kano and Trans-Amadi in Enugu. Non-fiscal measures
were also pursued to further create an attractive investment atmosphere. Among these was infrastructural development
which was not only continued where the colonial power left
off but was pursued with extra vigour. In fact, in terms of
the allocation of government expenditure over this period,
except for 1963-4 [13], transport and communications maintained a consistent lead not only in the economic sector but
in relation to all other sectors as well.

Capping all these was the absence of governmental controls
on the amount, character and location of investment and on
the repatriation of profits [14]. Exchange and other monetary controls had to await the establishment of a Central
Bank in 1962. This later control, however, served more as a
symbolic role than as a real control on the business activities of foreign commercial firms. The basic machinery for
exchange controls was on the statute books as a mere precau-
tion and was hardly applied in checking the repatriation and
remission of profits, etc.

With these policies and the government's firm guarantee
against nationalisation Nigeria could not but be a haven for
foreign investments. This situation was further encouraged
by the fact that there was hardly any attempt to control the
influx of foreign businessmen and professionals. The Immigration Act of 1963 did little to control such influx due to
laxity in its implementation. The cumulative effect of all
these incentives and the government's *laissez-faire* or passive attitudes to foreign business activities in Nigeria can
be seen in the fact that while foreign businessmen contributed 67.7 per cent of paid-up capital in Nigerian industries in 1963, by 1966 the percentage had risen to 70.2 per
cent [15].

While the government believed that its open door policy to
international capital was indispensable to its development
strategy, it also saw the need to protect and encourage domestic industries, irrespective of ownership. Apart from the
fact that most of the policies discussed above served this
purpose, the major policy instrument in this regard was support for import-substitution industries. This support necessitated a gradual increase in tariff rates and the institu-
tionalisation of restrictions such as import quotas [16].
The fact that, of all industrial plants established in the
country between 1961 and 1965, 80 per cent could be traced

to import-substitution activities [17] reflects a measure of government commitment in this regard.

The Approved Manufacturers Scheme initiated by the government was another measure aimed at encouraging domestic industries. This stipulated that government ministries and departments were to make their purchases from Nigerian industries where the products concerned were 'reasonably comparable in price and quality with imported goods' [18]. The provision of industrial sites, the gradual increase in tariff rates, and increasing governmental control over exchange and other monetary controls as the Central Bank became more efficient, were all geared towards encouraging domestic industries. In any case, the major effort at helping indigenous businessmen was through the provision of credit facilities in the form of loans. A measure of the government's serious concern can be seen in the estimated 4550 such loans granted by Regional Loan Boards alone by 1962. Whether these were adequately used is, however, a different matter [19].

THE DEVELOPMENTALIST PHASE

As a result of the unprecedented windfall gains from oil revenue and the control of the state by an élite group imbued with a high dose of nationalist sentiment, Nigeria's development strategy from the early 1970s started witnessing an aggressive assertion of state intervention in the process of capital accumulation. This was because the combination of oil revenue and nationalism gave the national bourgeoisie a measure of autonomy and thus some bargaining power in its dealings with the foreign bourgeoisie. In any case, while the bureaucratic bourgeoisie's 'developmentalist' strategy was aimed at squeezing the foreign sector and expanding its own stake in the economy at the same time, the national bourgeoisie shares with the foreign bourgeoisie an interest in maximising the exploitation of the working classes and in maintaining production and labour discipline. In the last analysis, however, the success of this 'establishment nationalism' depends on the avoidance of confrontations with the foreign sector and the labour force.

In Nigeria, the launching of the Nigerian Enterprises Promotion (Indigenisation) Decree in 1972 marked the beginning of a conscious attempt at increasing the roles of the state and the budding indigenous capitalist class in the process of capital accumulation in the economy (see Chapter 7). When it was launched the aim of the indigenisation programme was described as making for 'greater and more effective partici-

pation by Nigerians in the economic life of the nation'
[20]. More recently, however, the political nature of the
programme has been highlighted. In the 1979 budget speech
it was stated that the objective of the decree was not
merely the transfer of shares to and the earning of dividends by Nigerians, but that

> the main spring of the indigenisation was *political*. It
> was designed as a strategy for getting Nigerians them-
> selves to determine their own economic future by using
> equity ownership as a springboard into the boardroom
> where policies are discussed and determined and into
> management where they are implemented [21].

The firms that were subject to the decree were initially
divided into two categories: Schedule I was for firms reserved exclusively for Nigerian ownership, with Schedule II
(those requiring larger capital outlays) consisting of firms
of whose equity capital up to 40 per cent should be sold to
Nigerian partners. Following the report of the Indigenisation Review Panel in 1976 a third category of firms was
added; this addition also witnessed the re-allocation of
firms within the three schedules. The first schedule which
now experienced an increase in the number of firms included
was still reserved for Nigerians; Schedule II firms were required to sell 60 per cent of their shares to Nigerians;
while Schedule III firms were required to place 40 per cent
of their equity shares at the disposal of Nigerian investors. On the argument that the programme has slowed down the
inflow of foreign capital in some sectors of the economy,
the post-1979 civilian government initiated a further review
which involved the reclassification of some economic activities from Schedule I to II and from II to III and vice
versa [22].

The important thing, however, is that this indigenisation
programme was the forerunner of other measures aimed at increasing state and indigenous involvement in the economy.
Starting with the take-over of 40 per cent of shares in all
commercial banks, ostensibly to encourage them to lend to
Nigerians wishing to avail themselves of opportunities provided by the indigenisation decree, the process of expanding
state control of the 'commanding heights of the economy' was
gradually extended to other sectors of the economy. By 1976
government share-ownership in all foreign-owned banks was 60
per cent [23] while it was announced early in 1980 that
henceforth the federal government would fill 50 per cent of
the directorships in the eleven major commercial banks in
which it has a substantial shareholding [24]. With the

promulgation of the Insurance Decree of 1976 and the Nigerian Reinsurance Decree of 1977 government control of the insurance business was firmly established as government now owns 60 per cent of shares in all foreign-owned insurance companies.

It was, however, in the all-important oil industry that the most significant acts of state intervention took place. The significance of this intervention becomes better appreciated with the realisation that it coincided with a period when the oil industry was becoming the most dynamic sector of the Nigerian economy, contributing heavily to government revenue. For instance, while in 1966 the oil sector made up only 5.8 per cent of the country's Gross Domestic Product (GDP), this had almost tripled to 14 per cent in 1973. Similarly, over the same period, oil's contribution to export earnings rose from 32.4 per cent to 83.1 per cent, respectively. In terms of government revenue, the oil sector's contribution rose from 11.1 per cent in 1966 to 67.3 per cent in 1973 and today stands at over 80 per cent. This situation has been crucial in advancing the government's increased self-confidence in the pursuit of its development strategy and foreign policy.

Although as early as 1962 the government had acquired a 30 per cent interest in Agip, massive governmental involvement in the oil industry was to await the mid-1970s. In 1974 a 55 per cent share acquisition agreement was concluded between government and the oil companies. By 1980, however, government's share in the oil companies had reached the 60 per cent mark and even 80 per cent in the former Shell-BP (which was then the largest oil company operating in Nigeria). In 1971 the government took over 60 per cent ownership of the oil refinery in Port Harcourt and it is the sole owner of the two recently constructed and larger refineries in Kaduna and Warri. Similarly, it has 60 per cent of the shares in the proposed liquefied natural gas (LNG) project.

With the setting up of the Nigerian National Oil Corporation (NNOC, now renamed Nigerian National Petroleum Corporation, NNPC), government involvement in the oil industry became more pervasive and firmly established. The Corporation was charged not only with the exploration and marketing of oil for the government, but also with managing the state's share in the oil companies. In addition, all available acreages not covered by existing licences at the time of its establishment were transferred to it. Unlike government policy in other sectors of the economy it was not until 1979 that indigenous private companies were officially granted licences for oil exploration and to the best of my knowledge so far only one indigenous company has availed itself of this policy [25].

To carry the impact of state participation in the oil industry to the 'boardrooms' of the oil companies, the government has decreed since 1969 that an increased number of Nigerians were to fill the managerial, professional and supervisory posts in the oil companies. For all these grades put together, the number of Nigerians was not to be less than 75 per cent, while in each grade the percentage of Nigerians should not be less than 60 per cent [26].

While extending state and indigenous participation in the economy, the post-1970 governments have all continued the policy of nurturing a domestic capitalist class. Mention has already been made of the indigenisation programme. Another programme in the same category is the Small Scale Industries Credit Scheme (SSIC) [27]. With a relative abundance of financial resources this scheme (though initiated during the Second Plan Period, 1970-5), has been given greater emphasis in the Third and Fourth Development Plans; in the 1975-80 plan it was allocated ₦50 million and ₦380 million in the Fourth Plan.

Fiscal measures such as the Approved Users Scheme which made for the importation of needed raw materials at relatively reduced duty rates were effected to facilitate the operation of small-scale and other domestic industries. Further fiscal measures were enacted in the 1975, 1977 and 1978 budgets specifically aimed at promoting and protecting domestic production. The 1975 budget announced the abolition of excise duties for locally produced goods, relaxed foreign exchange controls and reduced import duties. The expatriate quota was relaxed, limits on payments to non-resident directors of Nigerian companies abolished, while tax on company profits was reduced from 60 per cent to 40 per cent. The 1977 and 1978 measures were specifically concerned with the protection of indigenous entrepreneurs. Some goods that competed with domestic ones were banned or placed under licence, while the 40 per cent prescribed minimum for commercial bank lending to indigenous entrepreneurs was raised to 50 per cent. In continuation of the policy of creating a congenial atmosphere for industrial and commercial activities the civilian government recently announced that a firm could now distribute as much as 60 per cent of its after-tax profit or the equivalent of 25 per cent of its paid-up capital.

A recent development in the development strategy has been the emphasis on export promotion. The government has put forward a series of incentives in this regard. These include the provision of preferential credit allocations by commercial banks; the setting up of rediscounting facilities for export of manufacturers and semi-manufacturers; the setting up of an Export Development Fund, with an allocation of ₦1 million in the Fourth Plan, for direct grants and financial assistance to indigenous exporters; and the Export Credit Guarantee Scheme with an allocation of ₦4 million to provide insurance cover for exporters [28].

CONTINUING DEPENDENCE ON THE WORLD CAPITALIST SYSTEM

The increased self-confidence of the Nigerian bourgeoisie has not only led to the extension of state and indigenous participation in the process of capital accumulation in the economy, but has also led to a drastic reduction in its dependence on the former colonial overlord. This has been replaced by a deliberate policy of diversification of contacts whose resultant effect has been continuing dependence and further integration into the world capitalist economy. Below I note two cases of this policy of diversification.

In the first case, while a few years back British companies predominated in the award of contracts in the country, in the crucial oil pipeline contracts awarded between 1975 and 1976 there was a conscious government policy to see that awards were diversified. The Soviet firm Tsvetmepromexport won the contract for the construction of two pipelines from Warri; Montubi Montaggi of Italy for the construction of pipelines from Kaduna to other parts of the northern states; and the US International Group for pipeline construction in the eastern states, while pipes were supplied by Japan's Mitsui [29].

The second case involves foreign currency holdings. While as late as 1970 70 per cent of Nigeria's currency holdings were in sterling, by 1976 this was down to 28.2 per cent. This contrasts sharply with the changing fortunes of the US dollar. In 1970 only 10 per cent of Nigeria's reserves were in dollars; by 1976, however, the proportion was 43.5 per cent. A Deutschmark account opened in 1974 held 12.3 per cent in 1976 while the French franc account opened the same year held 4.1 per cent by 1976. Nigeria currently has also reserve holdings in the Canadian dollar, Japanese yen, Dutch guilder and Swiss and Belgian francs [30].

That these measures have served to increase the relative autonomy of the government may not be in doubt; but simultaneously they have increased (particularly in the first case) Nigeria's dependence on the world capitalist system, since the major actors and the range of activities involved are circumscribed within that system. More recent happenings and other aspects of the development strategy have served to bring this out more clearly.

Given a rising import bill (set in trend by increased oil revenues from 1973) by 1977, when oil revenues began falling, the government had to go a-borrowing to keep its development projects afloat. On the argument that 'the Euro-dollar has no ideological colour' [31] the bulk of the 1978 loan was from Western financial institutions and Western capitalist countries. A breakdown of this $2 billion loan [32] shows $0.20 billion consisting of bond issues; $1 billion consisting of a Eurodollar syndicate loan; $0.60 billion consisting of official export credits; and $0.20 billion consisting of loans from the World Bank and the European Investment Bank. In 1979 a $100 million loan agreement was signed with Morgan Grenfell leading a syndicate of Western banks [33]; ₦270 million came from a group of West German and Austrian banks [34]; $1.75 billion came from two syndicated Euro-currency loans; while the World Bank earmarked $500 million annually for loans to Nigeria [35]. Further loans in 1980 included a $50 million Eurodollar facility; $131 million from the World Bank [36] — presumably part of the $500 million annual loan to Nigeria; $103 million from a consortium of West German banks; $63 million from the West German government; and $28 million from the International Development Agency (IDA).

There are several things worth noting about these loans. First, while Nigeria has since independence (with the possible exception of the 1973-7 period) laid a heavy premium on the importation of money-capital in its development efforts, before the late 1970s most of these loans and grants came from bilateral sources, particularly from Britain.

Second, although Nigeria has also been borrowing from international financial institutions such as the World Bank for quite some time [37], the current levels of borrowing are in a class of their own. In the first place, their size alone sets them apart from past borrowing; consequently, their effect on the economy would be more far-reaching than hitherto. Let me elaborate further, Nigeria's foreign debt in 1961 was only ₦85.5 million; in 1970 it was ₦178.8 million; and it was ₦352.2 million in 1977. While debt servicing was 4.1 per cent of the value of exports in 1970 this had fallen to 2.3 per cent in 1976 [38]. The fact that external borrowings are continuing — and all indications point to their continuation — means that the debt servicing figure will likely rise over the years, setting in trend the well-known vicious circle of dependence on external finance [39] from which oil has so far saved Nigeria. In Nigeria's case this vicious circle may not go on repeating itself *ad infinitum.*

The continuing flow of revenue from oil or any other export commodity, a drastic reduction in government spending
and a reappraisal of development priorities may lead to a
break in the circle as indeed oil revenue did for the country from 1971-6. Alternatively, a complete overhaul and
reorientation of Nigeria's socio-economic system, one that
challenges external dependence and emphasises instead a do-
it-yourself philosophy, would also break the circle. A
second feature of these loans is that they involve agents of
international monopoly finance which are central to the
operation of the global capitalist economy. This means not
only the further integration and dependence of Nigeria on
this system but also the development in Nigeria of a stake
in the successful operation of this system making it a
central element in the country's development strategy.

In fact the same conclusion is reached when looking criti-
cally at the so-called attempt to give Nigerians control of
their economy. In the case of the indigenisation programme,
the setting of a limit on individual shareholding [40] and
the demand that 10 per cent of equity shares be sold to
company employees, while good measures in themselves, have
served to scatter the Nigerian stake while the foreign
component remains consolidated. First, in other words, day-
to-day control still lies in the hands of expatriate managers. Second, the resultant partnership between foreign and
domestic capitalist forces means the foreign companies now
have greater security of tenure but also have local capital
at their disposal. And third, this partnership puts labour
in a more precarious position. Not surprisingly, the
Financial Times of London interpreted the indigenisation
programme in this light. It stated that the programme might
'help smooth labour relations' for, 'no longer can industry
be seen as an alien presence, as a manifestation of economic imperialism. This could help the government back-up
industry in the face of unreasonable demands (sic) from
labour' [41].

In the case of the oil industry, mention has already been
made of the fall in oil revenues in the 1977-8 period. This
had a mellowing effect on government's dealings with the
foreign oil companies: in 1977 favourable provisions (meant
to act as incentives to increased exploration activity) were
announced. These included a provision that the government
would bear the cost of exploration and drilling whether
successful or not. Tax rates for companies not yet producing
oil were reduced by about 24 per cent, to rise to the normal
level when production begins. The existing royalty rate of
20 per cent was graduated downwards, while an annual allow-

ance was approved to 'enable oil companies to clear their
assets in five equal annual installments' [42]. This situation indicates that despite the fact that the government
had increased state involvement in this major sector of the
economy, in the last analysis government depends on these
same oil companies to sustain the state component in this
crucial industry. The oil tankers owned by the NNPC are not
only managed by external firms; the NNPC itself depends on
the foreign oil companies for advice and expertise in car-
rying out its exploration and seismic surveys. Furthermore,
the oil companies have developed ingenious ways of circum-
venting and defeating government indigenisation policies
and efforts to transfer technology to Nigerian employees
[43].

Another prominent feature of Nigeria's development strategy which has made for its further integration and dependence is its import-substitution policy. Although this
policy has been carried over from the first indigenous
government, like all other post-independence policies, it
has undergone some modifications reflecting prevalent governmental ideology, predilection and decision-making. First,
there seemed to be an overemphasis on the assembly of cars
and trucks [44]. Second, Nigerian interests have a significant percentage (predominant in some) of the share-ownership
in these plants [45]. Third, in each of the agreements
establishing these plants, the foreign partner was required
to initiate a process of 'transfer of technology' to the
Nigerian employees. It was further stipulated that these
plants be locally incorporated and manufacture all component
parts in the country by 1991. Apart from the fact that such
plants were in keeping with the tastes and needs of the
élite, the Nigerian government seemed overly optimistic
about the readiness of their external partners to transfer
technology to them.

That this belief was central to government development
thinking is seen in the case of the petroleum industry discussed earlier (see Chapters 2, 6 and 7). Assuming indeed
that technology was transferred to Nigerian employees, to
the extent that the operational dynamics of such transferred
technology is informed by the ethics of capitalist development, to that extent it furthers the cause of Nigeria's
entrenchment in the global capitalist system.

While this dependence is in keeping with the development
strategy of the élites, it also serves class, fractional
and personal interests. Given the ideological identity between Nigeria and external élites, euphemisms like 'international interdependence' and 'partners in progress' are used
to mask the underlying structure of dependence. While this

serves class interests, fractional interests are also served simultaneously, as the bureaucratic bourgeoisie (which controls the state) also uses ideology to maintain its hegemony not only against other classes, but also against its budding commercial counterparts. An example of this was seen during the Gowon era. In anticipation of the government decree reducing capital allowances to oil companies and requiring them to introduce posted prices, the oil companies lobbied the various state governments with the result that, with but one exception, all of them made representations to the Head of State to dissuade him from promulgating the decree [46], in spite of the evident benefits of such a decree for the country. Counter-pressure from indigenous businessmen (who hoped to benefit) and from top civil servants were crucial in the eventual promulgation of the decree.

In fact, with the benefit of hindsight, government policy, which until September 1979 precluded the granting of exploration licences to indigenous businessmen, might have been geared towards maintaining the ascendancy of the bureaucratic bourgeoisie. Material benefits could also accrue to members of this bourgeoisie from corrupt practices in the award of licences and contracts; material benefits which would be both greater and safer when derived from external rather than internal sources. A case of the advancement of personal interest was exemplified in 1974. This resulted in the government's rejection of what Asiodu termed an excellent LPG/ethylene/ammonia/sponnage iron project to utilise about 4 10 million cubic feet of gas a day at Bonny (which is currently being burnt off) as a result of the 'manoeuvres by some interested individuals' [47].

CONCLUSION

To sum up, the philosophy that has informed development policies in Nigeria since independence has been characterised by a desire for capitalist development on a general basis. I have noted that in the early post-independence years, Nigerian policy-makers conceived of their participation in the global capitalist system basically in terms of the continuation of politico-economic links established with their erstwhile colonial power during the colonial era.

From the mid-1970s, however, I indicated a toning down of the emphasis on the continuation of colonial links; rather, the emphasis now was on partnership in participation in the world capitalist system. Similarly, while the desire for the protection and advancement of indigenous enterprises and entrepreneurs featured even in the first pre-independence

years, over time, structural changes in the Nigerian economy and an increasing nationalist fervour have infused an
element of aggressiveness in that quest [48]. In short, by
1979 participation in the global capitalist system and the
strengthening of a domestic capitalist political economy
were central elements in Nigeria's philosophy of 'development'; a situation that, given common interests between
national and external bourgeois factions, has rather mistakenly been termed 'ideological ambiguity' [49].

NOTES AND REFERENCES

1. This development strategy is discussed in greater detail
   in conjunction with others in S. G. Tyoden, 'State,
   Class and Capital Accumulation in the Periphery',
   Nigerian Political Science Association, Kano, April
   1981.
2. James F. Petras, 'New Perspectives on Imperialism and
   Social Classes in the Periphery', Journal of Contemporary Asia, 5 (3), 1975, p. 298.
3. Ibid., p. 299.
4. Sir Abubakar Tafawa Balewa, Nigeria Speaks (London:
   Longman, 1964) p. ix (emphasis added).
5. Ibid., p. 5.
6. Of all loans acquired by Nigeria between 1960 and 1966
   Britain provided 54 per cent.
7. It should be pointed out that while other capitalist
   states were gradually developing a stake in the Nigerian
   economy — a development that was encouraged by
   Britain's inability to satisfy Nigeria's capital demands
   resulting from the launching of the First National
   Development Plan — Britain still retained her dominance
   in all spheres of economic activity.
8. The government had stated, 'our policy is not to go all
   out spending public funds trying to establish industries
   in all parts of the country. Our policy is to encourage
   private enterprise', quoted in R. O. Ekundare, 'The
   Political Economy of Private Investment in Nigeria',
   Journal of Modern African Studies, 10 (1), March 1972,
   p. 39.
9. The Six Budget Speeches 1958–1963, by Chief F. S. O.
   Okotie-Eboh (Lagos: Federal Ministry of Finance, n.d.)
   p. 63.
10. T. A. Oyejide, Tariffs and Industrialisation in Nigeria
    (Ibadan University Press, 1975), p. 44.

11. P. C. Asiodu, 'Industrial Policy and Incentives in Nigeria', Nigerian Journal of Economic and Social Studies (NJOESS), 11 (2), 1969, p. 329.
12. The Six Budget Speeches, p. 6.
13. During this period, the allocation for the administrative sector took the lead. This is accounted for by the establishment of more government departments particularly of more foreign missions, the creation of the Mid-West region, and increasing indigenisation and expansion of the country's armed forces.
14. A. O. Philips, 'The Significance of Nigeria's Income Tax Relief Incentives', NJOESS, 11 (2), 1969, p. 329.
15. Industrial Survey of Nigeria 1963-1966 (Lagos: Federal Office of Statistics).
16. Oyejide, Tariffs and Industrialisation in Nigeria, p. 44.
17. O. Aboyade, 'Industrial Location and Development Policy: the Nigerian case', NJOESS, 10 (3), 1968, pp. 277-8.
18. The Six Budget Speeches, pp. 5-6. A detailed analysis of the scheme is given by Sayre P. Schatz, Nigerian Capitalism (Berkeley: University of California Press, 1977) ch. 10.
19. Schatz, ibid., treats this aspect of government policy adequately in chapter 12.
20. 'Caring for the People', Answers on the 1974/1975 Federal Budget, (Lagos: Federal Ministry of Information, 1974) p. 17.
21. 'Consolidation Budget', 1979-1980 Budget Speech (Lagos: Federal Government Printer, 1979) p. 4 (emphasis added).
22. The manufacture of jewellery and related articles, watch repairing, garment manufacture and rice milling, hitherto reserved for Nigerians was moved to Schedule II; i.e., foreigners can now have 40 per cent equity shares in such firms. Tin smelting and processing was moved from Schedule II to III, while the manufacture of metal containers, fertiliser production, cement manufacture, sugar plantation and processing and agricultural plantations were moved from Schedule III to II.
23. Government's share in Barclays (Union) Bank is now 80 per cent.
24. West Africa, 28 January 1980.
25. That is Nigus Petroleum, whose partner is Crown Central Petroleum Corporation of the US. While that was the official policy, Henry Stephens and Sons, a Nigerian company, was awarded oil concessions in 1972 and 1975.
26. Petroleum Decree, 1969, schedule 1, section 37.
27. Under the scheme loans of up to ₦50,000 could be granted to an individual intent upon setting up a small-scale

manufacturing or servicing venture. Each state government operates its own scheme under federal government guidance.

28. West Africa, 16 March 1981.

29. 'Nigeria' in Colin Legum (ed.), Africa Contemporary Record: Annual Survey and Documents, 1975-1976, vol. 8 (London: Africana, 1977) pp. 804-5.

30. Ibid.

31. This was the argument of the Commissioner for External Affairs, Joseph Garba, based on the premise that even socialist states borrow on the Eurodollar market.

32. Bilateral loans worth $0.14 billion were also received from Hungary, Poland and Czechoslovakia.

33. These include Bank of America, Banque Belge, Banque de Paris et des Pays Bas, Banque National de Paris, Credit Lyonnais, Societé Générale, International Westminster Bank, Gulf International Bank and Abu Dhabi Investment Company.

34. New Nigerian, 5 February 1979.

35. Nigeria Standard, 2 August 1979. It has been estimated that World Bank projects in Nigeria in 1979 alone were worth $182 million (West Africa, 1 October 1979).

36. An agreement was recently concluded for another loan of $349 million from the World Bank. This brings the total for the year to $480 million.

37. Nigeria started borrowing from the World Bank in 1958. By 1978 the Bank had lent Nigeria up to $912.4m. See J. P. Olinger, 'The World Bank and Nigeria', Review of African Political Economy, 13, May-August 1978, pp. 101-7.

38. Financial Times, 30 August 1979.

39. This refers to a situation where a worsening balance of payments position leads to external borrowing which momentarily alleviates the problem only to have it recur in a more acute form as the loans run out. Coupled with the need for debt servicing, this leads to further borrowing, momentary relief and the whole circle repeats itself.

40. It was stipulated that an individual could not hold more than 5 per cent equity capital or ₦50,000 (whichever is greater) in any enterprise.

41. Financial Times, 30 August 1978.

42. West Africa, 30 May 1977.

43. See Terisa Turner, 'The Transfer of Oil Technology and the Nigerian State', Development and Change, 7 (4), 1976, pp. 353-90.

44. There are at least seven car and truck assembly plants in the country: Fiat (trucks), Leyland (trucks), Peugeot (cars), Volkswagen (cars), Mercedes-Benz (trucks), Steyr Daimler (trucks/tractors) and Nissan (trucks and cars). The diversity of foreign partners involved is worth noting. They include Italian, British, French, German, Austrian and Japanese concerns.

45. For instance, Nigerian interests hold 60 per cent of the shares in Peugeot, Mercedes and Leyland plants and 40 per cent in Volkswagen.

46. P. C. Asiodu, Nigeria and the Oil Question (Ibadan: Nigerian Economics Society, 1979), p. 23.

47. Ibid. For further discussion on the centrality of fractional and personal interests in the evolution of Nigeria's oil policy, see Terisa Turner, 'Commercial Capitalism and the 1975 Coup' in Keith Panter-Brick (ed.), Soldiers and Oil (London: Frank Cass, 1978) pp. 166-7 and her 'Multinational Corporations and the Instability of the Nigerian State', Review of African Political Economy, 5, January-April 1976, pp. 63-79.

48. While there were differences in style and approach between particularly the Gowon and the post-Gowon regimes, as could be seen in the activities of both regimes, I am of the view that these differences do not overshadow the fundamental continuity in ideology and policy that runs through these regimes.

49. Gavin Williams, 'Nigeria: a Political Economy,' in his edited work Nigeria: Economy and Society (London: Rex Collings, 1976) p. 33. See P. C. W. Gutkind and P. Waterman (eds), African Social Studies: a Radical Reader (London: Heinemann, 1977) p. 285. Mistaken because Nigeria's economic nationalism does not indicate in any way a questioning of capitalist development or of participation in the global capitalist system or, indeed, of the participation of agents of monopoly capital in Nigeria's political economy.

9 Nigeria: Foreign Policy Alternatives

MARK W. DELANCEY

INTRODUCTION

Observers divide the history of Nigeria's foreign policy into two major periods, with the civil war years as an inter-
lude. The policy of the period of civilian rule from 1960
until the coups of 1966 is described as 'conservative' and
cautious. Nigeria was seen as a 'sleeping giant'. But once
the war was successfully completed and the huge revenues
from the sale of petroleum began to pour in, Nigerian foreign policy became more 'active', bold and, to some writers,
even radical. The content of the policy had not changed
greatly; nonalignment and the primacy of African affairs
have been constant themes, for example. But the behaviour,
the actions undertaken to support policy changed greatly
(see Chapters 2, 6 and 11).

Post-war Nigeria was actively involved, often assuming a
leadership position, in the international politics of
Africa. Since its return to civilian rule, these two models
from the past — the conservative and the active — have
served as examples for the future. No serious alterations
in content have yet taken place; here the continuity that
has existed since 1960 passes on into the present and the
future. But which behaviour the civilian leaders will select
— the conservative, passive model or the more active model
of the years of military rule — has not yet become clear.

PRE-WAR CIVILIAN RULE AND FOREIGN POLICY

Studies in the foreign policy of the period of pre-war civilian rule generally attribute the passivity of that policy
to one or both of two factors: the difficult, almost chaotic
domestic scene left no time for an active foreign policy and
the personality, knowledge, or attitudes of Prime Minister
Balewa would only allow a passive policy [1].

Certainly the first years of Nigeria's independence were years of hectic domestic activity. The whole process of establishing a new government must be seen as a time- and energy-consuming process. In addition, the fledgling government was faced with some difficult problems and pressures from its citizens. The demands for economic development and for a rapid improvement in the material standard of living were (and are) a vast challenge (see Chapter 8). Equally important were challenges to the structure of the government and the need for the development of national cohesion. Initially the government faced these problems with rather limited sources of income at its disposal; petroleum was a minor export in the early 1960s. Eventually these problems and the seeming inability of the government to solve them led to a breakdown of the political system. A general strike, political violence and thuggery, coups and then a civil war as a major section of the country aimed at secession were among the many domestic events of the last years of this period.

Ibrahim Gambari, a Nigerian scholar, has described four negative factors in this pre-war political system: (1) a national consensus had not yet emerged; (2) the regional governments were too powerful and each had its voice in foreign affairs; (3) ethnic and ideological splits among the population were severe; and (4), 'the federal government did not provide decisive leadership even at the most crucial times'. The last factor was attributed to the difficulties of ruling by coalition and to the personality of Balewa [2].

A lack of leadership was seen as an aspect of domestic political problems and the quality of leadership was blamed by several writers for Nigeria's rather reserved foreign policy during the first civilian regime. One study of this period concluded that Balewa 'was out of touch with the realities of the Nigerian and African political systems'. He did not understand Africa's problems and Nigeria's possible role in the solution of these problems. The traditionalism of his Nigerian culture and Islamic faith were important influences on him [3]. Another indigenous writer suggested that Balewa underestimated Nigeria's capabilities (cf. Chapter 6). He was 'naive' and followed 'pro-Western' policies. 'It would be fair to charge that, under his leadership, Nigeria suffered subconsciously from a curious inferiority complex which usually placed her on the "response" rather than on the "challenge" end of the response-challenge continuum' [4]. One of the most authoritative students of Nigerian foreign policy, Olajide Aluko, has summarised these arguments:

Because of the external environment in which the country
found itself in October 1960, and the domestic situation
with which the leaders had to cope, especially the constant threat to national unity, the social instability
and difficult federal structure of the country, its
military weakness, and the background and outlook of its
leaders, the country adopted a cautious note in foreign
policy [5].

Rather than provide an additional description of Balewa's
foreign policy [6], let me simply identify two elements
which the critics generally note as evidence of its passivity and conservatism — its non-alignment and its Southern
Africa policies.

At independence, the Nigerian government announced the
adoption of a policy it called 'neutralism', which by 1961
was referred to as 'nonalignment'. Almost all African states
have described their foreign policy with this latter term
and a single definition of it is not possible. During the
Balewa years, it meant a general pro-Western orientation
with very close ties to Britain and rapidly strengthening
ties to the United States. This was coupled with a not well-
disguised dislike for communism and a coolness toward communist regimes: 'From independence in October 1960 to the
coup of January 1966, Nigeria's policy of non-alignment
exhibited a great deal of partiality in favour of the United
States (and the rest of the Western powers), but against the
USSR' [7]. However there were disagreements between Nigeria
and the Western powers, the most obvious being opposition to
French nuclear tests in the Sahara which led to a Nigerian
diplomatic break with France in 1961 [8].

Critics of the Balewa policy attacked this pro-Western
orientation; one claimed that it was 'an incontrovertible
historical fact which makes nonsense of and exposes the bla-
tant hypocrisy underlying the declared policy of non-
alignment' [9]. These comments focus particularly on the
first few years of Balewa's regime when Nigeria and Britain
were very close in foreign trade, finance and military affairs. For example, in 1961 an Anglo-Nigerian Defence Agreement was signed. However popular resistance in Nigeria to
this led to a mild disengagement between the two states and
to a broadening of Nigeria's relations with other powers;
but not to a separation or to a strong divergence from
Nigeria's pro-Western orientation [10].

There was a hesitancy to open relations with communist
states and once normal relations were established strict
limitations were placed, for example, on the size and activities of the Soviet staff. No foreign aid was received or

requested from the USSR until after the 1966 coup. Scholar-
ships offered by the Soviet Union were generally declined,
travel by Nigerians in Eastern Europe was discouraged, and
for some years there was a ban on the importation and distribution of communist literature [11].

However as time elapsed there was some movement toward
more nonaligned behaviour and diplomatic relations were
opened with several Eastern bloc states. Also there were
attempts to diversify Nigeria's trading partners, if not to
include the Soviet Union at least to become less dependent
upon economic ties to the UK [12].

Nigerian government statements on continuing colonial rule
in the Portuguese colonies, Rhodesia and South Africa indicated a strong dislike for colonialism and racism; but
government actions were not aimed at rapid change in the
situations that prevailed in those territories. Indeed on
the entire question of decolonisation, Nigerian policy was
placid about the timing of independence for those states
still under colonial rule. The chaos in the Congo (Zaire) in
the early 1960s was seen as a result of premature independence and it was stated that colonial rule in Africa need
not end immediately, but perhaps in eight or ten years,
after suitable preparations were made in each territory.
Nigeria cooperated with the United Kingdom in the Rhodesian
situation consulting with, rather than confronting, the
British.

Nigeria did perform actions on behalf of the Africans
still under colonial or racist rule, but for the most part
these actions consisted of diplomatic contacts with the
colonial powers and activities within the confines of the
United Nations. South African citizens and a low-level Portuguese diplomatic post were allowed to remain in Nigeria
until the coup, even though many African states had by then
broken relations with South Africa and Portugal [13]. After
1963 Nigeria provided aid through the OAU to Southern African liberation movements, but no special consideration was
given to the training or assisting of the members of such
groups within Nigeria. The leaders of these movements were
discouraged from visiting Nigeria to consult with Nigerian
leaders [14].

MILITARY RULE, CIVIL WAR AND OIL: CHANGES IN THE NIGERIAN
POLITICAL SYSTEM

The military take-over of the government in 1966 and the
civil war which soon followed (lasting until 1970) was a
period in which Nigeria underwent dramatic and significant

domestic political and economic changes and these, in turn, resulted in significant changes in external behaviour.

The most obvious domestic change was in leadership. Not only was there a change from civilian to military leaders but there was also a change in the beliefs, attitudes and background of those in foreign policy decision-making positions. The northern-based conservatives were replaced by persons of a more aggressive and (after the second coup) more youthful character. Such changes occurred also in the second echelon, among those advising the men in charge [15].

There were also important structural changes in the political system. Although the federal character was maintained, the four regions eventually became nineteen smaller and weaker states. There was also a significant increase of power, including financial control, for the central government. In effect the balance of power was now in favour of the centre. And in foreign policy there was now only one voice: the Lagos voice [16].

The war and its successful conclusion had an important psychological effect upon the Nigerian leadership and perhaps upon the population as a whole. The war was a large undertaking and winning it was convincing proof to many that Nigeria and Nigerians were a capable people. The war served as a major national task — a national goal — for which most of the people of the country could unite in a common effort. For the victors this common and successful effort did much to build confidence in the nation and to overcome to some degree the sort of colonial mentality that was a hangover from the years of British rule [17]. It helped to break the bonds of psychological dependence upon the British. Some might argue that it went beyond this to engender a growing sentiment of Nigerian chauvinism.

The vanquished also came out of the war with a strengthened sense of confidence and pride. They had fought a hard battle and, although they lost, they had won respect for themselves, both for the manner in which they fought and for their technological achievements during the war. They did not view their fight as having been in vain for many felt that their point had been proven even in defeat. The manner in which the post-war reconciliation was conducted was so positive that reintegration of the defeated and the victor occurred rapidly [18].

Another effect of the war was the rapid growth of the Nigerian military, which now numbers between 150,000 and 175,000. What had been a colonial order-maintaining force had become the largest army in sub-Saharan Africa. It is reported to be inadequately trained and supplied but the Nigerian Army can claim to be stronger than any other

military force in black Africa [19] — see Chapters 2, 5,
6 and 10.

Perhaps the most dramatic and most visible change in
Nigeria has been the growth of crude oil production for and
sales in the world market. At the time of independence
Nigeria had barely begun to exploit its petroleum resources;
most of them were as yet unknown. But since then there has
been almost constant and rapid growth in the number of barrels extracted per day, and there have been great increases
in the sales price of that petroleum [20] — cf. Chapter 1.
Nigeria now sells to many states including most of West
Africa and there are plans to increase the number of local
refineries, first to supply home needs and then to export
refined products. However the oil boom has not been without
negative economic effects, such as inflation and a severe
decline in agricultural production.

This oil boom has had several significant influences on
Nigeria's foreign affairs. Most certainly, it has provided a
sense and a reality of economic independence. Nigeria was
able to pay for its civil war without going into debt; the
government ended the US aid programme; and with its new
income fuelling internal economic growth, industrialisation
underway and a huge population, Nigeria has become an attractive location for investments from abroad. These provide
a weapon for Nigerian policy-makers. The combination of
world thirst for oil and the desire for investment locations
and markets has provided Nigeria with bargaining power in
terms of the behaviour of buyers of oil and would-be investors: 'The phenomenal growth of the economy, largely as a
result of the oil boom ... has strengthened Nigeria's position in her relations with the superpowers ... Neither of
the superpowers can now use foreign aid as a means of political leverage on Nigeria ... Heavy American dependence on
Nigeria's oil [means] that Nigeria [is] free not only to
criticise the United States but also to put pressure on her'
[21]. The recent acquisition of wealth also gives Nigeria
the wherewithal to assist and influence neighbouring and
other African states [22]. However the power of this oil
weapon, both for international political and national economic purposes, is tempered by the ups and downs of the oil
market.

Nevertheless Nigeria came out of the civil war with a
stronger economic system; a political system that had become
more centralised; a larger and more potent military force;
and a greater sense of unity, purpose and national pride.
That is, the negative factors outlined by Gambari in the
pre-war period had been alleviated. The war and events in
the international environment surrounding the war also had

important educational effects for those ruling the country;
lessons were learned that have had significant ramifications
for Nigeria's foreign policy and behaviour. Olajide Aluko
describes such lessons: 'The first is that the country's
survival as a sovereign, independent state can no longer be
taken for granted.' This might be considered as the lesson
of *realpolitik*, the ending of naivety. Balewa had believed
that Nigeria's independence was secure and therefore there
was no need for a large military establishment and police
force or even for a strong central government.

'The second major lesson of the war is the need to have
friendly governments in neighbouring countries.' Here there
were the positive lessons of supportive behaviour from
neighbours such as Cameroon and the negative lessons of support for the rebels from Dahomey (Benin), Sao Tome and
Gabon. Although Aluko does not suggest it, part of this lesson includes the realisation that it may be necessary to
become involved in the affairs of neighbouring states if one
is to maintain or install friendly regimes therein. Such
involvement may include the granting of aid and the provision of advice as well as the lending of support of a more
substantial nature to regimes in power or counter-regimes
presently out of power.

'The third major lesson of the war is the fact that the
existence of the minority white-dominated regimes in
Southern Africa is a direct threat to Nigeria's security.'
There was ample evidence that the colonial and racist regimes of Southern Africa — Portugal, Rhodesia and South
Africa — were involved in the provision of support to the
Biafran secessionists. These regimes saw a united, economically developing Nigeria as a threat in the long run to the
maintenance of their particular form of rule and, in the
case of South Africa, to their hope of continental domination. The experience of the war taught that such regimes
must be numbered as major opponents of Nigeria and as critical targets of action for Nigerian diplomacy.

'The fourth lesson of the civil war is that there is dan-
ger in relying excessively on one power bloc or on the same
group of countries, and on relying entirely on external
sources for arms.' The Nigerian government quickly discovered that the traditional supplier of arms, the UK, and its
allies were not reliable; the US absolutely refused to sell
arms to the Nigerian government during the war [23]. Because
these states had their interests (and strong pressure groups
involved in the support of these interests), they were not
in a position to respond positively to all of Nigeria's support requests. So the Nigerians had to turn to the Soviet
bloc for support, and it was readily forthcoming. The

concepts of dependence and nonalignment took on new significance for Nigerian leaders. The West was unreliable; the
East was helpful. There were important benefits to be gained
by disengaging from the West to a greater extent and developing more complete and normal relations with the East [24].

MILITARY RULE AND FOREIGN POLICY

These changes in Nigeria's internal environment — political
and economic — and the lessons learned from the war had
important effects upon Nigeria's foreign policy behaviour
during the rule of the military. The state became an aggressive opponent of the Rhodesian and South African racist regimes, an eager believer and activist in African — especially West African — affairs and a much more nonaligned
state than in the past. Of course this is not simply a matter of new knowledge leading to new behaviour: Nigeria was
more capable of playing an active role than in the past.
Some might argue that Nigeria's booming capitalist economy
made a more active, perhaps 'imperialistic', policy a necessity. Let me briefly examine some of the actions of the
post-war military government in international affairs in an
effort to more fully understand the second model of Nigerian
foreign policy behaviour: the active rather than the conservative.

At what point a state moves from 'aligned' to 'nonaligned'
behaviour is open to debate, complicated by the necessity of
examining economic, political and cultural relations (at
least). However it is clear that Nigeria in this second
period was more nonaligned than prior to the war. In terms
of equality of diplomatic relations; acceptance of aid and
technology; exchanges of students, government officials and
other personnel; and attempts to expand trade and investment, Nigeria made a concerted opening to the East. This was
most clear during the war when the purchase of Soviet and
Eastern bloc weapons and the provision of Soviet advisers
was very significant [25]. But it continued with cultural
exchanges; the provision of Soviet medical teams for rural
areas; and Soviet, Polish and other East European instructors in Nigerian schools, colleges and universities. Soviet
trade with Nigeria increased (in automobiles, for example)
and the Soviet Union was involved in several major development projects such as an iron and steel industry, an oil
pipeline network and a training institute for petroleum
technicians. There was also some diplomatic cooperation, as
in the Angolan civil war and in the entire issue of Southern
Africa [26].

Nigeria's nonaligned stance was further underlined by the
opening of diplomatic relations with the People's Republic
of China (PRC) in February 1971 and by the severing of relations with Taiwan. In spite of PRC support for Biafra
during the war, relations between Nigeria and the PRC developed a more normal course; economic and trade agreements,
high-level official visits and full diplomatic relations
were undertaken [27].

These actions were not paralleled by any dramatic breaks
or turns away from the West, however. Relations with the UK,
although not without occasional conflicts, remained close;
trade and investment from Britain remained high; and cultural ties were as strong as ever. After the murder of
Murtala Mohammed, the successor to General Gowon as Head of
State, relations between the states appeared to decline to
a new low but, as Aluko argues, this appearance was deceiv-
ing. The Nigerian blustering against Britain was largely for
domestic political purposes and no significant long-term
change in any aspect of relations took place [28]. Furthermore, relations with the US seemed to reach a new low during
the reign of the inept (Africa-wise) Henry Kissinger and the
severe and important conflict between the US and Nigeria
over the Angolan civil war. Yet once the man and the issue
passed from the scene a strong, positive and cooperative
relationship was quickly apparent. Large numbers of American
instructors were recruited for Nigerian universities and US
investments in Nigeria and Nigerian oil sales to the US
continued to expand. Of greater significance was US-UK-
Nigerian cooperation in an effort to find a peaceful solution to the Rhodesian situation.

Underlying the maintenance of these links with the leading
Western states were a wide variety of financial and commercial ties. Western investments increased rapidly. Not only
the British and Americans but also the French were heavily
involved in Nigeria's economy; in 1978 Nigeria was France's
largest market in sub-Saharan Africa and the fourth largest
foreign location for French investments [29]. This involvement with the major capitalist powers is in keeping with the
predilections of the Nigerian rulers, as was convincingly
demonstrated during the process of writing a new constitution for the country.

A three-step procedure led to a new document which clearly
states a preference for a 'mixed economy' with substantial
room for Nigerian and foreign capitalists to operate [30].
During a year of public debate on the first draft of the
Constitution a major source of disagreement was its ideological underpinnings; to a large extent this was a debate
between adherents of socialism and capitalism. Support for

socialism appeared to be limited to the intellectual community, mostly university professors [31]. The prevailing ideological orientation in Nigeria is capitalist, or as Sayre Schatz states, 'nationalist nurture-capitalism with state-capitalist, welfare and accelerated-development tendencies' [32]. Schatz brings together many of the arguments of this chapter when he states:

> The particular form of Nigeria's postwar nurture capitalism was shaped by a postwar ebullience compounded of the surprisingly good economic — and political — state of the country at the end of the war, of a flowering of national self-confidence, of a bright postwar idealism, and of a more assertive nationalism [33].

Nigeria has always been a Western-oriented government (and it has remained so with the return of civilian rule), but it was not the naive follower of Western policy that it was prior to the civil war. Because of the effects of that war and because of changes in the international economic situation, Nigeria was now willing and able to oppose the Western powers when a conflict of interest occurred. This was made quite clear during the Angolan civil war when Nigerian and American interests and actions were in opposition to each other (see Chapter 3).

The Angolan case is only one example of a large number of international actions undertaken by the Nigerian military government. In Southern Africa, in West African regional affairs and in continental issues, Nigeria became the most active black African state; Nigeria was striving to be a continental power and a force to be reckoned with in international affairs beyond the continent as well (see Chapters 6, 10 and 11).

As Angola approached independence there were various attempts to bring the three African political groups — UNITA, MPLA and FNLA — into some sort of national coalition and to avoid the outbreak of civil war. However on 11 November 1975 the Portuguese passed sovereignty on to the Angolan people, but not to any government. There then followed a diplomatic campaign for recognition by the various political parties and an increase of involvement in Angolan affairs by external powers, African and non-African.

Nigeria withheld recognition of any government in the hope that a national coalition would form but this hope became irrelevant when evidence of South African military intervention inside Angola on behalf of UNITA-FNLA became clear. On 25 November Nigeria recognised the MPLA as the government of Angola and began a diplomatic campaign to bring other

African governments to the MPLA side [34]. The United States was actively supplying UNITA-FNLA and campaigning internationally for recognition of this alliance. But Nigerian recognition of the MPLA was a key factor in Africa's collective swing to the MPLA and the eventual international recognition of that party as the government of Angola [35].

Nigeria's motivations in the Angolan crisis are not absolutely clear. The new regime of Murtala Mohammed had stated that it wished to have a more active African policy than that of the Gowon regime and this was an opportunity to take action. One Nigerian writer has also suggested that competition with Zaire for continental leadership was involved; Zaire supported the UNITA-FNLA coalition [36]. Reaction to South African involvement was also a major factor [37].

Nigeria's actions in Angola (and in the attempts to find Zimbabwean and Namibian settlements) are indicative of a very different perception of Nigeria's proper role in Southern African affairs. This new behaviour, so different from that of the pre-war Balewa regime, is further exemplified by Nigeria's leading role in the African boycott of the 1976 summer Olympics in Canada. The ostensible object of protest was the participation of New Zealand in the games. A New Zealand rugby team had violated the calls of the UN, OAU and the Supreme Council of Sport in Africa to boycott all South African sports events. But more than a protest against New Zealand, the African action was a major publicity programme to make better known to the world the depth and breadth of African feelings about South African racism; it was an important achievement for African unity. Tanzania withdrew from the Olympics without sending a team to the games; other African states did send teams. But just prior to the opening of the games, Nigeria announced its withdrawal [38]. The next day twenty-two African states were absent from the opening ceremonies. In the following days the number of states joining the boycott rose to twenty-nine (including several non-African states). Only two African countries — Ivory Coast and Senegal — remained in the games [39].

One of Nigeria's greatest successes was its leadership of African and other developing states in the renegotiation of the agreements between them and the European Economic Community (EEC). Not only did Nigeria conduct much of the negotiating but it also forged a position of unity among the African governments prior to entering the negotiations [40].

Nigeria played a leading role in other aspects of continental affairs. In 1977 Lagos was the site of FESTAC, the Second World Black and African Festival of Arts and Culture, which included 15,000 performers from almost sixty countries

and thousands of visitors from all parts of the world.
FESTAC 'was intended to symbolise Nigeria's sense of leadership of black peoples in and out of Africa' [41].

Nigeria became an important mediator in African disputes.
For example, Nigeria served as mediator in the conflict between Zaire and Angola over the Shaba crisis, in the disagreements between Uganda and Tanzania, in the Western
Sahara crisis, in the effort to effect the release of French
and Swiss nationals held by rebels in Chad, and in the confrontation between Ethiopia and Somalia [42] — see Chapters
5, 6 and 10.

Nigeria also became a small-scale source of foreign aid,
particularly in the West African region. Recipients since
the end of the civil war included Sahel relief, and grants
or loans to Benin, Botswana, Ethiopia, Guinea-Bissau, Mali,
Mozambique, Niger, Somalia, Togo and Zambia. More recent
recipients have included Angola, Gambia and refugees from
Zimbabwe and South Africa. In addition, Nigeria provided
loans to the World Bank and the IMF [43].

It is in West African affairs, though, that Nigeria has
become most active. Here the prime achievement was the formation and operationalisation of ECOWAS, the Economic Community of West African States, which embraces all states in
the area from Senegal to Nigeria [44]. Nigeria's role in
ECOWAS has had a dual face; on one side it was the founder
and prime mover behind the organisation, and with good purpose: 'Nigeria was prepared to take the initiative for a
variety of reasons. With a booming economy Nigeria saw many
advantages in the creation of a common market in the West
African subregion' [45]. But on the other side, Nigeria's
size and economic power were vastly greater than those of
the other members; there was fear on their part of Nigerian
domination. 'To date, all the evidence indicates that the
Nigerians have acted in an exemplary fashion ... Yet it
cannot be denied that Nigeria is one of the foremost of the
new "middle powers" ... It is this wholly expected rise to
power that may be of some concern to smaller members of
ECOWAS' [46].

Bilateral trade agreements were made with most West
African states; aid was given to several countries in the
region; and several joint development projects were undertaken. With respect to the last category, examples are
jointly owned sugar and cement factories in Benin, an oil
refinery in Togo and Ghana, and iron ore projects in Guinea
[47]. Several authors have noted Nigeria's use of its crude
oil in facilitating the formation of ECOWAS in particular
and the improvement of inter-state relations in West Africa
in general. Nigeria has used oil in bilateral trading

agreements and has sold crude to West African states at concessionary prices [48].

Nigeria's desire to assume a leadership position in West
African politics caused the state's military rulers to become involved in the maintenance and establishment of
friendly governments in neighbouring states [49]. For many
years there had been serious domestic conflict in Chad,
and there was evidence of a breakdown of the central government and a full-scale civil war. The major rebel group,
FROLINAT or the National Front for the Liberation of Chad, a
northern Chad group, received major support from Libya and
Nigerian intervention appeared to be in part an effort to
offset the establishment of Libyan influence over the entire
country. As the situation deteriorated in March 1979,
Nigerian efforts to bring the various leaders together in-
tensified. An accord was reached, part of which included
the provision of a Nigerian peace-keeping force of 800 to
1000 men to monitor the ceasefire and Nigerian assistance
in the governing of Chad for a transition period [50].
Several sources suggest that Nigerian troops were sent even
prior to the Kano conference [51]. Later reports, prior to
Gaddafi's apparently decisive involvement, indicated that
an internal settlement had been reached which included the
appointment of Mohammed Shawa as Head of State and Head of
Government. Shawa was 'recently selected as leader of the
Popular Movement for the Liberation of Chad, a political
grouping usually described as having Nigerian backing' [52].

FROM CONSERVATISM TO ACTIVISM: CONSTRAINTS ON NIGERIAN
INFLUENCE

I have drawn two models of Nigerian foreign policy — initially the rather quiet, conservative policy that characterised the civilian regime of Balewa and secondly, the activist, Africa-oriented, more nonaligned model with efforts at
regional leadership of the post-war military regimes.

One might argue that the dichotomy established between
these two models is artificial; we may have witnessed a development process rather than an abrupt change. Nigeria's
independent, active foreign policy may be a matter of time
following the formal granting of independence: time in which
to gain experience in international relations, time to gain
confidence from 'small beginnings', time to settle critical
domestic questions in order that more energy could be expended in international affairs. A study conducted in the late
1960s indicated then that Nigeria was already one of the
most active of African states in the opening and maintenance

of diplomatic relations with other African countries: only three (Egypt, Ethiopia and Ghana) had established relations with more African governments than had Nigeria [53].

In discussing the general concept of decolonisation, I. William Zartman has stated that:

> Eur-African (and other North-South) relationships are caught up in an evolutionary process, as various forms of bilateral, metropolitan influence are replaced with multilateral relations. In the process, political independence is only the first step, and the 'last' step of complete independence is probably never attainable in an increasingly interdependent world ... Thus, there is a natural progression to the removal of colonial influence [54].

Dependence theorists present a different view: 'The dependence approach suggests that given Africa's subordinate place in the international hierarchy, its foreign policies are largely determined by external forces ... Given established inequalities any reduction in inequality is unlikely' [55]. But these theorists do suggest the existence of 'middle' powers or 'semi-peripheral' states:

> A subimperial state exists at the 'centre' of the periphery; it is a client-state that is able to exert dominance in one region of the Third World. Thus it can exploit the process of regional integration while at the same time remaining dependent on a greater, metropolitan power. A subimperial country exerts a regional hegemony akin to the global dominance of an imperial power, but at a subsystemic level. It plays an important intermediate role in a sphere of influence by dominating a region while still being subordinate to major actors at the centre of global feudal networks [56].

Most dependency theorists (at least in the African context) argue that sub-imperial status is a dead-end. The essence of the dependency relationship is the domination of the interests of the ruling élite of the sub-imperial power by the ruling élite of the imperial power and the inability or the lack of desire of the former to break away from the latter. But Kenneth W. Grundy stresses the potential for the growth and development of sufficient strength for such a middle power to break away from its dependence relation: 'This mini-empire, far from being an object of derision and scorn, may eventually challenge a core-state, at first in regional terms ... and then, conceivably in even broader terms' [57].

Nigeria's progression from its strong ties with and dependence upon the United Kingdom at the onset of independence,
to a strongly pro-West but more diversified dependence
through the remainder of the civilian era, to its present
policy of a 'Western-leaning', nonaligned stance that allows
for rather severe conflict with the West (as over Angola)
and includes movement toward regional domination and continental leadership, appears to be in keeping with Zartman's
concept of decolonisation. But the very special circumstances of Nigeria's human and mineral resources and the effects
of its civil war suggest that decolonisation operates only
under very limited conditions and that the pessimism expressed by Shaw and other dependency writers has more general
validity in African international relations.

Whether or not Nigeria will ever move beyond the 'sub-
imperial' category to an even more independent position is
doubtful, but not impossible (see Chapters 2, 6, 8 and 11).
It may be that the current international environment gives
Nigeria an opportunity (by utilising its high income from
oil to push through the development of its internal economic
structure and consolidate its external political and economic dominance of West Africa or perhaps sub-Saharan Africa)
to move to a more independent position. In this, Nigeria may
look for support to other 'middle powers', as suggested by a
$3 billion bilateral trade agreement with Brazil [58].

But Nigeria suffers from several serious problems which
may render useless any efforts to develop its internal economic structure and external influence, problems which may
leave the state in a dependent position. Among these are
doubts about the internal stability of the country and the
ease with which external powers (or domestic sub-élites) may
again stir up ethnic and regional disputes [59]. The furor
over the inclusion of Islamic courts in the first draft of
the new Constitution [60] and then over their exclusion from
the final draft [61], the shutdown of several northern universities because of their students' unhappiness over the
proportion of university admissions given to northern candi-
dates, and the long-term dispute over the acceptable manner
in which national funds (essentially oil revenues) should be
allocated to the states [62] suggest that a potential for
serious internal conflict remains. The recent disturbances
in Kano indicate that violence remains a tool to be used by
Nigerian politicians. Also there appears to be a recrystal-
lisation of the three old ethnic parties and a north-south
divide between government and opposition.

The 1981 glut on the world oil market makes clear the
dangers of relying on oil as a single source of income. A

previous glut caused severe reductions in expenditure during the 1975-80 development plan period [63]. Dependence on a monocrop or monomineral economy has been a threat to the independence of many African states as, for example, Kwame Nkrumah's Ghana and its dependence on cocoa exports. Nigeria's oil resources might be depleted before its internal economic structure has developed. World supplies are rising and demand dropping as conservation takes effect, and as alternative sources of energy come into use Nigeria's income drops drastically; in the first months of 1981 oil production was cut by over 60 per cent and government revenue was down by 30 per cent [64]. Meanwhile the periods of oil boom have been linked to the decline and decay of Nigeria's other, mostly agricultural, exports (see Chapter 1).

Nigeria's population growth and rapidly declining agricultural productivity make it a net importer of foods and its position will probably become much worse. The International Food Policy Research Institute in Washington reports that Nigeria may face a drastic food shortage within the next decade, similar to that which has been seen in India in the past. Nigeria's food deficit in 1990 may represent 35 to 39 per cent of the country's total food needs [65]. Such a situation would place Nigeria in a weakened position *vis-à-vis* food exporting states.

NIGERIA'S ALTERNATIVE FUTURES

These two models from Nigeria's past — the passive period just after independence and the more active era of post-war military rule — provide possible directions for today's civilian government to follow. But as yet it is not clear which model the Nigerian rulers will be capable of following. The political campaigns that preceded the election of the Shagari government gave little evidence upon which to make a prediction. Foreign policy was not an issue. And once in power, the Shagari government has yet to establish a constant pattern of foreign policy behaviour. Domestic distractions, such as the Kano riots and the need to establish a new system of government, and a worrisome economic situation in view of changes in the world petroleum market, have left little time for concerted foreign policy development. There are indications that an active role is still desired, but internal problems continue to push Nigeria back towards a passive role.

The view is widespread in Nigeria that because of its size (or because God wills it), Nigeria should be the leader of

Africa. This view has roots that go back even beyond independence, and it has found expression among foreign observers of African affairs as well as among Nigerians (see Chapter 11).

Nigeria has been viewed as a leader or a potential leader
by outsiders for many years. Phillips concluded his early
study of Nigerian foreign policy with the statement that
'Nigeria has begun to enter the life of the world community,
not merely as another new state but as probably the most
important state in Africa' [66]. And James Coleman discussed
the belief of Nigerian leaders, held even prior to independence, that their state should lead Africa [67]. More recently, James Mayall noted that 'since the civil war ... the
Nigerian government has consistently, discreetly, asserted
its leadership in inter-African affairs' [68]. And Jean
Herskovits has recently written of Nigeria's 'quietly growing leadership in the Third World' [69] and of Nigeria as
'a leader on the African continent' [70]. Much of this literature argues that as Nigeria is the leader of Africa it
behoves US policy-makers to stay on good terms with its
rulers as a means of influencing African affairs to
America's benefit [71].

The evidence is abundant that Nigerian politicians see
(and have seen) their country as an African leader. Prime
Minister Balewa is quoted as saying that Nigeria has a 'destiny as the leader of Africa' [72]. Jaja Wachuku, the ex-
Minister of External Affairs, stated that Nigeria 'must lead
Africa ... and we are not going to abdicate the [leadership]
position in which God almighty has placed us' [73]. And the
Permanent Secretary of that Ministry agreed in 1967: 'Because of Nigeria's population, location and human and
natural potential, the world naturally looks up to her to
provide responsible leadership in Africa' [74]. More recently, a presidential candidate, Chief Obafemi Awolowo, claimed
that under his party's rule 'Nigeria would be Africa's
leading light' [75]. As Aluko has indicated, a critical
change occurred in Nigerian foreign policy with the coup
that ousted General Gowon. Only after that time did Nigerian
rulers, both to the public and to foreign diplomats, state
their intention to be the leaders of Africa [76].

It is relevant to take notice of a provision that appeared
in the first draft of the new Nigerian Constitution. This
draft was replete with references to the preservation of
Nigerian sovereignty but nowhere is there any suggestion
that such sovereignty might be renounced in favour of some
larger-scale sovereignty, such as an African union or federation. Such statements are not unknown in African constitutions [77], but the only approach in this draft was in

paragraph 100/7/b which made provision for 'admitting
another State or part thereof from outside Nigeria as part
of the Federal Republic of Nigeria' [78]. Does this suggest
a role for Nigeria as some sort of imperial power in Africa
following a policy of 'Manifest Destiny' in swallowing up
neighbouring 'states or parts thereof'?

This one-sided approach was removed from the final draft,
but a similar sentiment did appear previously in Nigeria:
Balewa stated that 'Nigeria is big enough and does not need
to join others. But if others wish to join Nigeria, their
position would be made clear to them in such a union' [79].
And a 1961 editorial in the then influential West African
Pilot noted that 'Nigeria will not be a party to the dis-
memberment of the neighbouring countries, but when any of
them chooses to dismember itself, any part that would desire
to join Nigeria could do so and would be welcomed' [80].

Many Nigerian political scientists also view the country
as a leader of the African continent. This appears more or
less subtly in many of the Nigerian-authored articles referred to in this chapter (see Chapters 2, 6, 10 and 11). In a
section titled 'Recapitulation and Reflection' in his book,
Gordon Idang, for example, states that Nigeria 'is entitled'
to a position of leadership in Africa. And he claims that if
the country's leaders follow the correct policies, it 'will
make this large and potentially great African state a model
for other developing countries' [81]. From time to time this
view has been coupled with rather strong outbursts of popular chauvinism; for example, Bolaji Akinyemi has described
popular support for a Nigerian annexation of Fernando Po in
1962 [82]. In more recent years, the border dispute with
Cameroon has raised calls from the peoples living near the
border for the annexation (or the liberal defining of the
border) of some parts of that country. Occasionally one
hears expressions of a desire to retake all of those parts
of Cameroon that were once governed by the British and attached to Nigeria. Such statements are not made by government officials; indeed, until recently the government had
been very circumspect in this respect [83].

Two events soon after the return to civilian rule suggest
that there is considerable support within the Nigerian public (and certainly among the Nigerian press) for Nigeria to
play the active role in African affairs. First, there was
strong public reaction to Libyan intervention in Chad in
1980-1. Press and other elements of the public called for
military action to drive the Libyans out of Chad. Others,
including government officials, turned to diplomatic action
including cooperation with Chad's neighbours and with
France, the ex-colonial power in Chad. Some observers sug-

gested that although a military response to Libya's expan-
sionism was considered by the government, the Nigerian armed
forces were deemed not adequate to the situation. Only relatively few voices have argued that it was appropriate for
Libya to intervene in order to drive out the last remnants
of French colonial/neo-colonial rule and to establish law
and order in Chad for the first time since its independence.
But many have noted that Nigeria had suffered a major diplomatic embarrassment.

Second, there was a fierce reaction in Nigeria to a border
incident with Cameroon in which five Nigerian troops were
killed in a clash with Cameroon military forces, apparently
within Cameroon territory, in May 1981. There were immediate
demands from Nigeria that Cameroon should apologise, pay
damages and punish those soldiers involved. These demands
also mentioned reconsideration of border agreements made between the Cameroon government and the previous military
governments of Nigeria. In Cameroon there was no official
mention of the incident. But Nigerian radio, easily heard in
Cameroon, made no secret of the business and the rumour market in Cameroon was soon very active. Cameroon's ploy was to
keep the event as quiet and low-key as possible, preferring
to settle it quickly and without great stress; and without
allowing Cameroon public opinion to become a factor in the
settlement of the dispute. Nigerian policy was quite the
opposite, with the government calling in the world press and
with Nigerian radio stations (government-controlled) calling
for severe penalties for Cameroon, including the use of
military force. The Nigerian press, which is not government-
controlled, called for revenge and made extremely insulting
statements about Cameroon's leaders. Even after Cameroon
apologised and agreed to pay damages the pressure was kept
up. Nigeria emphasised the importance it attached to this
affair by keeping its President home during the OAU's annual
meeting in Nairobi. Diplomats in Yaounde felt that war was
very close, and Nigerian jets did buzz the new Cameroon oil
refinery in Victoria. When war did not occur, however, the
Nigerian press attacked their own government for its coward-
ice.

In fact this is not a simple reaction to a border incident, for other events show that this was part of a Nigerian
plan to bring about a renegotiation of the border settlement
reached between President Ahidjo and the previous military
governments of Nigeria. In January 1981, during what appeared to have been an amiable visit of President Shagari to
Cameroon, the Nigerians requested that the border agreement
be renegotiated. They argued that the military governments
had no legal right to have entered into such an agreement

and that, therefore, it was null and void. Soon after, the number of minor border incidents, including the imprisonment of a Cameroon administrator by Nigeria, began to increase.

This suggests that the killing of five Nigerians — an unfortunate incident — was only an excuse and not the cause, for the Nigerian government to reopen the border issue. This, in turn, suggests that apologies and payment of damages will not be sufficient to end the bilateral situation. That Nigeria was willing to put its military power to use, clearly as a threat and possibly as a reality, suggests a toughness in foreign policy that has not always been present in the past. There is some evidence to suggest that Nigeria may be willing to use this weapon in future foreign policy initiatives. In a recent article the respected and influential Director of the Nigerian Institute of International Affairs, A. Bolaji Akinyemi, wrote: 'We may now be witnessing a new era [in Africa] where military capability is going to be used to advance policy objectives by African states in relationships with other African states ... It seems, then, expedient for the Nigerian government to make up its mind. The missionary stage, the hortatory stage, of its militant foreign policy is over. It should be prepared to use military means to do two things — (1) either to stop other African states ... or, (2) using military means to achieve its own foreign policy objectives in Africa' [84]. The military may itself be impatient after the embarrassment of Nigeria's failure in Chad *vis-à-vis* the Libyans and the lack of revenge for its lost men in Cameroon.

Nigeria has many of the physical characteristics of a continental or middle power [85]. It has a large population, an economy that is powerful compared to its neighbours and one that is growing rapidly, mineral resources and a growing industrial capability, and a large military force. Underlying these characteristics, there appears to be a widely held assumption among Nigerians that Nigeria either already is, or is destined to become, a leader of Africa.

In spite of certain causes of internal weakness, it is probable that Nigeria's new civilian rulers will follow the model established by the military rulers, the model of an active power, playing the role of an influential state in West African, African and Third World affairs (see Chapters 6, 10 and 11). I suspect that the public, the military, the press and other groups will urge this role and that Nigeria's economic position will dictate it. Whether this activist role will be played as a 'sub-imperial' power with continuing dependence on external superpowers as in the dependency model, or as an 'imperial' power in its own right

struggling for dominance on the continent and for independence in world affairs, is a matter of debate for the
theorists. In general, Nigerians and Nigerian politicians
seem to be striving for the latter.

NOTES AND REFERENCES

1. The major study of this period notes that Nigerian
   foreign policy appeared to 'speak with too many voices'.
   See Claude S. Phillips, Jr, The Development of Nigerian
   Foreign Policy (Evanston: Northwestern University Press,
   1964) p. 81.
2. See Ibrahim A. Gambari, 'Nigeria and the World: a Growing Internal Stability, Wealth and External Influence',
   Journal of International Affairs, 29 (2), Fall 1975,
   pp. 1975, pp. 157-8. Another factor was 'the absence of
   nationally-oriented political parties'. See Julius E.
   Okolo and Winston E. Langley, 'The Changing Nigerian
   Foreign Policy', World Affairs, 135 (4), Spring 1973,
   p. 315.
3. See A. B. Akinyemi, Foreign Policy and Federalism: the
   Nigerian Experience (Ibadan University Press, 1974),
   pp. 200-1. That foreign policy was almost entirely an
   executive function (and to a large extent of Balewa's
   making) is argued in R. A. Akindele, 'Nigerian Parliament and Foreign Policy, 1960-1966', Quarterly Journal
   of Administration, 9 (3), April 1975, pp. 279-91.
4. R. A. Akindele, 'The Conduct of Nigeria's Foreign
   Relations', International Problems, 12 (3-4), October
   1973, pp. 61-2.
5. Olajide Aluko, Ghana and Nigeria 1957-70: a Study in
   Inter-African Discord (London: Rex Collings, 1976)
   pp. 20-1.
6. Studies of this period are numerous. In addition to
   Akinyemi, Foreign Policy and Federalism, Aluko, Ghana
   and Nigeria, and Phillips, The Development of Nigerian
   Foreign Policy, see Gordon J. Idang, Nigeria: Internal
   Politics and Foreign Policy (1960-1966) (Ibadan University Press, 1973). Also see L. Gray Cowan, 'Nigerian
   Foreign Policy' in R. O. Tilman and T. Cole (eds), The
   Nigerian Political Scene (Durham: Duke University Press,
   1966) pp. 115-43.
7. Olajide Aluko, 'Nigeria and the Superpowers', Millenium,
   5 (2), Autumn 1976, p. 132.
8. See Phillips, Development of Nigerian Foreign Policy,
   pp. 124-6.

9. R. A. Akindele, 'On the Operational Linkage of External and Internal Dimensions of Balewa's Foreign Policy', Odu: a Journal of West African Studies, 12, July 1975, p. 114.

10. For a fuller discussion see Olasupo Ojedokun, 'The Anglo-Nigerian Entente and Its Demise, 1960-62', Journal of Commonwealth Political Studies, 9 (3), November 1971, pp. 210-33. Also see Phillips, Development of Nigerian Foreign Policy, passim. Henry L. Bretton argues that this close Anglo-Nigerian relation was a product of the transfer of power from colonial to independent state. Through educational and economic ties, 'a group of Nigerians had been trained to accept the system and its implications'. Power and Stability in Nigeria (New York: Praeger, 1962) p. 24.

11. Aluko, Ghana and Nigeria, pp. 187-8.

12. Olasupo Ojedokun, 'The Changing Pattern of Nigeria's International Economic Relations: the Decline of the Colonial Nexus, 1960-1966', Journal of Developing Areas, 6 (4), July 1972, pp. 535-54. Also see Douglas G. Anglin, 'Nigeria: Political Non-alignment and Economic Alignment', Journal of Modern African Studies, 2 (2), June 1964, pp. 147-63.

13. Aluko, Ghana and Nigeria, pp. 92-3 and 177-80.

14. Akinyemi, Foreign Policy and Federalism, pp. 100-9.

15. See Victor A. Olorunsola, Societal Reconstruction in Two African States (Washington: University Press of America, 1977).

16. For brief discussions of these changes see Gambari, 'Nigeria and the World'; Okolo and Langley, 'The Changing Nigerian Foreign Policy'; O. Aluko, 'The Civil War and Nigerian Foreign Policy', Political Quarterly, 42 (2), April-June 1971, pp. 182-4, and 'Nigeria's Role in Inter-African Relations', African Affairs, 72 (287), April 1973, pp. 156-9; and Jean Herskovits, 'One Nigeria', Foreign Affairs, 51 (2), January 1973, pp. 392-407.

17. It is possible that such a war, although not fought directly against the colonial oppressor, serves a function similar to that suggested by Frantz Fanon in The Wretched of the Earth (Harmondsworth: Penguin, 1967).

18. Herskovits, 'One Nigeria', pp. 394-401.

19. See Africa Research Bulletin, November 1978, p. 5030C, November 1977, p. 4613B, and February 1976, p. 3905C.

20. For a brief summary of the growth of oil production and its effects on Nigeria, see Guy Arnold, Modern Nigeria (London: Longman, 1977) pp. 50-64. For greater depth, refer to Douglas Rimmer, 'Elements of the political

economy' in K. Panter-Brick (ed.), Soldiers and Oil
(London: Cass, 1978) pp. 141-65 (but especially pp. 149-
53). Scott R. Pearson, Petroleum and the Nigerian Economy (Stanford University Press, 1970) is a earlier analysis.

21. Aluko, 'Nigeria and the Superpowers', p. 138.

22. For further discussion see James Mayall, 'Oil and
Nigerian Foreign Policy', African Affairs, 75 (300),
July 1976, pp. 284-316.

23. Oye Ogunbadejo, 'Nigeria and the Great Powers: the
Impact of the Civil War on Nigerian Foreign Relations',
African Affairs, 75 (298), January 1976, pp. 18-21 dis-
cusses US policy.

24. Aluko, 'The Civil War and Nigerian Foreign Policy',
pp. 178-80. The author also describes a fifth lesson:
'the importance and the value of publicity in the conduct of external relations' (p. 180). Also see Olajide
Aluko, 'Nigerian Foreign Policy' in his collection, The
Foreign Policies of African States (London: Hodder &
Stoughton, 1977) pp. 163-95.

25. For discussions of Soviet policy see Robert Legvold,
Soviet Policy in West Africa (Cambridge, Mass.: Harvard
University Press, 1970) and the note by George Obiozor,
'Soviet Involvement in the Nigerian Civil War' in
U. G. Damachi and H. D. Seibel (eds), Social Change and
Economic Development in Nigeria (New York: Praeger,
1973) pp. 230-4.

26. Oye Ogunbadejo, 'Ideology and Pragmatism: the Soviet
Role in Nigeria, 1960-1977', Orbis, 21 (4), Winter 1978,
pp. 803-30 and his 'Nigeria and the Great Powers', pp.
23-7. For comparison of US and Soviet relations with
Nigeria see Aluko, 'Nigeria and the Superpowers'.

27. Ogunbadejo, 'Nigeria and the Great Powers', and S.
Salahuddin Ahmad, 'Nigeria-China Relations: an Approach
to Positive Neutrality', Pakistan Horizon, 26 (1), 1973,
pp. 48-54.

28. Olajide Aluko, 'Nigeria and Britain since Gowon',
African Affairs, 76 (304), July 1977, pp. 303-27.

29. Africa Research Bulletin, 15 (3), 15 April 1978,
p. 4798A and Africa Research Bulletin, 15 (1),
15 February 1978, p. 4726A.

30. Nigeria — Report of the Constitution Drafting Committee
Containing the Draft Constitution, Volume 1 (Lagos:
Federal Ministry of Information, 1976).

31. Discussed in Mark W. DeLancey, 'Selected Aspects of the
Public Debate on the Drafting of the Nigerian Constitution', International Studies Association, Toronto, April
1979, and 'Public Opinion on the Draft Constitution' in

S. E. Oyovbaire (ed.), <u>Political Issues in the Nigerian Draft Constitution</u> (Zaria: Nigerian Political Science Association, 1977) pp. 147–75.

32. Sayre P. Schatz, <u>Nigerian Capitalism</u> (Berkeley: University of California Press, 1977) p. 7.
33. Ibid., p. 21.
34. Arnold notes that several Nigerian officials visited various African capitals to win support for the MPLA. As examples of Nigeria's influence, he suggests that Ghana, Libya, Niger and Chad moved to the MPLA side among other states as a result of Nigerian efforts (<u>Modern Nigeria</u>, p. 137).
35. Although it must be admitted that negative African reaction to Ford–Kissinger diplomacy helped the MPLA to some extent.
36. Peter Enaharo, 'OAU and Angola: Power Politics', <u>Africa</u>, 54, February 1976, p. 13. For other Nigerian opinions, see Mark W. DeLancey, 'Some Nigerian Views on the Angolan Conflict', <u>Bulletin of the Southern Association of Africanists</u>, 4 (2), June 1976, pp. 39–53.
37. Arnold, <u>Modern Nigeria</u>, p. 137.
38. 'Taiwan, Nigeria Quit Olympics; More Withdrawals Threatened', <u>New York Times</u>, 17 July 1976, p. 17.
39. Nigeria's attempt to repeat the boycott at the 1978 Commonwealth Games in Edmonton, Canada failed. No team followed Nigeria's withdrawal and call for a boycott. See 'Nigeria Denied Support in Boycott Decision', <u>New York Times</u>, 28 July 1978, p. 18 and 'Games Boycott Shocker', <u>Daily Times</u>, 28 July 1978, p. 1.
40. See Olajide Aluko, 'Nigeria and the European Economic Community', <u>International Studies</u>, 13 (3), July–September 1974, pp. 465–73.
41. John Darton, 'Nigeria, Africa's West Coast Giant', <u>New York Times</u>, 13 February 1977, IV, p. 3.
42. Olajide Aluko, 'Nigeria's Role in Inter-African Relations', pp. 154–5, describes earlier Nigerian mediation roles.
43. Arnold, <u>Modern Nigeria</u>, p. 139; Mayall, 'Oil and Nigerian Foreign Policy', p. 326; <u>Africa Research Bulletin</u>, January 1978, p. 4695B, February 1978, p. 4700B, and April 1978, p. 4802A; and Okoi Arikpo, 'Nigeria and the OAU', <u>Nigerian Journal of International Affairs</u>, 1 (1), 1975, pp. 8–10.
44. Nigeria's role in founding this organisation is briefly described in Aluko, 'Nigeria's Role in Inter-African Relations' and Mazi Ray Ofoegbu, 'The Relations Between Nigeria and Its Neighbours', <u>Nigerian Journal of International Studies</u>, 1 (1), July 1975, pp. 28–40.

45. John P. Renninger, <u>Multinational Cooperation for Development in West Africa</u> (New York: Pergamon, 1979) p. 31; and also see p. 48.
46. Ibid., p. 45.
47. Mayall, 'Oil and Nigerian Foreign Policy', p. 326.
48. Ibid., and Olajide Aluko, 'Oil at Concessionary Prices for Africa: a Case Study in Nigerian Decision-making', <u>African Affairs</u>, 75 (301), October 1976, pp. 425-43.
49. A role suggested by Aluko, 'Nigerian Foreign Policy', pp. 165-6.
50. A student of Nigerian foreign policy has recently suggested that Nigeria is not acting as a regional power. To support this contention, he claims that 'there is no sign that Nigeria is prepared to play a significant role in any regional crisis'. Raymond W. Copson, 'African International Politics — Under-development and Conflict in the 1970's, <u>Orbis</u>, 22 (1), Spring 1978, p. 241.
51. 'Nigerian Troops for Chad', <u>Daily Times</u>, 9 March 1979, p. 1; 'Chad: Nigeria Takes Major Role', <u>Africa News</u>, 16 March 1979, p. 2; 'Chad: Peace Accord Signed in Kano', <u>Africa News</u>, 23 March 1979, p. 11; Winfred Carey, 'Nigeria to Mediate in Chad's War', <u>New York Times</u>, 1 March 1979; and 'Chad Leaders Sign Peace Treaty', <u>Daily Times</u>, 17 March 1979, p. 1.
52. Geoffrey Godsell, 'Chad Opts for Power Sharing', <u>Christian Science Monitor</u>, 8 March 1979.
53. David H. Johns, 'The Normalisation of Intra-African Diplomatic Activity', <u>Journal of Modern African Studies</u>, 10 (4), December 1972, pp. 597-610.
54. I. William Zartman, 'Europe and Africa: Decolonisation or Dependency?' <u>Foreign Affairs</u>, 54 (2), January 1976, p. 326.
55. Timothy M. Shaw and M. Catherine Newbury, 'Dependence or Interdependence: Africa in the Global Political Economy' in Mark W. DeLancey (ed.), <u>Aspects of International Relations in Africa</u> (Bloomington: African Studies Program, Indiana University, 1979) p. 41.
56. Timothy M. Shaw, 'Kenya and South Africa: "Subimperialist" States', <u>Orbis</u>, 21 (2), Summer 1977, p. 376.
57. Kenneth W. Grundy, 'Regional Relations in Southern Africa and the Global Political Economy' in DeLancey (ed.), <u>Aspects of International Relations in Africa</u>, p. 95. This argument is also presented in Grundy, 'Intermediary Power and Global Dependency: the Case of South Africa', <u>International Studies Quarterly</u>, 20 (4), December 1976, pp. 553-80. Henry Bretton argues that no such power exists in tropical Africa in his <u>Patron-Client Relations: Middle Africa and the Powers</u> (New York: General Learning Press, 1971) p. 1.

58. 'African Update', Africa Report, May–June 1979, p. 29.
    For an analysis of Brazil as a middle power see Annette
    B. Fox, The Politics of Attraction (New York: Columbia
    University Press, 1977).
59. For example, see Terisa Turner, 'Multinational Corpora-
    tions and the Instability of the Nigerian State', Review
    of African Political Economy, 5, January–April 1976,
    pp. 63–79; also published as 'Commercial Capitalism and
    the 1975 Coup' in Panter-Brick (ed.), Soldiers and Oil,
    pp. 166–97.
60. Discussed in DeLancey, 'Selected Aspects of the Public
    Debate' and 'Public Opinion on the Draft Constitution'.
61. 'Walkout Protest over Sharia', West Africa, 3170, 17
    April 1978, p. 737 and 'Obasanjo Warning to Assembly
    Members', West Africa, 3171, 24 April 1978, pp. 776–9.
62. Winfred Carey, 'Resentment Growing in Nigeria's North',
    New York Times, 17 March 1979; 'JAMB Today, None
    Tomorrow', West Africa, 3221, 9 April 1979, pp. 625–7;
    and S. E. Oyovbaire, 'The Politics of Revenue Alloca-
    tion' in Panter-Brick (ed.), Soldiers and Oil, pp. 224–
    49.
63. 'A Valuable Pause for Nigeria', West Africa, 3188,
    21 August 1978, p. 1627.
64. 'Cost of the Oil Glut to Nigeria', West Africa, 3343,
    24 August 1981, p. 1947.
65. 'Nigeria Faces Dearth of Food', Sun, 1 January 1978.
    Also see I. William Zartman, 'Coming Political Problems
    in Black Africa' in Jennifer Seymour Whitaker (ed.),
    Africa and the United States (New York University Press
    for Council on Foreign Relations, 1978) p. 91.
66. Phillips, Development of Nigerian Foreign Policy,
    p. 145.
67. James S. Coleman, 'The Foreign Policy of Nigeria' in
    J. E. Black and K. W. Thomson (eds.), Foreign Policies
    in a World of Change (New York: Harper & Row, 1963)
    p. 400.
68. Mayall, 'Oil and Nigerian Foreign Policy', p. 325.
69. Jean Herskovits, 'Nigeria: Africa's New Power', Foreign
    Affairs, 53 (2), January 1975, p. 315.
70. Jean Herskovits, 'Dateline Nigeria: a Black Power',
    Foreign Policy, 29, Winter 1977–8, p. 188.
71. Ibid., and Jennifer Seymour Whitaker, 'U.S. Policy
    Toward Africa' in her collection on Africa and the
    United States, p. 236.
72. Quoted in Coleman, 'The Foreign Policy of Nigeria',
    p. 400.
73. Quoted in Aluko, Ghana and Nigeria, p. 75. Also see the
    remainder of his chapter (pp. 72–121) on Nigerian-
    Ghanaian competition for leadership of Africa.

74. E. O. Ogbu, 'Nigeria's Foreign Policy', <u>Administration</u> (Ibadan), 2, October 1967, p. 24.
75. Quoted in 'UPN Will Make Nigeria Africa's Light', <u>Daily Times</u>, 10 April 1979, p. 37.
76. Olajide Aluko, 'The 'New' Nigerian Foreign Policy', <u>Round Table</u>, 66, October 1976, p. 411.
77. As discussed briefly in Mark DeLancey, 'Early Attempts at West African Unity', <u>Indian Journal of Politics</u>, 7 (1), 1973, pp. 47-55.
78. <u>Report of the Constitution Drafting Committee Containing the Draft Constitution</u>, Volume 1, p. 41.
79. Quoted in Phillips, <u>Development of Nigerian Foreign Policy</u>, p. 90, and R. A. Akindele, 'Nigeria's Foreign Relations', <u>International Problems</u>, 12 (3), 1973, pp. 102-13.
80. As quoted in Akinyemi, <u>Foreign Policy and Federalism</u>, p. 148.
81. Idang, <u>Nigeria</u>, pp. 159-60.
82. Bolaji Akinyemi, 'Nigeria and Fernando Po, 1958-1966: the Politics of Irredentism', <u>African Affairs</u>, 69 (276), July 1970, pp. 236-49; revised version appears as 'Fernando Po and the Cameroun: the Politics of Irredentism' in his <u>Foreign Policy and Federalism</u>, pp. 110-48. Also see Phillips, <u>Development of Nigerian Foreign Policy</u>, pp. 127-9.
83. Akinyemi, <u>Foreign Policy and Federalism</u>, p. 147, notes that the Premier of Northern Nigeria wished to claim for Nigeria all parts of Cameroon that were once part of the Fulani Empire.
84. A. Bolaji Akinyemi, 'Chad: the Lessons for Nigeria', <u>Nigerian Forum</u>, 1 (1), March 1981, pp. 12-13.
85. A rank ordering of thirty-two black African nations on a measure of power has Nigeria ranked first. See B. W. Tomlin and M. A. Kuhlman, 'Relative Status and Foreign Policy', <u>Journal of Conflict Resolution</u>, 21 (2), 1977, p. 202.

10 Nigerian Foreign Policy in the Year 2000

OLAJIDE ALUKO

In a Lagos lecture on 'Nigeria in World Affairs' in the mid-1970s, Ali Mazrui predicted that at the end of this century Nigeria would have greater diplomatic influence than either Britain or France even though she might not be as technologically developed as them [1]. Mazrui's prediction must be regarded as too bold and perhaps misleading. Bold because a variety of factors, and the forces of the unforeseen, could frustrate this prediction. Misleading because it tends to separate the level of industrial technology from the diplomatic weight of a country. While it is arguable that diplomatic influence does not necessarily correspond to the level of technological development, it is also true that a country with a low level of technological and industrial development can hardly have much diplomatic weight.

Apart from the above specifics in relation to Nigerian foreign policy in the year 2000, there are obvious general difficulties in writing about the future. These are most serious in international relations. For here states are involved in coping with external circumstances over which they have neither control, nor perfect knowledge. Moreover these external circumstances can undergo drastic change. Even at home where governments seem to be in greater control, major changes can occur in political, economic and social fortunes far beyond what any analyst will have foreseen.

All this makes writing about the future of foreign policy a risky enterprise even for futurologists. While theologians will say that tomorrow belongs to God, G. K. Chesterton said that 'the most plausible and depressing prophecy of all is that the future will resemble the past' [2]. Taking a cue from this and recognising the common social science axiom that the future is largely a function of the past and the present, I can try to examine what may be Nigeria's foreign policy options at the end of this century. In order to do this properly, I shall first examine several issues of the past and present, namely: current policy goals and the determinants of policy both external and internal.

CURRENT POLICY GOALS

The current goals of Nigerian foreign policy are not very
different from those of the recent past. Section 19 of the
1979 Federal Constitution states the objectives of the
country's foreign policy. These are to 'promote African
Unity, as well as total political, economic, social and
cultural liberation of Africa and all other forms of international co-operation conducive to the consolidation of
universal peace and mutual respect and friendship among all
peoples and States, and ... combat racial discrimination in
all its manifestations'. While this list is useful it is not
a comprehensive guide. For section 19 of the Constitution
has lumped too many objectives together, some of which are
unrealisable such as the 'total political, economic, social
and cultural liberation of Africa' [3]. Moreover, it does
not include some of the salient objectives of Nigerian
foreign policy in Africa.

None the less, from the provisions of the Constitution as
well as from the pronouncements and practices of Nigerian
leaders, the objectives of the country's foreign policy can
be classified into five, namely: the promotion of African
unity; the elimination of colonialism, racism and apartheid
from the continent; a determination to play the leadership
role in Africa; the promotion of regional and sub-regional
economic groupings in Africa; and the promotion of a peaceful and just world. I shall elucidate further on each of
these briefly.

Right from the first years of independence Nigeria has
been committed to the promotion of African unity. This could
be seen in the attempt of Sir Abubakar to bring the Monrovia
and the Casablanca groups of states together during the
1961-3 period. Since the formation of the OAU Nigeria has on
the whole continued to back the Organisation. Its position
has been that a continent that is made up of as many mini-
states as Africa will remain an easy prey for the great
powers if it is not united. Furthermore, Lagos believed that
only a united continent with a single spokesperson could
reasonably work out any economic arrangement with the big
powers; hence the decision of the then federal military
government in 1973 to join, and lead, the rest of Africa
together with the Caribbean and the Pacific states (ACP) in
negotiations with the EEC during the 1973-5 period.

Likewise, the elimination of colonialism, racism and
apartheid in Africa has long been central to Nigerian

foreign policy. It should be remembered that the Balewa
government played an important role in the events that led
to the withdrawal of South Africa from the Commonwealth in
1961. However since the end of the Nigerian civil war in
1970, the government has brought greater vigour and commitment to the campaign against colonialism, racism and apartheid in Southern Africa. It is pertinent to note the critical role of Nigeria in Angola between 1975 and 1976, and in
Rhodesia (now Zimbabwe) between 1971 and 1980.

Since the early years of independence Nigeria has played a
key role in the formation of economic groupings in West
Africa in particular and in the continent in general. These
were made at two levels — bilateral and multilateral. In
1964 both the River Niger Basin Commission and the Chad
Basin Commission were established at the initiative of
Nigeria. And it was the bilateral agreement between Nigeria
and Togo in April 1972 that paved the way for the formation
of the Economic Community of West African States (ECOWAS)
in May 1975. At the continental level Nigeria has done much
to make the OAU specialised commission on economic and
social matters work, though to little avail. And it was
largely a Nigerian initiative that led to the first African
economic summit in Lagos in April 1980.

A desire to play the leadership role in Africa and to be
the continent's spokesperson in international affairs has been
one of the main objectives of Nigerian foreign policy, even
though the country's leaders have rarely elaborated on this
goal (see Chapters 2, 6, and 11). Even a modest leader such
as the country's first Prime Minister, Sir Abubakar, believed that it was Nigeria and not Ghana that should speak
for Africa [4]. Recently the Nigerian Defence Minister,
Alhaji Akanbi Oniyangi, said that 'We [Nigerians] are also
generally agreed that Nigeria should provide the leadership
role in Africa ... By and large our people would want
Nigeria to become and remain a dominant power in our sub-
region, and on the African continent as a whole' [5]. And
Peter Enahoro, the publisher of <u>Africa Now</u> magazine has
described Nigeria as 'the power base of Africa' [6], by
which he seemed to mean that Nigeria has become the leader
and spokesperson of Africa.

The promotion of a peaceful and just world is also an
important objective of Nigerian foreign policy. Nigeria's
active participation in the nonaligned movement is a good
example of this. The same could be said of Nigeria's vigorous and positive role in the Group of 77, the North-South
dialogue and OPEC, especially in the contribution of funds
to assist the less developed oil-importing states. Similarly, the participation of some units of the Nigerian armed

forces in the UN military operation in the Congo in the
early 1960s and in Lebanon (in UNIFIL) since the late 1970s
are clear examples of Nigeria's commitment to international
peace.

Like the foreign policy of any other country, Nigerian
foreign policy is largely a result of an interplay between
external and internal factors. Significant changes in any of
these factors can bring about shifts in foreign policy [7].
Thus I shall consider the major external and internal environments shaping Nigerian foreign policy, possible changes
in them in the mid-term future, and consequences for foreign
policy options at the end of this century.

DETERMINANTS OF POLICY: EXTERNAL ENVIRONMENT

At the global level there are two types of pressure that
have been influencing Nigerian foreign policy over the last
twenty years. The first arises from the Cold War — the continuing rivalry and competition between the superpowers —
and the second arises from Nigeria's membership in the UN.

Nigeria became independent in 1960 at the height of the
Cold War. Although it seems as if the worst of the Cold War
is now over, the intense competition between the US and the
USSR has continued, with the nuclear angel blazing his flam-
ing sword over the whole world threatening the extinction,
and at the same time protecting the future, of this troubled
planet. In these circumstances, Nigeria's policy option was
clearly and definitely that of nonalignment. For to have
aligned with either side would have cost Nigeria embarrassment at home and a loss of self-respect abroad.

It is doubtful whether this intense competition between
the superpowers will disappear by the end of this century.
If the past trend is anything to go by, the rivalry may not
lead to hot war between them but the bilateral competition
will continue. And as long as this is the case, Nigeria's
policy orientation towards them will be based on nonalignment.

Nigeria's membership of the UN has imposed some obligations on her under the UN Charter. Apart from participating
in all UN-sponsored conferences on economic and social
matters, such as UNCTAD, FAO, UNESCO, etc., Nigeria has
sent some detachments of her armed forces to participate in
the UN military operation in the Congo (ONUC) and now in
Lebanon (UNIFIL). Short of a major mishap to the world, such
as a nuclear holocaust, the UN will remain in existence in
the year 2000. And if it does then Nigeria's membership of
it will continue; and this is bound to shape her policy

options in the future as in the past.

At the regional level pressures influencing Nigeria's foreign policy have arisen from two main points: first, the existence of the OAU and Nigeria's membership in the Organisation; and second, the continued occupation of Namibia by South Africa along with continued existence of apartheid in the Republic of South Africa itself — and two minor points: first, the Commonwealth and second, ECOWAS. Membership in the OAU has imposed certain obligations on Nigeria including such principles as respect for the sovereign equality of states, non-interference in the internal affairs of member states and the sanctity of frontiers inherited from the former colonial powers. Although some African states — such as Ghana under Nkrumah, Tanzania's 'invasion' of Uganda in 1978 and 1979, and Somalia's incursion into Ethiopia during 1977 and 1978 — have breached these principles, all Nigerian governments since independence have tended to comply with these basic OAU principles in the interest of peace and order in Africa. It was said, though not really convincingly, that this was why the Mohammed government did not take any military action in January 1976 against the Equatorial Guinean government for killing fifteen Nigerian nationals on the premises of the Nigerian embassy in Malabo.

Nigeria has taken a number of steps to keep the OAU united. These included her decision in mid-1973 to reverse her earlier decision not to enter into any multilateral arrangement with the EEC. In the event she opted not only to join the other ACP states but also to lead them in their negotiations with the EEC in what later became the first Lomé Convention. Although during the latter part of the 1970s the Obasanjo government took some stands against the majority of OAU member states — see, for instance, the decision to recognise the MPLA regime in Angola in Chapter 3 — on the whole the overriding consideration has been to keep both Africa and its continental organisation united. As far as I can tell, the OAU will continue to exist by the end of this century. In that case, Nigeria's continued membership of it will continue to have some influence on her foreign policy.

Another factor that has continued to shape Nigeria's foreign policy on the continent has been the continued existence of white-supremacist regimes in Southern Africa. In order to end these, Nigeria has since independence taken a number of measures against them, especially in spearheading their exclusion from most UN conferences and agencies, in the field of propaganda against the white redoubt, and in the provision of material, moral, financial and diplomatic support to all the liberation movements in the sub-region. Moreover, Nigeria has for years been putting pressure on

South Africa's Western economic partners to end their oil, financial and military ties with Pretoria.

Although Nigeria's efforts have neither had much effort on the basic apartheid philosophy of South Africa nor have they made Pretoria to want to scuttle out of Namibia, Nigeria has continued to provide assistance to, and to widen her range of support for, the liberation movements in South Africa and Namibia. In addition she has continued to put pressure on the Western powers to review their relationships with Pretoria if they want to continue to enjoy cordial relations with her. As long as there is no fundamental change in the socio-economic and political arrangements in those territories under white regimes, Nigeria is unlikely to change her policy towards them. On the contrary, in the future she may add more ammunition to her armoury in her campaign against them.

While the Commonwealth is not strictly a regional organisation, I shall say something about it for two reasons. First, Nigeria has remained a member of it since her independence in 1960, and during the state visit of President Shehu Shagari to London in February 1981 he said that his country continued to value ties with the Commonwealth. Second, her membership has imposed some rights and duties on her, however slight. The obligations arising from membership in the Commonwealth include such things as regular contributions to the Commonwealth Secretariat in London — to which Nigeria contributes an annual average of ₦35,000 — and to the Commonwealth Special Technical Fund — to which Nigeria contributes an annual average of ₦13,000 [8]. Furthermore, another obligation is informal political consultation among all the Commonwealth member states.

Despite the turbulent history of the Commonwealth especially since 1961, I can reasonably expect that the Commonwealth will not have disappeared by the year 2000. Although there have been some critical opinions expressed about Nigeria's continued membership in the Commonwealth, short of a major root-and-branch change within the country before the end of this century, Nigeria will continue to retain her membership of it. And if she does, it follows that she has to accept the associated obligations.

On the sub-regional level — that is, West Africa — pressures have been intense. While this sub-region, and especially neighbouring states, was not considered to pose any threat to the security of Nigeria until recently, Gowon regarded it as the first line of defence of the country's territorial integrity, sovereignty and independence: he regarded it as the core area of concentration for Nigerian diplomacy. The decision of the Gowon government in 1974 to

sell oil at preferential rates to African states was largely
in response to pressures from West Africa [9]. This largely
accounted for Gowon's bold initiatives that eventually led
to the formation of ECOWAS in May 1975. His successors, such
as Obasanjo, tried on the whole to build on this foundation;
hence the non-aggression pact signed by all the ECOWAS states
in Dakar in 1979 as well as the protocol of free movement
for all ECOWAS citizens for a period of ninety days signed
at the same Dakar Summit. All things being equal, ECOWAS is
likely to survive until the year 2000. In which case,
Nigeria's policy will continue to be influenced by it.

DETERMINANTS OF POLICY: INTERNAL ENVIRONMENT

Internal pressures influencing Nigerian foreign policy arise
mainly from her economic resources, her military capability
and her political structure. I shall deal with each of these
briefly, concentrating on likely changes in each of them and
the effect of these on foreign policy.

With a population estimated at about eighty million over
an area of about 356,700 sq. miles, Nigeria is potentially
strong economically. She is, moreover, well endowed by nature. Apart from a variety of agricultural products such as
cocoa, palm products, cotton, coffee, groundnuts, rubber and
logs, the country has a large number of valuable and strategic mineral resources such as tin, columbite, tantalite,
wolfram, gold, lead, zinc, coal, iron, uranium, lignite,
natural gas and crude oil.

However although since the mid-1970s Nigeria has become
the sixth oil-exporting country, other sectors of the economy have been depressed. Indeed agriculture has sharply declined. A country that was not only able to feed its citizens but also to export food to other West African countries
even during the civil war (1967-70) has now become a net
importer of food. In 1979 Nigeria spent about ₦1.7 billion
or about 13 per cent of all its import bill for that year on
food [10]. In addition Nigeria has since the late 1970s been
importing palm oil, groundnuts, logs, etc., which used to
form a significant proportion of her foreign exchange earnings in the immediate years after independence.

Furthermore, the level of industrialisation continues to
be low; for instance, the manufacturing sector contributed
only 7 per cent of GDP in 1980. The quality of modern infrastructural facilities in the country is even worse than at
independence. It can be said that in almost all senses the
Nigerian economy is underdeveloped, being based largely on
the exportation of primary products and the importation of

finished goods and technical know-how. The balance of payments position of the country was in deficit from 1975
until 1979; and the surplus of ₦1.5 billion [11] recorded in
1980 was in the main caused by the Iranian revolution and
the subsequent Gulf War.

The consequences of this continuing economic weakness for
the country's foreign policy have been considerable. It set
limitations on the amount of financial resources Nigeria
could make available to the African Development Bank, the
OAU Secretariat and as aid to less fortunate African countries. It has also restricted the number of experts Nigeria
could provide to other African countries under her technical
assistance programme.

I cannot say categorically what will be the state of the
country's economic status and strength at the end of the
century. But unless proper, sound planning takes place and
unless there is a considerable improvement in the management
of the country's agricultural sector, the end of the century
may see Nigeria spending a greater percentage of her total
import bill on food. The upshot of this would be further
limitations on the country's foreign policy options. If,
however, the economy becomes more industrialised and more
buoyant by the year 2000, then the Nigerian government will
be able to play a more dynamic role in Africa and in the
rest of the world.

Militarily, Nigeria's position has not been strong especially when compared to that of the great powers. In size
the country's armed forces total 146,000 and are adequate
for both the internal and external requirements of the
country. But they are ill-equipped. Although the army has
recently acquired some tanks — sixty-four T-55 medium-range
tanks, and fifty Scorpion light tanks — it has no
single mechanised battalion. Moreover, most of the arms,
ammunition and equipment used by the Nigerian armed forces
are supplied from external sources [12]. The country has,
since the end of the civil war, been spending an annual
average of 11 per cent of GDP on the armed forces, which is
one of the highest for a country not fighting a war. However
a very large proportion of this — estimated by General T.
Y. Danjuma, Nigerian Chief of Staff from 1975 until 1979, at
about 90 per cent of total government estimates for the
army — was devoted to the payment of salaries and personal
emoluments leaving very little for the purchase of modern
equipment. There is no evidence that there has since been
a major change in the percentage of the army budget devoted
to salaries and other personal allowances at the expense of
materiel.

The Nigerian Navy, consisting of about 8000 men and women,

is in even worse shape. It has no single destroyer, not to
talk of a submarine. It has a couple of frigates but these
are not even adequate to patrol Nigerian territorial waters.
And about half of its other boats are not even serviceable.
The situation has got so bad that it was recently reported
that officers and men were quitting the navy in large numbers [13]. Likewise, the state of the Nigerian Air Force
(NAF) is hardly better. While the Air Force is also 8000
strong, it is also ill-equipped. Half of its twenty-one
combat aircraft are said to be unserviceable. Although the
NAF has some medium-range military transport planes — the
Hercules C-130 — not all of them are in good condition. Nor
does the air force have modern sophisticated communications
equipment, such as radar, etc.

  While it is difficult to say something about things such
as the level of leadership, discipline and morale within the
armed forces, they can hardly be high. Also the level of
military technology within the armed forces is very limited.
Similarly, their network intelligence is rather poor. It is
a combination of all these factors that enabled Libya to
move hundreds of tanks and other pieces of heavy military
equipment into Southern Chad without being detected by the
Nigerian armed forces.

  Given all this, then, the country's armed forces can
hardly be counted upon as an effective instrument of foreign
policy. They cannot adequately supply and support an active
military campaign hundreds of miles beyond the country's
borders, not to mention Southern Africa which is several
thousands of miles from the Nigerian shore. However if the
military capability of the country improves in the present
decade and in the next one, then the armed forces will become an important instrument in the conduct of the country's
foreign relations.

  The contemporary political structure of the country hardly
makes for a dynamic foreign policy. The civilian administration that has been in power since October 1979 is made up of
a coalition of two rather incompatible parties — the
National Party of Nigeria (NPN) and the Nigerian Peoples'
Party (NPP) — reminiscent of the federal coalition of the
NPC and the NCNC of the 1960s. While the President, Shehu
Shagari, belongs to the NPN, the Minister for External
Affairs, Ishaya Audu, belongs to the NPP. This cannot but
create some problems in foreign policy decision-making. A
few decisions, such as the recognition of the Islamic
League, permission for it to open an office in Lagos and
acceptance of observer status in the Conference of Islamic
States, were taken without the knowledge of the Minister
[14].

Furthermore, while the 1979 Constitution vests the control and the conduct of the country's external relations in the executive, there are severe constitutional constraints on the exercise of these powers. To cite a few examples, the President of the country cannot declare war between Nigeria and any other country without the approval in a resolution of both Houses of the National Assembly in a joint session (Section 5 (3)(a) of the Constitution). Under Section 5 (3) (b) the President cannot send any member of the armed forces on combat duty outside Nigeria without the approval of the Senate. Under Section 12 (1) no treaty between Nigeria and any other country can come into force unless the National Assembly has enacted it into law. And under Section 74 (2) no money can be spent by the President from the Consolidated Revenue Fund without the authorisation of the National Assembly. It was under this provision that President Shagari was queried by the National Assembly for making an independence grant of ₦10 million to Zimbabwe in April 1980. Finally, the appointments of heads of diplomatic missions cannot be valid without Senate approval under Section 157 (4); it took the President eighteen months to get the list of most of his non-career heads of mission approved by the Senate.

Apart from these constitutional constraints, there are other real political problems. While the federal coalition parties control ten states in the federation, the remaining nine states are dominated by three other political parties. All this is a reflection of the vast diversities in tradition, history, geography, culture, language and even religion in the country. One of the consequences of these diversities has been to impose caution and constraint on Nigerian policy-makers at home and abroad. Indeed, Ambassador Gabriel Ijewere has said that even under the military these diversities dictated compromise in external policy [15]. If Nigeria's foreign policy was cautious under the military, it is even more so now. For instance, the Shagari government cannot easily get troops dispatched to any other African country as the Obasanjo government did in March 1979 when it sent one or two battalions to Chad.

Some of these constitutional provisions are extremely restrictive. If the country is to be able to respond quickly and effectively to external issues, some of these restrictions will surely have to be amended or even scrapped. Furthermore, in order to be able to pursue a vigorous foreign policy a greater degree of political cohesion must be established at home. It would be a futile exercise for Nigeria to preach African unity abroad while she remained hopelessly divided at home. But if the political and consti-

tutional evolution of the country can occur in a progressive
way — emphasising unity rather than division and effective
rather than weak government — then Nigeria will find it
easier to pursue her goals of African unity and world peace.
The country has got men and women with the necessary political imagination, vision and intellectual ability to bring
this about. If these people were to take charge of the
country's affairs in the near future, then the country's
foreign policy would be more effective in the year 2000 than
it has ever been.

POLICY OPTIONS

From the above, the outline of the policy options at the end
of this century seem to be clear. First, some of the present
policy goals such as the self-preservation of the country,
the promotion of African unity, the encouragement of a just
and peaceful world as well as the support of regional and
sub-regional economic groupings in Africa will continue to
be important in the year 2000. Second, the same is likely to
be true in regard to the elimination of apartheid and racism
in Southern Africa unless the unexpected happens and South
Africa collapses before the end of this century either
under her own contradictions or a combination of those and
external pressures; this, however, is a remote possibility
as of now. And third, if the country remains united and suc-
ceeds in establishing a stable internal political order,
then the role of leadership on the continent will undisput-
ably be that of Nigeria at the end of the century.
  Major changes in external and internal environments can
affect the country's foreign policy either way. But as was
indicated earlier, it is unlikely that there will be sudden
fundamental changes in the external environment of the
country by the end of this century. In which case, Nigeria's
policy towards the great powers will continue to be based on
a policy of nonalignment, and she will continue to play an
active role in the nonaligned movement. She will continue to
retain her memberships in both the UN and the OAU and will
continue to be active in both. Accordingly, her policies
will continue to be influenced by the obligations arising
from such memberships. This will be true of the Commonwealth
too, if by the year 2000 the Commonwealth still exists and
if Nigeria still retains her membership. Likewise, by the
year 2000, if things go well, ECOWAS will have become a common market in which Nigeria will play a major role. However,
if none of the African countries have given up their sovereignty and independence by then, Nigeria will have to con-

tinue to intensify her policy of promoting functional cooperation among West African and other African states.

By contrast to the external environment, the internal
situation could undergo radical change. For instance, the
political structure could be altered by either a revolution
or a coup. If either of these were to happen then the consequences for the country's foreign policy would be hard to
predict. However if change were to occur within the present
political system and to retain the territorial unity of the
country, then the foreign policy would not be totally different from the past. For there are powerful pressures
within Nigeria that have a way of taming any new regime and
leading it into a peculiarly Nigerian pattern of behaviour
in both external and internal matters.

If the economic capability of the country were to improve
considerably, as projected by the recently launched, fourth
five-year plan [16], then the ability of Nigeria to use economic power in the conduct of her external relations would
improve considerably. Indeed some Nigerian leaders have said
that if the country's economic position were to be a little
better than what it is now, then she would be able to play a
more formidable role in Africa and the rest of the world
than the Libya of Gaddafi [17]. In working out the Kano
agreement in March 1979 and the Lagos agreement in August
1979 over Chad, the then federal military government had to
spend a lot of money. Part of the failure of the Shagari
government to get directly involved in Chad in the middle of
1980 before Libyan troops entered in large numbers was said
to be attributable to lack of funds [18]. Similarly, if the
military strength of the country were to improve, then the
country's armed forces would be a more important arm of the
country's foreign policy in the future. Part of the failure
of the mission of Nigerian troops in Chad in 1979 was
ascribed to lack of adequate logistical facilities and support. It will be recalled that the Nigerian troops had to be
flown out of Ndjamena hurriedly with the help of French
forces.

If the financial and economic resources of Nigeria were to
permit, more money would surely be made available to the
armed forces. Indeed this has already started to happen
since the massive Libyan involvement in Chad from December
1980. Nigeria has placed orders for more modern equipment,
arms, ammunition, combat aircraft and naval boats. Greater
emphasis is being given to the training of the armed forces
and to their conditions of service. If all these improve-
ments can continue steadily, and if they are accompanied by
a stable political order and a socially just society at
home, as well as by the development of a viable economic and

industrial base, then I expect that by the year 2000 the country's foreign policy is likely to be more dynamic, more consistent and more effective than ever before.

NOTES AND REFERENCES

1. For details see Ali A. Mazrui, 'Nigeria in World Affairs', Nigerian Journal of International Affairs, 2 (2), 1976.
2. Quoted in Bernard Crick's article on prediction in The Sunday Times (London), 30 December 1979.
3. The Constitution of the Federal Republic of Nigeria, 1979 (Kaduna: New Nigerian, 1979) section 19, p. 10.
4. For details see Olajide Aluko, Ghana and Nigeria, 1957–70: a Study in Inter-African Discord (London: Rex Collings, 1976) passim.
5. Akanbi M. Oniyangi, 'Closing Address' to the 9th Annual Conference of the Nigerian Society of International Affairs at the University of Ife, 20 February 1981.
6. The Punch (Lagos), 11 April 1981.
7. The personality of leaders is not unimportant. However their personal influence is limited by both external and internal environments as well as by the machinery or bureaucracy of foreign policy decision-making. On the latter and the attempts by Obasanjo and Yar 'Ardua to exercise individual power see Chapter 4 and Olajide Aluko, Essays in Nigerian Foreign Policy (London: Allen & Unwin, 1981).
8. See The Estimates of the Federal Government, 1979–81 (Lagos: Government Printer, 1979).
9. See Aluko, Essays in Nigerian Foreign Policy.
10. See West Africa, 15 September 1980.
11. Daily Times (Lagos), 16 February 1981.
12. For details see The Military Balance, 1980/81 (London: International Institute for Strategic Studies, 1980) pp. 53–4.
13. See Sunday Punch (Lagos), 5 April 1981.
14. Interview, April 1981.
15. Gabriel O. Ijewere, 'Two Decades of Independence in Nigeria, with Special Reference to Nigeria in International Relations', text of paper presented on the occasion of the 20th independence anniversary of Nigeria (Lagos: Ministry of External Affairs, September 1980); reprinted as 'Nigeria in International Relations', Review of International Affairs, 32 (738), 5 January 1981, pp. 26–30.

16. For details see <u>Outline of the Fourth National Development Plan, 1981-85</u> (Lagos: Federal Ministry of Planning, 2980).
17. Interview, April 1981.
18. Ibid.

11 Nigeria in the World System: Alternative Approaches, Explanations and Projections

TIMOTHY M. SHAW and OROBOLA FASEHUN

Our country is the largest single unit in Africa ... we
are not going to abdicate the position in which God
Almighty has placed us ... The whole black continent is
looking up to this country [Nigeria] to liberate it from
thralldom.

Jaja Wachuku [1]

Our uneven relationship with Europe, and now including
Northern America, remains basically unchanged. We continue
to be trading posts which supply primary products in exchange for processed goods. The existence of import substitution industries does not detract from this fact.
These trading posts are run and maintained by our citizens. These agents can be grouped into four: (a) Intellectual trading post agents, (b) Commercial trading post
agents, (c) Bureaucratic trading post agents, (d) Technical trading post agents. The activities of these agents
constitute impediments to Black African development.

Lt. General Olusegun Obasanjo [2]

Nigeria is at an historic conjuncture, one that poses problems as well as offering opportunities for both political
analysts and activists. The country is now two decades old
and just another two decades away from the twenty-first
century. In its first twenty years of *de jure* independence,
the territory and political economy of Nigeria were administered by several elements within the reconstituted ruling
class; initially by combined political-entrepreneurial fractions but for the most part by three distinct military
administrations.

Nigeria is starting its third decade under an essentially
conservative set of civilian governments at federal and
state levels. At the level of (political) superstructure
they largely reflect the interests of the local bourgeoisie,
with its bases in the (economic) substructure. The former

superstructural level has exhibited considerable change
since independence whereas the latter substructural level
has revealed more continuity. Such uneven rates of development have increased tensions between different social groups
both inside and outside the bourgeoisie. They have also
generated debate over development strategy and foreign
policy as Nigeria enters the 1980s.

This chapter represents an attempt to identify alternative
approaches to Nigeria in the world system at a time when the
traditional school is under attack from a more radical approach, itself reflective of increasingly diverse interests
within the political economy (including elements within the
last military regime, as reflected in Olusegun Obasanjo's
opening quotation). We attempt to contribute to this debate
— with its implications for policy and prediction — by
presenting an overview and evaluation of the alternative
modes of analysis as well as by identifying the different
futures projected by each of them. We turn first, however,
to an introduction to the widespread assumption that Nigeria
is Africa's great power [3]; an assumption reflected in
Jaja Wachuku's opening citation. This necessitates a critical evaluation of prevalent premises about Nigeria's capability and potential. The very different manner in which
these have been treated — whether they lead to influence or
dependence — serves, we hope, as an appropriate and suggestive introduction to alternative modes of analysis, explanation and projection for Nigeria's foreign policy.

NIGERIA'S GREATNESS: BELIEFS AND BASES

Despite shifts in both sub- and superstructure since independence, one characteristic of Nigeria's international position has been taken as a constant by almost all analysts
— its greatness. Whilst the basis of this greatness has
been seen to change, its presence has been commonly accepted
or assumed by Nigerian and non-Nigerian scholars (and
decision-makers) alike. This awareness of Nigeria's power
and potential is a reflection of a widespread perception
held by national leaders about their country's external
position. The perception is held particularly strongly in
the case of Nigeria's role in continental affairs [4]. So
regardless of time-period or regime in power — whether
during the incipient stage of Nigeria's independence or in
the post-war era — there is a near-unanimous consensus
amongst Nigerian leaders and scholars that Nigeria is destined to 'lead Africa'.

Writing as early as 1962, L. Gray Cowan, in a seminal

article on Nigerian foreign policy, reflects this sense of
manifest destiny: 'Nigeria has been expected to assume a
decisive role in African politics' [5]. In his first book on
Nigeria in world politics, A. Bolaji Akinyemi even detects
the possibility of a continental 'Pax Nigeriana' [6], while
Olajide Aluko concludes a 1973 study of Nigerian in African
affairs thus: 'Nigeria cannot readily give up the bid to
play a leading role in the OAU' [7].

The postulated bases of Nigeria's own conception of its
national role as Africa's great power, as well as analysts'
assumptions about its self-image, have varied over time.
Initially they were usually a reflection of its geographical
size (territory and population) and political pluralism
(parliamentary and federal rule). Occasionally its stature
was taken to be a reflection of its relatively diverse and
developing economy. And for a while its greatness was seen
to be an attribute of the national psyche — its concilia-
tory treatment of defeated parties after the civil war. But
with the advent of military rule, political order and the
high price of oil, Nigeria's greatness has been largely conceived as an attribute of its oil revenue. Jean Herskovits
reflects this consensus about the centrality of oil, an
issue to which we return later in the chapter: 'Oil has in-
vigorated what was once called "Africa's sleeping giant".
It permitted Nigeria to finance its civil war and thus
strengthened the country's international independence. Oil
made possible an unparalleled post-war recovery' [8]. Oil is
now seen to overshadow all other factors as the determinant
of Nigeria's rate of development and dominance: all other
attributes of prosperity and power cited in the literature
— expressways, motor vehicle assembly plants, communications facilities, even plans for a nuclear reactor — are
treated as oil-derivatives. Together, however, they reinforce Nigeria's claims to leadership in continental affairs.

By contrast, Nigeria's continued and expanded incorporation within the global economy because of oil-based interaction and industrialisation is seen by a few, radical scholars as constituting an intensification of dependence. In
treating the impact of Shell-BP in Nigeria, for instance,
Ikenna Nzimiro argues that 'the Nigerian golden age of oil'
has served to transform the political economy into a more
capitalist one, characterised by a variety of new class
formations and relations. Nzimiro emphasises the mutual
interests of the new indigenous ruling class and multinational companies which were advanced by capitalist influence being allowed to grow during the first post-colonial
republic:

Where foreign multinational corporations invade a country,
and where this invasion is accepted by a ruling class that
is predisposed to the capitalist ideology of the bourgeoisie who control these corporations, such a country
faces political and economic insecurity ... the national
interest is subsumed under foreign interest [9].

Thus the radical school because of its concerns goes beyond
the narrow state-centric focus of the traditionalists. Instead of assuming Nigerian sovereignty and capability, de-
cisiveness and effectiveness it concentrates on capabilities
and contradictions [10]. As we shall see, the radicals focus
on transnational class relations, on the national political
economy in the world system, and on constraints and inequalities [11]. The challenge posed to established assumptions
by both different analytic approaches and novel empirical
trends has forced a reconsideration amongst traditional
scholars. The mid-1970s onwards have constituted an important and exciting period for both analysis and interaction.

1975: TURNING POINT AND/OR CONJUNCTURE?

The series of interrelated changes within both the world
system and the Nigerian political economy have together made
a reconsideration of national foreign policy concepts and
content an imperative. The need for such a re-evaluation has
increased with shifts in global politics — the rise of new
middle powers — and global economics — the price and
supply of energy and the elusiveness of a post-Bretton Woods
financial order. Ray Ofoegbu's work is representative of the
attempts being made to revise analysis of Nigeria's foreign
policy within (as well as outside) the largely traditional
and diplomatic perspective:

Existing works on Nigeria's foreign policy contain lapses
which I have endeavoured to avoid ... They devote a disproportionate amount of time and space to issues of domestic politics, constitutional development, and domestic
economy, and are thus unable to provide adequate analysis
of the substantive issues of foreign policy. Secondly,
they generally tend to ignore the development of the
Nigerian Foreign Office. Thirdly, they ignore the nexus
between defence and foreign policy [12].

Whilst Ofoegbu laments the deficiencies of the established
literature in terms of content, Gavin Williams regrets its
continued inadequacies in terms of concepts. The former is

representative of revisionist thought within the traditional
international relations genre whereas the latter is representative of revisionist thought within the radical political economy mode:

We have tried to offer an alternative approach to that
adopted in the research and analysis of Nigeria which
currently predominates in official and academic circles.
Against the narrow concerns of disciplinary specialisa-
tions we seek to draw on the intellectual resources of
several traditions, and, in particular, the classic and
Marxist traditions of political economy in the analysis
of substantive issues. Against the concern with the
management of society and containment of conflict, we are
concerned with the emancipation of people [13].

However the persistence, if not the powerfulness, of the
traditional perspective has in many ways been reinforced by
Nigeria's new-found national affluence and continental influence. There is a widespread consensus in the orthodox
literature that the Murtala/Obasanjo period marks a turning
point in foreign policy orientation and expectation. From
being a dilettante or a debutante until 1975, Nigeria with
civil war over and oil revenue flowing emerged as a dominant
power in Africa. Akinyemi reflects this new, optimistic mood
of the mid-1970s:

Nigeria would no longer wait to be part of an OAU consensus before stating Nigerian positions ... On the contrary,
Nigeria was now adopting a strategy of staking out
Nigerian initiatives and providing a leadership of ideas,
thus setting out the parameters of the ensuing debate
[14].

If 1975 is seen as a (political and diplomatic) turning
point at the level of superstructure by the majority of
(traditional) analysts, it is seen as an historic conjuncture (of political economy) at the level of substructure by
the minority of (radical) analysts. This distinction is
revealed particularly in how the two schools define Nigeria
as a NIC. Both sets of scholars agree with popular perceptions and statements that Nigeria is a leading power on the
continent — a semi-industrialising state at the semi-
periphery with sub-imperial potential (and, at times, pre-
tensions) [15] — but they disagree over whether it is best
characterised as a Newly Influential Country (a traditional-
superstructural position) or a Newly Industrialising Country

(a radical-substructural position).

This disagreement is most profound at the level of explanation. For in terms of description there is a larger measure of agreement: Nigeria is increasingly active and decisive in regional and continental affairs over a variety of issues, such as Chad, Ghana, Sahara and ECOWAS regionally and Angola, Zimbabwe and South Africa continentally. Ironically, its new activism in Africa (a change in style) overlays a persistence in its status quo orientation (a continuity in substance). Nigeria's greatness is reflected in its activist stance combined with its role of a 'status quo mediator' in Africa [16]. Such sub-imperial potential, pretentions and capabilities serve to reinforce orthodox (realist) approaches to analysis.

As already indicated, most analyses of the role of Nigeria in Africa have been conceived and conducted within the traditional power politics paradigm. This realist perspective is, of course, associated with leading students of international relations in Europe and the United States such as Hans Morgenthau [17]. In the Nigerian case, the power politics approach of intellectuals is, as we shall see, largely compatible with the assumptions and aspirations of leading decision-makers and entrepreneurs; i.e. that Nigeria has, does and will wield power, particularly in regional and continental affairs. This self-consciousness and self-image has grown in the mid-1970s when, according to Ibrahim Gambari, Nigeria 'decided that it had to pay more attention to Africa and to take a leading role in the continent' [18]. Gambari also reflects popular perceptions of the benefits of such an activist role by arguing that 'Nigeria has gained important dividends within the continent from its diplomatic initiatives and exertions in Africa' [19].

Other analysts have formulated this rational state-actor model on which the power politics approach is predicated more forcefully, whilst recognising the continental limits of its scope. Julius Okolo and Winston Langley have asserted, for instance, that

> the increased capability of Nigeria since the civil war
> has influenced its more assertive posture in foreign rela-
> tions in general and its relations with African states in
> particular. Because Nigeria recognises that it still has
> limited power potential *vis-à-vis* many other states in the
> international system, however, it recognises that it must
> proceed with prudence [20].

We turn below to a more general critique and evaluation of this dominant approach and its less accepted alternative —

a more radical political economy perspective. Here, however, we note the former's emphasis on continuity of orientation as well as belated attempts to update its conceptual apparatus. Akinyemi has pointed to this paradox of conservative ideology and revisionist framework:

> In spite of this consistency, and in spite of the domestic upheavals that beset the country, Nigerian foreign policy scholars successfully applied Rosenau's linkage system of analysis to explain Nigerian foreign policy. What appears at first to be a contradiction dissolves in the explanation that none of the domestic upheavals has changed the ideological complexion of the governmental and business élites in Nigeria. The consistency then results from a realisation that the sum total of the policy continues effectively to serve the interest of this élite which is by and large conservative. Unless and until this ideological complexion changes, even the best of intentions at effecting changes in the foreign policy of Nigeria will only lead to a cosmetic job [21].

This type of awareness of constraints as well as capabilities and of social structure as well as national role points to the possibility of a new synthesis between at least some aspects (particularly the non-materialist ones) of the radical approach with certain features (particularly the revisionist ones) of the orthodox approach. Before examining this prospect further, however, we consider first the former's challenge to the latter in more detail.

RADICAL CHALLENGE

Although the majority of students of Nigerian foreign policy — nationals and foreigners alike — continue to work within the dominant traditional paradigm, many of their assumptions have been challenged in terms of both theory and reality in the mid-1970s. Their assertion of Nigeria as an independent and purposive actor is under increasing attack not so much because of the civil war and subsequent coups but essentially because of the continuing processes of dependence and underdevelopment. These are centred on and symbolised by increasing oil exports and food imports.

Whilst the orthodox school still sees Nigeria as an autonomous national actor in world politics, the alternative approach conceives of it as a set of dependent social formations, many of which have unequal transnational links with a variety of 'external' interests and institutions. The

latter perspective has received empirical and theoretical
support from several sources: (1) Nigeria's continued reliance on external trade, technology and finance; (2)
Nigeria's emergence as a semi-industrial state at the semi-
periphery; (3) the related process of class formation as
more national elements within the bourgeoisie develop to
challenge or balance the established comprador fractions;
and (4) the continued inability of successive ruling
classes to establish a comprehensive and reliable infra-
structure for sustained development. Whilst Nigeria has
enjoyed continuous growth and avoided the problems of national impoverishment so common on the continent, it none
the less continues to confront a variety of significant
structural conditions that cannot be readily or incremen-
tally alleviated.

The political economy of Nigeria may be moving towards an
historic conjuncture, then, as the second republic dawns.
The radical approach attempts to capture this movement and
moment, focusing as it does on sub- rather than superstructure. As Segun Osoba suggests:

> The essence of the deepening crisis of the Nigerian
> national bourgeoisie ... is that its failure to retain and
> use an adequate proportion of the nation's wealth for
> generating a credible quantity of economic and social
> development in the country has robbed succeeding bourgeois
> regimes in Nigeria of even minimal legitimacy and author-
> ity in the eyes of the overwhelming majority of Nigerians
> [22].

Given this crisis — which is not necessarily resolvable in
a rapid or decisive way — the national ruling class has
attempted to accelerate local industrialisation and accumulation, with significant repercussions on Nigeria's position
in the global political economy. As we shall see, the national fraction in the local bourgeoisie is beginning to
challenge the more established transnational fraction.
Nigeria may be in the process of shifting away from peripheral capitalism (itself a result of historical incorporation within the world system) and towards semi-peripheral
capitalism in which national and transnational elements come
to a new balance in their relationships (see Chapters 2, 7
and 8).

Despite the apparent unpreparedness of the majority of
scholars within the international relations community in
Nigeria to question the assumptions of the dominant paradigm
— despite current changes in Nigeria's internal and external situation — some intellectuals and some leaders have

begun to do so, as indicated in Obasanjo's opening citation. Their scepticism about the 'realist' school's assertion of Nigeria as an independent and purposive actor has been based on empirical data and theoretical disposition [23]. Their alternative 'radical' formulation is founded on the premise of Nigeria as a dependent state and society, one whose international actions and internal formations are significantly constrained by its place in the world system.

The challenge to the orthodox realist school from the radical faction is not a homogeneous one, however. Rather, there are major debates within the emerging alternative approach itself, broadly along the common cleavage within the political economy genre: namely, between the more Marxist and the less Marxist. While there are distinctive streams within the radical political economy approach, however, they do share common features, especially when contrasted with the traditional school. First, they are based on the assumed interrelatedness of 'sectors' within the national system, whether they be economic, political or social in emphasis. Second, they recognise that no national system is wholly independent or autonomous; rather each has multiple linkages with other 'external' systems. And third, they go beyond state-centric assumptions to treat a rich variety of actors and interests as authoritative in international relations. Osoba reflects these analytic attributes well: 'the structural integration of the Nigerian economy and its national bourgeoisie into an international capitalist order constitutes a major constraint on the ability of the bourgeoisie, even if it were willing, to change radically this structure of dependence' [24]. Yet whilst radical scholars share this substantial set of premises in attempting to describe and explain the political economy of Nigeria, they do diverge on the related issues of whether its social formations exist in an antagonistic and dialectical relationship or not and whether national as opposed to transnational capitalism is possible. Clearly, treatment of these issues is important for *praxis* as well as for analysis as noted below in the next section on projections.

A non-Marxist political economy is well represented in the optimistic policy-oriented work of Sayre Schatz on <u>Nigerian Capitalism</u>:

> The Nigerian economy has entered the final quarter of the twentieth century ebulliently ... The people are vigorous, industrious, economically responsive. The population has a superabundance of the entrepreneurial attributes: willingness to work hard for economic gain, to take risks, to persevere and persist, to undertake new occupations and

new ways of doing things ... The new oil wealth was responsible for an exuberant application of an (established)
development orientation ... nurture-capitalism [25].

By contrast to this essentially uncritical form of political
economy, Osoba's work is characteristic of a more dialectical and materialist mode. He argues that the explanation
as to why underdevelopment has persisted and

national dependence has survived in our country can be
found in an analysis of the objective and subjective factors operating within the Nigerian society and on the
global scene to inhibit positive and decisive action by
successive bourgeois regimes in Nigeria. These factors can
be subsumed under four main categories: (1) the structure
of world imperialist economy into which Nigeria has been
effectively coopted; (2) the profitability of the Nigerian
bourgeoisie's role as commission agents; (3) contradictions within the ranks of the national bourgeoisie; and
(4) contradictions between the national bourgeoisie and
the masses [26].

Attentiveness to such issues has increased with Nigeria's
re-emergence in the mid-1970s as Africa's major power. As
already noted in the first section, Nigeria's potential
greatness was recognised in earlier periods based on its
substantial population, diverse resources and federal
system. Dramatic increases in oil production and price have
made respect for its power almost commonplace; but only a
few scholars have asked fundamental questions about what
oil- or naira-power means. Most have merely accepted massive
oil revenues as a source of enhanced internal growth and
external influence. Only a critical minority have treated
related problems or contradictions, asking whether reliance
on foreign energy technology and industrial planning is just
another form of dependence. Oil has become central within
both realist and radical approaches [27], but the former focuses on domestic revenue and international influence whereas the latter focuses on domestic distortions and international dependence.
    A related factor to that of oil is food. Nigeria is rather
representative of the growing difficulties faced by the
nouveaux riches in the world system; namely the need to
import increasing amounts of food, especially grain. Nigeria
has a rich and varied range of climatic zones and food po-
tentials. But the combination of dazzling oil income and
tempting taste-transfer has meant a growing reliance on
foreign wheat and other basic products. As noted below in

the fifth section, the amount of grain imported has a major
impact on domestic agricultural development and on balance
of payments. Just as the two approaches analyse oil differently so they treat food in contrasting ways.

From the orthodox perspective, food imports are a local,
transitory difficulty that will pass as modernisation and
industrialisation proceed. But from a more radical viewpoint, such imports are an aspect of structural dependence:
an exogenous economy lacks self-reliance and generates novel
forms of dependence on the world system [28].

So in addition to dependence on oil exports, the radical
perspective has drawn attention to the implications of dependence on food imports. Projections of Nigeria's reliance
on foreign grains based on Club of Rome data point to massive food imports if malnutrition is to be eliminated by the
end of this century: $11 billion deficit per annum on the
food trade by the year 2001 on such an assumption. If, however, a lower goal is set and more self-reliant agricultural
policies are followed in some sort of 'green revolution'
then the annual food import bill may be kept down to $6
billion [29].

In either case, however, Nigeria's political economy is
likely to become one centred on the exchange of oil for
food [30]; a contrast with earlier forms of incorporation
when vegetable oils were exchanged for consumer and capital
goods. Given that Nigeria's major oil consumer is also its
major grain supplier — the United States — the new food
trade becomes a central factor in foreign policy. So Patrick
Wilmot has called for greater self-reliance in this sector
if oil is to lead to influence rather than dependence:

> If the present Nigerian government is determined to pursue
> independent domestic and foreign policies it must, there-
> fore, ensure that it is not dependent on outside powers
> for essential food supplies ... Nigeria cannot effectively
> oppose imperialism if the imperialists control a signifi-
> cant proportion of its food needs [31].

We turn next, then, to a general conceptual overview of the
two distinct approaches to the analysis of Nigeria in the
world system — the traditional and the radical — both of
which include consideration of oil. But whereas the former
perspective treats it in terms of national income and
growth, the latter perspective considers it as a new source
of external dependence and dilemmas; the former concentrates
on distribution, the latter on production.

ALTERNATIVE APPROACHES

The radical challenge (typified in the work of Nzimiro,
Osoba and Williams) has not only stimulated a revisionist
response from previously traditionalist scholars (as illus-
trated by the recent writing of Akinyemi and Ofoegbu), but
it has also forced the majority in the realist school to
reconsider their assumptions and assertions and to become
more rigorous and self-conscious about their mode and level
of analysis. Table 11.1 presents an overview of the primary
characteristics of the two major approaches to description,
explanation and prediction [32].

As already suggested, the (dominant) traditional approach
to the study of Nigerian foreign policy is closely associated with the realist, power politics genre. It accepts the
realists' essential assumptions of (1) the state as the
primary and independent actor, and (2) international relations occurring at the level of superstructure, consisting
largely of diplomatic and strategic interactions. By contrast, the radical approach challenges this set of assumptions by (1) its association with political economy as a
form of enquiry; (2) its treatment of the 'state' as a dependent social formation having transnational linkages with
a variety of actors; (3) its recognition of substructure as
the salient determinant of behaviour; and (4) its focus on
economic and political rather than other issue areas.

These two distinctive approaches also differ about the
primary level of Nigeria's external relations, about the
definition of NICs, and about future policies and projections. The former, traditional mode concentrates on Nigerian
'dominance' in regional and continental fora, thus reflecting national leaders' own perceptions [33], whereas the
latter radical mode concentrates on Nigerian 'dependence' on
global exchange. As already indicated, these two schools
differ over how to conceive of NICs — influential or industrialising countries — and the former still advocates capitalism as the path to growth whereas the latter advocates
socialism as the path to development.

We turn to alternative future projections and policies in
the next section. Here we merely note (1) the essential
compatibility of orthodox 'development theory' with
Nigeria's emergence as a sub-imperial power and (2) the
major deficiencies of the traditional perspective. First,
on 'modernisation' and Nigeria's regional role, it is in-
structive to note that most middle powers continue to encourage a capitalist mode of production. Unlike the majority
of Third and Fourth World countries, the minority in the
semi-periphery has been upwardly mobile. For them, 'coopta-

Table 11.1   Alternative modes of analysis for Nigerian
Foreign Policy

	Traditional	Radical
Theoretical asso-ciations	Realism/power politics	Political economy
Level of analysis	Superstructure	Substructure
Mode of analysis	State-centric	Multiple actors/interests
Theoretical assump-tion	Independent actor	Dependent formations
Primary process	Sub-imperialism	Semi-industrialism
Primary issue areas	Diplomatic/strategic	Economic/political
Primary levels of interaction	Regional/conti-nental	Global
Ideology/strategy	Capitalism	Socialism
Direction/projec-tion	Growth	Underdevelopment
Expectation/pre-diction	Consensus	Contradictions

tion' and 'counter-penetration' are viable options because
of their attractiveness to transnational interests. The
'success stories' of, say, Brazil, Mexico, South Korea,
Taiwan and the Ivory Coast serve to salvage development
theory somewhat from the attack of the *dependentistas* [34].

And secondly, the traditional perspective is not only
rather complacent; it is state-centric, static, superstructural and less heuristic. The traditional, realist approach
still tends to exclude myriad non-state actors from its pur-
view. Unlike revisionist liberal scholars in Europe and
North America it has not incorporated transnationalism into
its framework; and unlike radical scholars it has excluded
international class linkages. The power politics perspective
is also largely static and unhistorical, ignoring Nigeria's
incorporation over time into the world capitalist system and
the impact of this on its modes and relations of production;
it overlooks processes of underdevelopment and class formation and their impact on foreign policy. Moreover, the orthodox scholar still focuses on super- rather than substructure and on contemporary events rather than underlying
trends. In short, the established perspective is neither
theoretical nor predictive; it seeks to describe and under-

stand rather than to explain and project.

Within this dominant, traditional paradigm the major concerns are with foreign policy success (or failure), activism (or passivity), cooperation (or conflict) and continuity (or change). Debate within it is limited largely to the
degree and direction of national influence and to the bases
and amounts of power. Work within the orthodox school is
largely concentrated on current affairs — chronology,
ideology, regime changes, crisis diplomacy and domestic factors. It accepts and contributes to Nigeria's new activist
African policy and overlooks most constraints and contradictions. Although a few scholars within this mode recognise
the dichotomy between continental influence and global dependence, awareness of substructural factors is minimal.

Fifteen years ago, Douglas Anglin examined, from an unorthodox perspective, the tensions between Nigeria's 'political nonalignment and economic alignment'; but he failed to
recognise the organic relationships existing between the
polity and economy, internal and external systems, and
super- and substructures. Thus Anglin concluded then, as
many traditionalists would still do today, that 'while external economic influences profoundly affect the Nigerian
domestic economy, their impact on Nigerian foreign policy is
not as great as might be supposed' [35]. From a more radical
political economy perspective such a conclusion would be
impossible, because within that genre it is taken for granted that economic and political forces are interrelated and
that 'domestic' decision-making is inseparable from transnational linkages and constraints. The alternative approach
is, then, more holistic and interdisciplinary, conceiving of
'Nigeria' as a set of social relations within the world
system. From this perspective, the Nigerian state and its
foreign policy represent the interests of dominant national
social forces in their relationships with transnational and
international interests [36]. And because the radical approach is more explicitly theoretical than the orthodox one,
it has predictive as well as explanatory purposes.

ALTERNATIVE FUTURES

The two distinctive modes of analysis already identified
differ not only on what and how to explain; each of them is
suggestive of divergent futures for the country. The alternative futures posited can be divided into (1) projections
about what is likely to occur and (2) strategies about what
should occur.

Given the promises of the nationalist movements and sub-

sequent efforts at national planning, notions about future
growth are quite commonplace in Nigeria. Moreover, expectations and dreams have been reinforced of late by popular
notions of oil- or naira-power.

The traditional perspective on Nigeria's economic and
international prospects assumes a unilineal path to prosperity and power. As already noted, the basis of this ineluctable trend towards affluence and influence has shifted from
population and federation in the 1960s to oil and industrialisation in the 1970s. But in both periods the premises and
promises of 'political modernisation' were widely accepted
amongst scholars and decision-makers: increases in (internal) stability and (international) status were taken for
granted. Gambari expresses the common assumptions and assertions of the traditionalists:

> In general, therefore, we may well see continued growth in
> the Nigerian economy, a fairly high degree of domestic
> peace and stability, a non-ideological approach to social
> engineering by the government, and a temporarily retarded,
> but none the less significant long-term rise in the coun-
> try's international stature [37].

Confidence in orthodox development strategy — growth and
modernisation — has been reinforced not only by oil but
also by Nigeria's emergence as a semi-peripheral state.
Although orthodox development theory stands discredited in
many parts of the world, it remains relatively untarnished
in the context of the minority of semi-peripheral states
that have experienced high levels of growth (if not of
development) over the last twenty years. This minority has
been upwardly mobile because of (1) size of domestic market
(e.g. Brazil or India) or (2) because of oil resources
(e.g. Saudi Arabia and Iran) or (3) because of entrepreneurial skills (e.g. South Korea and Taiwan). Together they constitute the Newly Influential Countries, many of which are
also Newly Industrialising Countries (NICs) as well. In
general the traditional approach focuses on the former,
superstructural conception of NICs whereas the radical approach focuses on the latter, substructural conception. The
former also conceives of the related status of 'sub-
imperialism' as an expression of diplomatic or military
power at the level of superstructure whereas the latter
conceives of sub-imperialism as an expression of economic and
class imperative at the level of substructure (see Table
11.1).

In addition to containing a different understanding of
NICs and sub-imperialism, the radical school offers a very

different picture of the future of Nigeria. Its projections
are largely informed by dependence rather than development
theory and assume uneven rather than unilineal change. Instead of steady progress towards modernisation and industrialisation, it expects an intensification of inequalities
and underdevelopment. So the radical perspective projects
a less promising future than the orthodox school, one of
dilemmas and tensions based on continued dependence and difficulties. As Biersteker and others demonstrate, the ubiqui-
tous activities of multinational corporations in Nigeria
have had a significant impact on 'displacement [of indigenous industry], the transfer of consumption patterns, and the
development of local comprador groups' [38].

Within the political economy genre there is a major debate
over 'what is to be done' in response to such dependence and
inequality that is reflective of the more versus less materialist divide already identified. The more orthodox
Marxist view of Nigeria's future is that social contradictions and antitheses will continue to multiply and intensify
until a revolutionary situation is created out of which a
new synthesis will emerge. As Osoba suggests:

the contradiction between the national bourgeoisie and the
masses in Nigeria hinges on the operation of international
finance capitalism that sustains the dependent domestic
capitalism of the national bourgeoisie. But the national
bourgeoisie is not able to resolve this contradiction in
favour of the masses of its people and against its foreign
imperialist principals. It is also not able to come out
openly and tell the Nigerian people that its true commitment is (sic) to domestic and foreign capitalist exploitation of the human and material resources of the nation ...
the only viable course of action for us is a revolutionary
one ... the national bourgeoisie has to be stoutly opposed
and overthrown [39].

The less or non-Marxist view of the future of Nigeria's political economy is that different policies could be identified and adopted to ameliorate the tensions and avoid conflict; i.e. reform could be implemented to avoid revolution
[40]. Schatz's work on Nigeria is representative of this
revisionist approach to 'redistribution with growth'. He
conceives of national 'development orientation declared at
the final quarter-century mark' as a form of 'nurture-
capitalism',

characterised by a highly ambitious programme of accelerated development, an enhanced government investment-role

with an element of state capitalism, and a concern for
mass welfare, particularly for the reduction of income
disparities and also of unemployment. We can call this
orientation one of nurture-capitalism with state capitalist, welfare and accelerated-development tendencies [41].

Schatz also identifies a major policy, political and
economic issue within such a reformist approach, namely the
balance between national and transnational capitalisms. The
question of the national (as opposed to the comprador) bourgeoisie is an important and lively one within the dependence
and underdevelopment school, particularly as it relates to
the emergence of the NICs within the semi-periphery. Here,
however, we merely cite Schatz's work on the tensions between more nationalistic and more transnationalistic elements within the Nigerian bourgeoisie.
  Schatz recognises that continued dependence on foreign
finance and firms is anathema in a period of nationalism and
suggests that policies of indigenisation are common responses favouring 'nationalistic nurturing' [42] over universal.
The capitalist mode of production *per se* is not threatened;
rather attention is paid to the conflict and balance between
national and transnational investments and interests. Schatz
foresees tension being resolved through discrimination in
favour of the former, national bourgeoisie:

> Though the foreign investors are the major source of
> dynamism in Nigeria's private sector, the role of indigen-
> ous private enterprise, already important, is sure to
> expand. Such an expansion will be brought about by the
> nationalistic element of nurture-capitalism with its pro-
> grammes to assist indigenous enterprise in particular,
> by the powerful antagonism toward dependence upon foreign
> corporations which partially underlies that nationalistic
> element, and by the increasing power and affluence of the
> Nigerian capitalist class buttressed by the new oil
> prosperity [43].

Within the radical school, then, both more and less materialist perspectives favour a greater degree of self-
reliance. But the intent and process of achieving this
differ from class conflict on the one hand to state strategy
on the other. For whereas the Marxist preference is for
socialism through self-reliance, the non-Marxist preference
is for (national) capitalism through self-reliance. However
the former approach denies the feasibility of the latter.
Osoba argues, for instance, that the latter policy — the
nationalist nurture-capitalism of Schatz — is an impossi-

bility because capitalism is by definition transnational and so dependence-inducing:

> The most distinguishing aspect of this power-sharing arrangement is that the Nigerian national bourgeoisie has always operated as a junior partner in relation to the British colonial authorities and British finance capital before independence, and in relation to the Euro-American metropolitan centres of world imperialism and their transnational corporations since independence. In other words, the power distribution between the Nigerian national bourgeoisie and the international bourgeoisie of the Western imperialist metropoles is akin to that subsisting between an agent and a principal in a capitalist market system [44].

Schatz points himself to some of the implications of continued dependence on transnational capitalism, but still sees nationalistic nurturing rather than socialism as the solution:

> Reliance upon international investment also entails pressures for particular orientations and policies within the capitalist framework. The country that needs foreign private capital feels impelled to create a climate attractive to those who provide it. In accord with this imperative, Nigeria has emphasised a set of conservative fiscal, monetary, balance-of-payments, and other economic policies [45].

The postulated choice between or conflict over more or less self-reliance and more or less capitalism provides a framework for distinguishing four alternative futures for Nigeria (see Table 11.2).

Table 11.2 Alternative strategies for Nigeria

Strategy	Capitalism	Socialism
Degree of incorporation:		
More incorporation	Transnational	State
Less incorporation	National	Participatory

Given the interrelated processes of industrialisation, accumulation, differentiation and class formation in Nigeria, we can suggest a categorisation of major advocates of each of these four development strategies, with the

bourgeoisie tending to favour alternative forms of capitalism and Marxists and radicals (if not the proletariat itself) favouring alternative forms of socialism (see Table
11.3).

Table 11.3 Advocates of alternative strategies

Transnational capitalism:	State socialism:
transnational bourgeoisie	Labour aristocracy
National capitalism:	Participatory socialism:
national bourgeoisie	workers and peasants

The alternative forms of capitalism identified by different bourgeois fractions are likely to be a major focus of
political and intellectual debate given the unlikelihood of
more fundamental forms of change [46]. This is related, on
the one hand, to the possibility of national capital accumulation and on the other hand, to the possibility of national
political stability. Therefore the identification of and
balance between different fractions is of more than academic
interest.

As the opening citation from the previous Head of State
indicates, 'trading outpost agents' in the country can be
divided into commercial/business, bureaucratic, technical
and intellectual groups [47]. Osoba suggests that the division between the first pair is central, particularly as it
affects relations with external actors:

> there exist among the bourgeoisie several contradictions
> of varying degrees of antagonism which undermine their
> cohesiveness and unanimity in the bargaining that they
> have to do as a class of commission agents with foreign
> monopoly capitalist interests. Some of the most antago-
> nistic contradictions exist between the bureaucratic bour-
> geoisie (whether military or civilian) and the business
> bourgeoisie. This is because the bureacratic bourgeoisie
> are the ultimate political decision-makers and ... they
> have some awareness of a constituency of accountability
> that they must periodically appease if not with positive
> action then at least by appropriate rhetorical pronounce-
> ments [48].

And a civilian bureaucratic bourgeoisie is more likely to be
sensitive to the pressures of accountability than a

military-based one.

Given the salient features of and debate over the Nigerian political economy in a global context, at least four alternative futures can be identified. These represent the logical projection of established modes of analysis and policy and over time would lead to distinctive and divergent national forms. They can be conveniently separated into traditional and radical types along the lines already suggested and subdivided into more optimistic and more pessimistic varieties, as indicated in Table 11.4.

Table 11.4   Alternative futures for Nigeria

	Traditional	Radical
Optimistic	Semi-industrialism	Revolution
Pessimistic	Stagnation	Repression

The major proponents and features of the two optimistic projections have already been identified: Schatz for semi-industrialisation and Osoba for revolution. These two scholars also recognize the possibility of less optimistic scenarios within each of their modes of analysis; i.e. stagnation and repression respectively. The semi-industrial and stagnation possibilities proposed in the traditional literature are compatible with the conceptualisation of Nigeria as a part of the semi-periphery. The more optimistic view on the one hand assumes that indigenisation and industrialisation lead to enhanced national accumulation and autonomy; on the other hand, the more pessimistic possibility assumes that these remain elusive and that growth is retarded because of external recession as well as internal stagnation [49].

The revolutionary and repressive projections of the radical school both assume that social contradictions continue to intensify. But the former is based on the expectation that these antagonisms will generate dramatic change resulting in a new synthesis; by contrast, the latter is based on the assumption that social tensions will bring forth an authoritarian response — a series of military moves, perhaps even fascism — to prevent revolutionary change. In general, of course, the alternative semi-industrial and revolutionary futures are favoured by the bourgeoisie (and the labour aristocracy?) and workers-peasants (especially the under- and unemployed?) respectively. Very few fractions would benefit from the two pessimistic possibilities although, with appropriate ideological trimmings, elements within the national bourgeoisie (particularly within its bureaucratic and military parts?) might hope to recapture their relative position through stagnation or fascism. Most scholars and leaders examine only the more optimistic projections, however, preferring to ignore the other gloomier possibilities.

Characteristic of the concentration on the optimistic scenarios is the work by Ofoegbu on Nigeria's diplomatic and political role and by Schatz on its economic and industrial potential. Such writing in the traditional mode is balanced by Osoba and Collins *et al.* within the more radical genre. The latter argue (in opposition to a non-materialist form of political economy) that national and military elements within the local bourgeoisie cannot generate conditions for development by administrative directives alone:

> The elimination of the 'comprador' state, serving foreign and local capitalist interests, requires the building of 'powerful organisations ...' Foreign capitalists and their local allies must be expropriated. The state should control industrial production and foreign trade, while encouraging the development of peasant and petty commodity production. Workers and peasants in Nigeria have demonstrated a capacity to resist oppression and exploitation in various ways. The overthrow of their exploiters requires the organisation of a socialist movement, behind a clear, popular programme for the social and economic reconstruction of Nigeria [50].

By contrast to this materialist and idealist dream of the radical optimists are the diplomatic and pragmatic propositions of a traditional optimist. In concluding his volume on changes in Nigerian foreign policy, Ray Ofoegbu called for a 'new philosophy of foreign policy for Nigeria' in which he

> recommended *action-orientation* as the foundation for a new foreign policy. We ... urged *dynamic style*. This can only come about if we plan foreign policy; cultivate a keen sense of timing; seize and sustain initiatives; and develop, professionally, a capacity to communicate effectively at home and abroad on our foreign policy positions. On the *substantive issues* of foreign policy, we have argued the case of discarding our preoccupations with the Cold War and its induced Non-Alignment philosophy of foreign policy. We are now in a new era of détente which demands more action and involvement in world affairs

from us [51].

In his book, Ofoegbu also touched on some of the sources of
foreign policy conceptualisation and conservatism in
Nigeria. We turn in our final section to a brief consideration of the sociology of the debate over Nigeria in the
world system.

SOCIOLOGY OF KNOWLEDGE: THE DEBATE OVER NIGERIAN FOREIGN POLICY

General Obasanjo was critical of the role of 'intellectual
trading outpost agents' in his FESTAC speech. We have already identified major distinctions and divisions amongst
students of Nigerian foreign policy, the majority of whom
remain remarkably orthodox in their mode of analysis and
prescription. Given Nigeria's position in the world system,
the role of intellectuals in examining, explaining and responding to its inheritance and potential is an important
aspect of its international relations [52]. Obasanjo suggested that there was a division of labour amongst the
intellectual and other 'trading outpost agents'; in general
scholars do seem to be reasonably comfortable with Nigeria's
contemporary global position and posture.
   Yet whilst the majority of students of Nigerian foreign
policy appear to be accepting of Nigeria's present situation
and status, more 'national' as opposed to 'transnational'
elements can be identified within the intelligentsia just as
they can be distinguished within the bourgeoisie in general.
Furthermore, there is an identifiable, articulate and expanding group of scholars who have adopted a more radical
mode of analysis and who seek to change, as well as to
understand, Nigeria's political economy. In general the
intellectual members of the bourgeoisie in Nigeria as elsewhere are uncritical about the bureaucratic and entrepreneurial fractions (even if inclined to opposition to military elements). Only a minority like Ake, Nzimiro and Osoba
advocate fundamental change [53].
   A central feature of the new activism and Afrocentrism
apparent in Nigerian foreign policy has been the distinctive
role of the Nigerian Institute of International Affairs
(NIIA) during the Mohammed and Obasanjo military regimes
[54]. Under the third military government the NIIA went
through a dramatic revival and reorientation, serving to
enhance debate and information about Nigeria's foreign
policy in a post-Gowon, post-OPEC and post-Bretton Woods
era. The remarkable transformation of its size, stature and

salience is a central feature of Nigeria's 'new' policy, as
Ofoegbu suggests in his own analysis of 'Nigerian intellectuals and foreign policy':

> No other Nigerian government relied on the NIIA as the
> third military government did; and no management of the
> NIIA has associated scholars of foreign policy and inter-
> national relations with the work of the Institute in
> research and policy planning, as the management of
> Director-General Bolaji Akinyemi [55].

In general, the NIIA, like its counterparts in Britain, US
[56], USSR, Canada, India and elsewhere, tends to espouse —
if it can be treated as a single institution — a rather orthodox view of international politics and global futures. So
major influences on the analysis and practice of Nigerian
foreign policy — Akinyemi, Aluko, Gambari, etc. — are
largely associated with traditional approaches and projections. More radical scholars — Ake, Nzimiro, Osoba, etc.
— do not have (and probably do not seek) the same degree of
access or visibility within the nation-state. Just as members of the Trilateral Commission constitute an intellectual
fraction within the transnational Western bourgeoisie [57],
so the majority of Nigerian students of the state's foreign
policy — notwithstanding nuances and niceties — essentially accept the assumptions, expectations and projections
of the present political economy and its dominant social
forces.
     In addition to intellectuals in Nigeria being associated
with other 'trading outpost agents' they also tend to suffer
from conceptual dependence and time-lag; a particular professional hazard facing all Third World scholars (cf. the
chapters in this book). In general, the approaches proposed
by the orthodox school reflect educational experiences in
Britain, the United States and elsewhere over the past one
or two decades. However, not only have orthodox realist
assumptions been largely superseded in such countries themselves; but they were always proposed with advanced industrialised states in mind [58]. Ake and Nzimiro have pointed
both to the general deficiencies within the established
'modernisation' literature and to alternative materialist
approaches to underdevelopment [59]. The latter are advocated to escape from both intellectual dependence and inappropriate frameworks. 'The crisis in the social sciences'
in Nigeria in particular and the Third World in general has
important implications for the study of foreign policy and
international relations. As Mansbach, Ferguson and Lampert
insist, we need to progress 'beyond conservatism in the

study of world politics':

> The time has come to cast aside what Wight terms 'the
> intellectual prejudice imposed by the sovereign state'.
> The conservative bias of the past, as Oran Young remarks,
> has too long precluded 'the analysis of a wide range of
> logically possible and empirically interesting models
> of world politics'. Since scholars are concerned with
> investigating global behaviour, it is reasonable to pro-
> pose that actors be identified and classified according
> to behavioral rather than legal or normative criteria
> [60].

The imperative of going beyond realist, state-centric
approaches is particularly crucial in the Third World for
developmental and intellectual reasons. First, issues of
political economy are central to any attempt to overcome an
inheritance of dependence and underdevelopment. And second,
scholars in the advanced industrialised states have already
come to recognise the claims of the alternative approach
(albeit usually adopting a non-materialist mode of political
economy). Joan Spero reflects this new awareness of the importance of international political economy:

> The mid-1970s reality of international relations is now
> undermining the separation of economics from the study of
> international politics ... as the postwar economic con-
> sensus disintegrates and as security issues recede,
> economic issues are re-emerging as the focus of interna-
> tional relations [61].

Questions of political economy would seem to be central if
African states and scholars wish to both understand and
overcome their inheritance of national and intellectual
dependence [62]. Given the immediacy of the multiple processes of underdevelopment in Nigeria and elsewhere, new modes
of analysis and of response may be expected to originate in
the (semi)periphery rather than in the centre. To continue
to follow orthodox 'international' paradigms is to run the
risk of perpetuating intellectual and existential dependence.

NOTES AND REFERENCES

1. Jaja Wachuku, first Minister of Foreign Affairs, in Nigerian Parliament, House of Representatives Debates, January 1960, column 54.
2. 'Opening Address to the Colloquium of the Second World Black and African Festival of Arts and Culture, Delivered by His Excellency Lt. General Olusegun Obasanjo', Colloquium in Black Civilisation and Education Proceedings, vol. 1 (Lagos: 1977) p. 19.
3 See the selected bibliography below for the frequency with which works on Nigerian foreign policy use terms such as 'great', 'major' or 'leading' power.
4. See, for instance, the strikingly titled but otherwise disappointing book by Joseph Wayas, Nigeria's Leadership Role in Africa (London: Macmillan, 1979).
5. L. Gray Cowan, 'Nigerian Foreign Policy' in R. O. Tilman and Taylor Cole (eds), Nigerian Political Scene (Durham: Duke University Press, 1962) p. 116.
6. A. Bolaji Akinyemi, Foreign Policy and Federalism: the Nigerian Experience (Ibadan University Press, 1974) p. 191.
7. Olajide Aluko, 'Nigeria's Role in Inter-African Relations with Special Reference to the Organisation of African Unity', African Affairs, 72 (287), April 1973, p. 162.
8. Jean Herskovits, 'Dateline Nigeria: a Black Power', Foreign Policy, 29, Winter 1977-8, p. 171.
9. Ikenna Nzimiro, 'The Political and Social Implications of Multinational Corporations in Nigeria' in Carl Widstrand (ed.), Multinational Firms in Africa (Stockholm: Almqvist & Wiksell, 1975) p. 210.
10. For a general comparison of the contents and claims of these two modes see Timothy M. Shaw, 'Foreign Policy, Political Economy and the Future: Reflections on Africa in the World System', African Affairs, 79 (315), April 1980, pp. 260-8. The notion of 'foreign policy' employed here is, of course, a broad one: all interactions with and policies towards 'external' actors, whether they be individuals, classes, other non-state actors, other states, regional institutions and universal organisations. This goes beyond official relations and ideologies to embrace a wide variety of 'transnational' linkages (see notes 58 and 61 below).
11. For a comparative discussion about the analytic and political debates over the intention and direction of Zambian foreign policy see Timothy M. Shaw, 'Dilemmas of Dependence and (under)Development: Conflicts and

Choices in Zambia's Present and Prospective Foreign
Policy', Africa Today, 26 (4), October/December 1979,
pp. 43-65.

12. Ray Ofoegbu, The Nigerian Foreign Policy (Enugu: Star,
1979) p. ix.

13. Gavin Williams, 'Introduction' in Gavin Williams (ed.),
Nigeria: Economy and Society (London: Rex Collings,
1976) pp. 3-4.

14. A. Bolaji Akinyemi, 'Nigerian Foreign Policy in 1975:
National Interest Redefined' in Oyeleye Oyediran (ed.),
Survey of Nigerian Affairs, 1975 (Ibadan: OUP, 1978)
p. 112. Olajide Aluko is one of very few scholars in
either traditional or radical schools to argue that the
Murtala/Obasanjo period represents a continuity rather
than a change (see Aluko, 'The 'New' Nigerian Foreign
Policy: Developments Since the Downfall of General
Gowon', Round Table, 66, October 1976, pp. 405-14).

15. For a succinct and suggestive introduction to the industrial, exchange, regional, military, social and theoretical implications of NICs see Raimo Vayrynen, 'Economic
and Military Position of Regional Power Centres in the
International System', Journal of Peace Research, 16
(4), 1979, pp. 349-69.

16. On this role see Orobola Fasehun, Nigerian Politics and
the Roles of Nigeria in the OAU, 1963-1976 (Unpublished
Ph.D. thesis, Rutgers University, January 1979). On
national role orientations in general see Kal Holsti,
'National Role Conceptions in the Study of Foreign
Policy', International Studies Quarterly, 14 (3),
September 1970, pp. 233-309.

17. On power politics see the classic study by Hans
Morgenthau, Politics Among Nations (New York: Knopf,
1967, fourth edn).

18. Ibrahim A. Gambari, 'Nigeria and the World: a Growing
Internal Stability, Wealth and External Influence',
Journal of International Affairs, 29 (2), 1975, p. 164.

19. Ibid., p. 165.

20. Julius E. Okolo and Winston E. Langley, 'The Changing
Nigerian Foreign Policy', World Affairs, 135, Spring
1973, p. 324.

21. A. Bolaji Akinyemi, 'Introduction' in his collection on
Nigeria and the World: Readings in Nigerian Foreign
Policy (Ibadan: OUP for NIIA, 1978) pp. x-xi.

22. Segun Osoba, 'The Deepening Crisis of the Nigerian
National Bourgeoisie', Review of African Political
Economy, 13, May-August 1978, p. 65.

23. As Gavin Williams notes, most analyses of Nigeria to date has been within established disciplines and theories: 'These limitations have led much academic research to evade the crucial questions of interpreting Nigerian society .. The central problems facing Nigeria, like all other societies, are no respecters of the conventions and conveniences of academia. They originate from specific historical events and make present history' ('Introduction', p. 1). See also his 'Editorial: Nigeria' in Review of African Political Economy, 13, May-August 1978, pp, 1-7.

24. Osoba, 'The Deepening Crisis of the Nigerian National Bourgeoisie', p. 69.

25. Sayre P. Schatz, Nigerian Capitalism (Berkeley: University of California Press, 1977) pp. 1 and 2.

26. Osoba, 'The Deepening Crisis of the Nigerian National Bourgeoisie', pp. 65-6.

27. As Bill Freund comments, because the oil industry is capital intensive, 'the impact of oil had very little direct effect on the mass of Nigerians; it was the vast sums that suddenly accrued to the Nigerian government which has (sic) been decisive' ('Oil Boom and Crisis in Contemporary Nigeria', Review of African Political Economy, 13, May-August 1978, p. 93).

28. For introductions to this world system perspective see Immanuel Wallerstein, The Modern World System: Capitalist Agriculture and the Origins of the European World Economy in the Sixteenth Century (New York: Academic, 1974) and The Capitalist World Economy (Cambridge University Press, 1979); and Daniel Chirot, Social Change in the Twentieth Century (New York: Harcourt Brace Jovanovich, 1977).

29. Barry B. Hughes and Patricia A. Strauch, 'The Future of Development in Nigeria and the Sahel: Projections from the World Integrated Model (WIM)' in Timothy M. Shaw (ed.), Alternative Futures for Africa (Boulder: Westview, 1981) pp. 179-200.

30. This exchange takes place largely at the international level. One definition for modern agriculture suggests that it is the transformation of oil (fertiliser, power for transportation and irrigation, etc.) into food at the national level. In which case, once Nigeria organises for its oft-promised green revolution it might be able to realise its considerable agricultural potential.

31. Patrick F. Wilmot, In Search of Nationhood: the Theory and Practice of Nationalism in Africa (Ibadan: Lantern, 1979) p. 123.

32. For comparable attempts to contrast traditional and radical approaches to regionalism, nonalignment, NIEO and foreign policy see Timothy M. Shaw, 'Towards a Political Economy of Regional Integration and Inequality in Africa', Nigerian Journal of International Studies, 2 (2), October 1978; 'The Political Economy of Nonalignment: from Dependence to Self-Reliance', International Conference on NonAlignment, Nigerian Institute of International Affairs, January 1980; 'Dependence to (Inter) Dependence: Review of Debate on the (New) International Economic Order', Alternatives, 4 (4), March 1979, pp. 557–78; and with Olajide Aluko, 'Introduction: the Political Economy of African Foreign Policy' in Timothy M. Shaw and Olajide Aluko (eds), The Political Economy of African Foreign Policy: Comparative Analysis (Aldershot: Gower, 1982).

33. On these see, for example, J. N. Garba, 'The New Nigerian Foreign Policy', Quarterly Journal of Administration, 11 (3), April 1977, pp. 135–46. See also Martin Dickson, 'Foreign Policy: New Dynamism', Financial Times Nigerian Survey, 1 October 1979, p. ix.

34. For more on Africa's middle powers see Timothy M. Shaw, 'Kenya and South Africa: "Sub-imperialist" States', Orbis, 21 92), Summer 1977, pp. 375–94, and 'Inequalities and Interdependence in Africa and Latin America: Sub-imperialism and Semi-industrialism in the Semiperiphery', Cultures et Developpement, 10 (2), 1978, pp. 231–63.

35. Douglas G. Anglin, 'Nigeria: Political Non-alignment and Economic Alignment', Journal of Modern African Studies, 2 (2), June 1964, p. 262.

36. For general theoretical work on the Third World state and foreign policy see Biplab Dasgupta, 'Interpretation of Foreign Policy: an Alternative Approach', International Round Table on Non-Alignment, Calcutta, November 1979, and Timothy M. Shaw, 'The Political Economy of African International Relations', Issue, 5 (4), Winter 1975, pp. 29–38.

37. Gambari, 'Nigeria and the World', p. 139. Cf. Geoffrey Hunt and Christos Theodoropoulos, 'Nigeria: Will Civilian Rule Bring Democracy?', African Communist, 79, fourth quarter 1979, pp. 88–101.

38. Thomas J. Biersteker, Distortion or Development? Contending Perspectives on the Multinational Corporation (Cambridge, Mass.: MIT Press, 1978) p. 161.

39. Osoba, 'The Deepening Crisis of the Nigerian National Bourgeoisie', pp. 74 and 77.

40. A further, more fascist variant of this reformist position is that an authoritarian response would serve to contain, if not remove, social pressures; see Claude Ake, Revolutionary Pressures in Africa (London: Zed, 1978) p. 107.

41. Sayre P. Schatz, Nigerian Capitalism (Berkeley: University of California Press, 1977), p. 46.

42. Ibid., p. 3.

43. Ibid., p. ix.

44. Osoba, 'The Deepening Crisis of the Nigerian National Bourgeoisie', p. 63. Contrast this statement with Obasanjo's opening quotation.

45. Schatz, Nigerian Capitalism, p. 266.

46. See Williams, 'Editorial' and 'Introduction'.

47. Cf. a somewhat similar focus and formulation proposed by Biersteker: 'the Nigerian example illustrates that there are different types of comprador groups. Although all organise the access of multinational corporations to the Nigerian market, there are important differences between investment compradors, commercial compradors and state compradors' (Distortion or Development?, p. 150).

48. Osoba, 'The Deepening Crisis of the Nigerian National Bourgeoisie', pp. 71-2.

49. Mark DeLancey, in one of the very few attempts to project alternative futures for Nigeria, suggests the utility of Zartman's dichotomy — decolonisation and dependency. He contrasts these within the context of Nigeria's emergence as a major power at the semi-periphery; and his work is largely within the traditional paradigm and excludes more radical scenarios. See Chapter 9.

50. Paul Collins, Terisa Turner and Gavin Williams, 'Capitalism and the Coup' in Williams (ed.), Nigeria, p. 192.

51. Ofoegbu, The Nigerian Foreign Policy, p. 96.

52. There is considerably more writing on Nigerian foreign policy than on the foreign policy of any other African state (except, perhaps, the 'special' case of South Africa). There are also more trained and professionally active social scientists in Nigeria (particularly in the fields of political science and international relations) than in any other country on the continent (let alone the large number of Nigerian scholars still in the diaspora!). Yet because of the widespread adoption of traditional modes of analysis, Nigerian scholars have yet to have a proportional impact on the frontiers of and debates within these sub-fields. See Mark W. DeLancey, 'The Study of African International Relations' in his

collection on Aspects of International Relations in
Africa (Bloomington: Indiana University, African Studies
Programme, 1979) pp. 1-38, especially 8-9.

53. Ikenna Nzimiro, in addition to proposing a typology of
class relations, alliances and contradictions for
Nigeria, is critical about the prevalence of conservatism in the universities, both institutional and intellectual He calls for a new tolerance of radicalism and
for a revival of creativity. See his The Crisis in the
Social Sciences: the Nigerian Situation (Mexico City:
Third World Forum, 1977, Occasional Paper no. 2) especially pp. 27-51.

54. For an interesting overview of this intense period of
change and continuity see A. Bolaji Akinyemi, 'Mohammed/
Obasanjo Foreign Policy' in Oyeleye Oyediran (ed.),
Nigerian Government and Politics under Military Rule
1966-79 (London: Macmillan, 1979) pp. 150-68; cf. note
12 above.

55. Ofoegbu, The Nigerian Foreign Policy, p. 43.

56. On the US case see Laurence Shoup and William Minter,
Imperial Brains Trust: the Council on Foreign Relations
and United States Foreign Policy (New York: Monthly
Review, 1977).

57. See Holly Sklar (ed.), Trilateralism: Elite Planning for
World Management (Boston: South End, 1979).

58. Typical of the new concerns amongst established scholars
for transnational, ecological, developmental and economic factors are Seyom Brown, New Forces in World Politics (Washington: Brookings, 1974); Robert O. Keohane
and Joseph S. Nye, Power and Interdependence: World
Politics in Transition (Boston: Little, Brown, 1977),
Joan E. Spero, The Politics of International Economic
Relations (New York: St. Martins, 1977); and David H.
Blake and Ronald H. Walters, The Politics of Global
Economic Relations (Englewood Cliffs: Prentice-Hall,
1976). See also Timothy M. Shaw, Towards an Internation-
al Political Economy for the 1980s: from Dependence to
(Inter)Dependence (Halifax: Centre for Foreign Policy
Studies, 1980).

59. See the powerful critiques in Claude Ake, Social Science
as Imperialism: the Theory of Political Development
(Ibadan University Press, 1979) especially pp. 1-98 and
Nzimiro, The Crisis in the Social Sciences, especially
pp. 17-26.

60. See Richard W. Mansbach, Yale H. Ferguson and Donald E.
Lampert, The Web of World Politics: Non-state Actors in
the Global System (Englewood Cliffs: Prentice-Hall,
1976) p. 31.

61. Spero, The Politics of International Economic Relations, p. 3. Blake and Walters are also critical of realist and state-centric approaches:

    the conceptual frameworks most frequently used by American analysts tended to relegate economic relationships to the periphery of inquiry; the interrelationships between domestic and international politics were not systematically examined; and the interests other than those of states (such as corporate, partisan or class interests) received almost no attention in studies of international politics. Marxist analyses dealing explicitly with interests and relationships that were of little concern to scholars representing the dominant analytical tradition of American scholarship on international politics were virtually ignored. These are some important reasons accounting for the poverty of conceptual frameworks useful in studying the politics of international economic relations (The Politics of Global Economic Relations, p. 4).

62. For one attempt to do so see Adebayo Adedeji, 'Development and Economic Growth in Africa to the Year 2000: Alternative Projections and Policies' in Shaw (ed.), Alternative Futures for Africa, pp. 279-303.

Bibliography on Nigerian Foreign Policy: Orthodox and Radical Literatures

OROBOLA FASEHUN and TIMOTHY M. SHAW

ORTHODOX

Realist Overviews

Agbi, S. Olu, 'Selected Issues in Nigeria's Foreign Policy
from Balewa to Obasanjo: Continuity and Change', Nigerian
Journal of Political Science, 2 (1), June 1980, 57-61.
Akinyemi, A. Bolaji, 'Introduction' in A. B. Akinyemi (ed.),
Nigeria and the World: Readings in Nigerian Foreign Policy
(Ibadan: OUP for NIIA, 1978) viii-xiv.
Akinyemi, A. Bolaji, 'Nigerian Foreign Policy in 1975:
National Interest Redefined', in Oyeleye Oyediran (ed.),
Survey of Nigerian Affairs, 1975 (Ibadan: OUP for NIIA,
1978) 106-14.
Akinyemi, A. Bolaji, 'Mohammed/Obasanjo Foreign Policy' in
Oyeleye Oyediran (ed.), Nigerian Government and Politics
under Military Rule, 1966-79 (London: Macmillan, 1979)
150-68.
Akinyemi, A. Bolaji, 'Foreign Policy, Defence and the New
Consciousness', Nigerian Forum, 1 (2), April 1981, 72-6.
Aluko, Olajide, Essays in Nigerian Foreign Policy (London:
Allen & Unwin, 1981).
Aluko, Olajide, 'The "new" Nigerian Foreign Policy:
Developments since the Downfall of General Gowon', Round
Table, 66, October 1976, 405-14.
Aluko, Olajide, 'Nigerian Foreign Policy' in Olajide Aluko
(ed.), The Foreign Policies of African States (London:
Hodder & Stoughton, 1977) 163-95.
Aluko, Olajide, 'Necessity and Freedom in Nigerian Foreign
Policy', Nigerian Journal of International Studies, 4
(1 and 2), January and June 1980, 1-15.
Anglin, Douglas G., 'Nigeria: Political Non-alignment and
Economic Alignment', Journal of Modern African Studies,
2 (2), June 1964, 147-63.

Coleman, James S., 'The Foreign Policy of Nigeria' in Joseph E. Black and Kenneth W. Thomson (eds), Foreign Policies in a World of Change (New York: Harper & Row, 1963) 379-406.

Gambari, Ibrahim A., 'Nigeria and the World: a Growing Internal Stability, Wealth and External Influence', Journal of International Affairs, 29 (2), Fall 1975, 155-69.

Gambari, Ibrahim A., Party Politics and Foreign Policy: Nigeria under the First Republic (Zaria: Ahmadu Bello University Press, 1980).

Garba, J. N., 'Towards a Dynamic Foreign Policy', Nigeria: Bulletin on Foreign Affairs, 6 (1), January 1976, 14-20.

Garba, J. N., 'The "New" Nigerian Foreign Policy', Quarterly Journal of Administration, 9 (3), April 1977, 135-46.

Herskovits, Jean, 'Nigeria: Africa's New Power', Foreign Affairs 53 (2), January 1975, 314-33.

Herskovits, Jean, 'Dateline Nigeria: a Black Power', Foreign Policy, 29, Winter 1977-8, 167-88.

Inwang, Edet, 'Nigeria – Foreign Policy: Seeking a Break-Even Point', South, 16, February 1982, 57-8.

Mackintosh, J. P., 'Nigeria's External Relations', Journal of Commonwealth Studies, 2, November 1964, 189-218.

Mayall, James, 'Oil and Nigerian Foreign Policy', African Affairs, 75 (300), July 1976, 284-316.

Ofoegbu, Ray, Nigerian Foreign Policy (Enugu: Star Printing, 1979).

Ofoegbu, Ray, 'Foreign Policy and Military Rule' in Oyeleye Oyediran (ed.), Nigerian Government and Politics under Military Rule, 1966-79 (London: Macmillan, 1979) 124-49.

Ogunbadejo, Oye, 'Nigeria's Foreign Policy Under Military Rule, 1966-79', International Journal, 35 (4), Autumn 1980, 748-65.

Ogunsanwo, Alaba, 'The Nigerian Military and Foreign Policy, 1975-1979: Processes, Principles, Performance and Contradictions', Princeton University Center for International Relations, 1980, Research Monograph no. 45.

Okolo, Julius E. and Winston E. Langley, 'The Changing Nigerian Foreign Policy', World Affairs, 135 (4), Spring 1973, 309-27.

Phillips, Claude S., The Development of Nigerian Foreign Policy (Evanston: Northwestern University Press, 1964).

Shagari, Alhaji Shehu, 'Annual Foreign Policy Address', Nigerian Forum, 1 (6), August 1981, 203-6.

Stremlau, John S., 'The Fundamentals of Nigerian Foreign Policy', Issue, 1! (1 and 2), Spring and Summer 1981, 46-50.

Wachuku, Jaja, 'Nigeria's Foreign Policy', University of Toronto Quarterly, 31 (1), October 1961, 62-82.

National

Akindele, R. A., 'Nigeria's Foreign Relations: Elite Attitudes and Government Policy', International Problems, 12
(3), 1973, 102-13.
Akindele, R. A., 'Nigerian Parliament and Foreign Policy,
1960-1966', Quarterly Journal of Administration, 9 (3),
April 1975, 279-91.
Akindele, R. A., 'The Conduct of Nigeria's Foreign Rela-
tions', International Problems, 12 (3-4), October 1973,
46-65.
Akinyemi, A. Bolaji, Foreign Policy and Federalism: the
Nigerian Experience (Ibadan University Press, 1974) espe-
cially 75-109 and 191-201.
Aluko, Olajide, 'Necessity and Freedom in Nigerian Foreign
Policy', inaugural lecture, University of Ife, 17 March
1981.
Aluko, Olajide, 'Oil at Concessionary Prices for Africa: a
Case Study in Nigerian Decision-making', African Affairs,
75 (301), October 1976, 425-43.
Aluko, Olajide, 'The Civil War and Nigerian Foreign Policy',
Political Quarterly, 42 (2), April-June 1971.
Aluko, Olajide, 'The Iyalla Reorganisation and the Admini-
stration of the Foreign Service' in C. Baker and M. J.
Balogun (eds), Ife Essays on Administration (University
of Ife Press, 1975) 135-146.
Aluko, Olajide, 'Public Opinion and Nigerian Foreign Policy
Under the Military', Quarterly Journal of Administration,
7 (3), April 1973, 253-69.
Aluko, Olajide, 'The Foreign Service', Quarterly Journal of
Administration, 5 (1), October 1970, 33-52.
Asobie, H. A., 'Bureaucratic Politics and Foreign Policy:
the Nigerian Experience', Nigerian Political Science
Association, Port Harcourt, March 1980.
Gambari, Ibrahim A., 'Domestic Political Constraints on
Progressive Foreign Policy for Nigeria', Nigerian Journal
of Political Science, 2 (1), June 1980, 24-35.
Herskovits, Jean, 'One Nigeria', Foreign Affairs , 51 (2),
January 1973, 392-407.
Idang, Gordon J., Nigeria: Internal Politics and Foreign
Policy (Ibadan University Press, 1973) especially 107-60.
Ofoegbu, Mazi Ray and Obuagu, S. A., 'Towards a New Philo-
sophy of Foreign Policy for Nigeria', in Bolaji Akinyemi
(ed.), Nigeria and the World (Ibadan: OUP for NIIA, 1978)
116-35.
Ogene, Francis, 'The Foreign Service the Nation Deserves',
Nigerian Forum, 1 (4), June 1981, 151-9.

Ogunbadejo, Oye, 'Foreign Policy Under Nigeria's Presidential System', Round Table, October 1980, 401-8.
Ogunbadejo, Oye, 'The Presidential System and Foreign Policy: Problems and Prospects in Nigeria', Australian Outlook, December 1980, 325-37.

Regional

Aluko, Olajide, Ghana and Nigeria, 1957-70: a Study in Inter-African Discord (London: Rex Collings, 1976).
Aluko, Olajide, 'Nigeria's Initiative on the West African Economic Community', Societe d'Etudes et d'Expansion Revue, November-December 1973, 870-80.
Ofoegbu, Mazi Ray, 'Nigeria and Its Neighbours', Odu, 12, July 1975, 3-24.
Ojo, Olatunde J. B., 'Nigeria and the Formation of ECOWAS', International Organisation, 34 (4), Autumn 1980, 571-604.
Osuntokun, 'Jide, 'Relations Between Nigeria and Fernando Po from Colonial times to the Present', in Bolaji Akinyemi (ed.), Nigeria and the World (Ibadan: OUP for NIIA, 1978) 1-12.
Udokang, Okon, 'Nigeria and ECOWAS: Economic and Political Implications of Regional Integration' in Bolaji Akinyemi (ed.), Nigeria and the World (Ibadan: OUP for NIIA, 1978) 57-80.
Weladji, C., 'The Cameroon-Nigerian Border', Abbia, June 1974, 157-72.
Yansane, Aguibou Y., 'State of Economic Integration in North West Africa South of the Sahara: the Emergence of ECOWAS', African Studies Review, 20 (2), September 1977, 63-87.

Continental

Adebesi, B., 'Nigeria's Relations with South Africa, 1960-1975', Africa Quarterly, 16 (3), 1977, 67-89.
Akinyemi, A. Bolaji, 'Nigeria and Fernando Po, 1958-1966: the Politics of Irredentism', African Affairs, 69 (276), July 1970, 236-49.
Akinyemi, A. Bolaji, Angola and Nigeria: a Study in the National Interest (Geneva: Graduate Institute of International Studies, 1978).
Akinyemi, A. Bolaji, with Margaret Vogt, 'Nigeria and Southern Africa: the Policy Options' in Douglas G. Anglin, Timothy M. Shaw and Carl G. Widstrand (eds), Conflict and Change in Southern Africa (Washington: University Press of America, 1978) 151-68.
Aluko, Olajide, 'Nigeria's Role in Inter-African Relations with Special Reference to the OAU', African Affairs, 72 (287), April 1973, 145-62.

Arikpo, O., 'Nigeria and the OAU', Quarterly Journal of
    Administration, 9 (1), October 1974, 44-59.
Fajana, Olufemi, 'Nigeria's Inter-African Economic Rela-
    tions: Trends, Problems and Prospects' in Bolaji Akinyemi
    (ed.), Nigeria and the World (Ibadan: OUP for NIIA, 1978)
    17-31.
Feustel, Sandy, 'Nigeria: Leadership in Africa', Africa
    Report, 22 (3), May-June 1977, 48-50.
Helleiner, Gerald K., 'Nigeria and the African Common
    Market', Nigerian Journal of Economic and Social Studies,
    4 (3), November 1962, 283-98.
Nnoli, Okwudiba, 'Nigerian Policy Towards Southern Africa',
    Nigerian Journal of International Affairs, 2 (1-2), 1976,
    14-34.
Ogunbadejo, O., 'General Gowon's African Policy', Interna-
    tional Studies, 16 (1), January-March 1977, 35-50.
Ogunbadejo, O., 'Conservatism and Radicalism in Inter-
    African Relations: the Case of Nigeria and Tanzania',
    Jerusalem Journal of International Relations, 4 (1), 1979,
    23-33.
Polhemus, James H., 'Nigeria and Southern Africa: Interest,
    Policy and Means', Canadian Journal of African Studies,
    11 (1), 1977, 42-66.
Spiliotes, Nicholas J., 'Nigerian Foreign Policy and
    Southern Africa: a Choice for the West', Issue, 11 (1 and
    2), Spring and Summer 1981, 41-5.
Wayas, Joseph, Nigeria's Leadership Role in Africa (London:
    Macmillan, 1979).
Whiteman, Kaye, 'OAU and the Nigerian Issue', World Today,
    24 (11), November 1968, 449-53.

Global

Akindele, R. A., 'Review article: on the Operational Linkage
    of External and Internal Dimensions of Balewa's Foreign
    Policy', Odu, 12, July 1975, 110-22.
Azikiwe, Nnamdi, 'Nigeria in World Politics', Presence
    Africaine, 4/5 (32/33), 1960, 19-30.
Haastrup, Adekokun, 'Nigeria's Role in World Affairs',
    Africa Quarterly, January-March 1965, 240-3.
Hanning, Hugh, 'Nigeria: a Lesson of the Arms Race', World
    Today, 23 (11), November 1967, 465-72.
Ijewere, Gabriel O., 'Nigeria in International Relations',
    Review of International Affairs, 32 (738), 5 January 1981,
    26-30.
Isong, C., 'Nigeria's External Finance', Nigerian Journal of
    International Affairs, 1 (1), July 1975, 47-58.

Kadzai, Ayuba, Nigeria's Global Strategy (Lagos: NIIA, 1976).

Legum, Colin, 'International Involvement in Nigeria, 1966-70' in Y. A Tandon and D. Chandarana (eds), Horizons of African Diplomacy (Nairobi: EALB, 1974) 45-85.

Obasanjo, Olusegun, 'Foreign Attitudes and Involvement' in his My Command: an Account of the Nigerian Civil War, 1967-70 (Ibadan: Heinemann, 1980) 146-58.

Ojedokun, Olasupo, 'The Changing Pattern of Nigeria's International Economic Relations: the Decline of the Colonial Nexus, 1960-1966', Journal of Developing Areas, 6 (4), July 1972, 535-54.

Ojo, Olatunde J.B., 'Commercial Representation in Nigeria's Overseas Missions: Its Nature, Functions and Problems', Nigerian Journal of International Affairs, 2 (1/2), 1976, 50-66.

Bilateral and Multilateral Relationships: Great Powers

Ahmad, S. S., 'Nigeria-China Relations: an Approach to Positive Neutrality', Pakistan Horizon, 26 (1), 1973, 48-54.

Ajayi, E. A., 'Nigeria-Soviet Aid Relations, 1960-1968', Nigeria: Bulletin on Foreign Affairs, 1, 1974.

Akinyemi, A. Bolaji, 'Nigerian-American Relations Re-examined' in Oye Oyediran (ed.), Survey of Nigerian Affairs, 1976-77 (Lagos: Macmillan for NIIA, 1981) 105-14.

Ale, Bassey, 'Influence Dynamics in Nigeria-US Aid Relationship, 1960-66', Nigerian Journal of International Studies 4 (1 and 2), January and June 1980, 36-55.

Aluko, Olajide, 'Nigeria and Britain Since Gowon', African Affairs, 76 (304), July 1977, 303-20.

Aluko, Olajide, 'Nigeria and the Superpowers', Millenium, 5 (2), Autumn 1976, 126-41.

Aluko, Olajide, 'Nigeria, the United States and Southern Africa', African Affairs, 78 (310), January 1979, 91-102.

Idang, Gordon J., 'The Politics of Nigerian Foreign Policy: the Ratification and Renunciation of the Anglo-Nigerian Defence Agreement', African Studies Review, 13 (2), September 1970, 227-51.

Klinghoffer, A. J., 'The USSR and Nigeria: the Secession Question', Mizan, 10, Winter 1968, 64-70.

Mazrui, Ali A., 'Nigeria and the United States: the Need for Civility, the Dangers of Intimacy, Orbis, 25 (4), Winter 1982, 858-64.

Morrison, D. L., 'The USSR and the War in Nigeria', Mizan, 11, Spring 1969, 31-8.

Obiozor, George, 'Soviet Involvement in the Nigerian Civil War', in U. G. Damachi and H. D. Seibel (eds), Social Change and Economic Development in Nigeria (New York: Praeger, 1973) 230-4.

Ogunbadejo, Oye, 'Nigeria and the Great Powers: the Impact of the Civil War on Nigerian Foreign Relations', African Affairs, 75 (298), January 1976, 14-32.

Ogunbadejo, Oye, 'Ideology and Pragmatism: the Soviet Role in Nigeria, 1960-1977', Orbis, 21 (4), Winter 1978, 803-30.

Ogunbadejo, Oye, 'A New Turn in US-Nigerian Relations', World Today, 35 (3), March 1979, 117-26.

Ojedokun, Olasupo, 'Anglo-Nigerian Entente and Its Demise, 1960-62', Journal of Commonwealth Political Studies, 9 (3), November 1971, 210-33.

Orjiako, Umunna, 'Anglo-Nigerian relations: 1979-1981', Nigerian Forum, 1 (2), April 1981, 49-56.

Panter-Brick, S. K., 'Soviet Views on Nigeria', Mizan, March-April 1967, 70-4.

Bilateral and Multilateral Relationships: Other Powers

Adebisi, B., 'Nigeria's Relations with South Africa, 1960-1975', Africa Quarterly, 16 (3), 1977, 67-89.

Akinsanya, A., 'On Lagos Decision to Break Diplomatic Relations with Israel', International Problems, 17, Spring 1978, 65-79.

Aluko, Olajide, 'Ghana and the Nigerian Civil War', Nigerian Journal of Economic and Social Studies, 12, November 1970, 341-60.

Aluko, Olajide, 'Israel and Nigeria: Continuity and Change in Their Relationship', African Review, 4 (1), 1974, 43-59.

Aluko, Olajide, 'Nigeria and the European Economic Community', International Studies, 13 (3), July-September 1974, 465-73.

Ojedokun, Olasupo, 'The Future of Nigeria's Commonwealth Relations', Nigeria: Bulletin on Foreign Affairs, 1 (4), May 1972, 8-17.

Olinger, John Peter, 'The World Bank and Nigeria', Review of African Political Economy, 13, May-August 1978, 101-7.

Olusanya, G. O., 'Nigeria and the Commonwealth', African Quarterly, 6 (4), January-March 1967.

Crises and Conflicts

Akuchu, G. E., 'Peaceful Settlement of Disputes: Unsolved Problems for the OAU (A Case Study of the Nigeria-Biafra Conflict)', Africa Today, 24 (4), October-December 1977, 39-58.

Cervenka, Zdenek, The Nigerian Civil War 1967-1970
(Frankfurt: Bernard & Graefe Verlag for Wehrwesen, 1971).
Cronje, Suzanne, The World and Nigeria: the Diplomatic
History of the Biafran War 1967-1970 (London: Sidgwick &
Jackson, 1972).
de St. Jorre, J., The Brothers' War: Biafra and Nigeria
(Boston: Houghton Mifflin, 1972).
Elaigwu, J. Isawa, 'The Nigerian Civil War and the Angolan
Civil War: Linkages Between Domestic Tensions and Inter-
national Alignments', Journal of Asian and African
Studies, 12 (1-4), January and October 1977, 215-35.
Henderson, Robert D'A, 'Nigeria: Future Nuclear Power?',
Orbis, 25 (2), Summer 1981, 409-23.
Henderson, Robert D'A, 'Choices and Changes in Nigeria's
Defence Policy in the 1970s', Journal of Modern African
Studies (forthcoming).
Lewis, Roy, 'Britain and Biafra', Round Table, 60, July
1970, 241-8.
Nweke, G. A., External Intervention in African Conflicts:
France and French-speaking West Africa in the Nigerian
Civil War, 1967-1970 (Boston University, African Studies
Center, 1976).
Ostheimer, John M. and Gary J. Buckley, 'Nigeria' in
Edward A. Kolodziej and Robert E. Harkavy (eds), Security
Policies of Developing Countries (Lexington: Lexington,
1982) 285-303.
Panter-Brick, S. K., 'The Right to Self-determination: Its
Application to Nigeria', International Affairs, 44 (2),
April 1968, 254-66.
Stremlau, John J., The International Politics of the
Nigerian Civil War (Princeton University Press, 1977).
Vogt, Margaret A., 'Nigeria's Defence: an Assessment',
Nigerian Forum, 1 (2), April 1981, 77-81.

Transnational

Akinyemi, A. Bolaji, 'Religion and Foreign Affairs: Press
Attitudes Towards the Nigerian Civil War', Jerusalem
Journal of International Relations, 4 (3), 1980, 56-81.
Booth, A. R., 'The Churches in the Nigerian War: the
Threat of Moral Imperialism', Round Table, 60, April 1970,
121-7.
Collins, J. D., 'The Clandestine Movement of Groundnuts
Across the Niger-Nigerian Boundary', Canadian Journal of
African Studies, 10 (2), 1976, 259-78.
Davis, Morris, Interpreters for Nigeria: the Third World
and International Public Relations (Urbana: University
of Illinois Press, 1977).

Fajana, Olufemi, 'Trade and Growth: the Nigerian Experi-
    ence', World Development, 7 (1), 1979, 73-8.
Fajana, Olufemi, 'International Trade and Balance of Pay-
    ments' in F. A. Olaloku et al., Structure of the Nigerian
    Economy (London: Macmillan, 1979) 224-54.
Hilton, A. C. E., 'Perceptions of Foreign Involvement in
    Nigeria' in K. P. Sauvant and F. G. Lavipour (eds),
    Controlling Multinational Enterprises (Boulder: Westview,
    1976).
Ijewere, G. O., 'The New International Economic Order and
    Nigeria's External Economic Policy', Ife International
    Relations Occasional Papers, 1, 1981, 72-96.
King, Mae C., 'Nigerian Foreign Policy and the African
    Diaspora: the North American Region', Nigerian Society
    for International Affairs, Zaria, January 1979.
Olofin, S., 'Ultra-import Biased Taste in Nigeria's External
    Trade Relations' in Bolaji Akinyemi (ed.), Nigeria and the
    World (Ibadan: OUP for NIIA, 1978) 32-43.
Shagari, Shehu, 'The World Monetary Crisis in Relation to
    Nigeria', Nigerian Journal of International Affairs, 1
    (1), July 1975, 59-70.
Wright, Stephen, 'Nigeria: the Politics of Sport', Round
    Table, 272, October 1978, 362-7.

RADICAL

Akeredolu-Ale, E. O., 'Private Foreign Investment and the
    Underdevelopment of Indigenous Entrepreneurship in
    Nigeria' in Gavin Williams (ed.), Nigeria: Economy and
    Society (London: Rex Collings, 1976) 102-22.
Biersteker, Thomas J., Distortion or Development? Contending
    Perspectives on the Multinational Corporation (Cambridge,
    Mass.: MIT Press, 1978) passim.
Callaway, Barbara, 'The Political Economy of Nigeria' in
    Richard Harris (ed.), The Political Economy of Africa
    (Cambridge: Schenkman, 1975) 93-135.
Collins, P., 'The Political Economy of Indigenisation: the
    Case of the Nigerian Enterprises Promotion Decree',
    African Review, 4 (2), 1974, 491-508.
Ekundare, R. O., 'The Political Economy of Private Invest-
    ment in Nigeria', Journal of Modern African Studies, 10
    (1), March 1972, 37-56.
Freund, Bill, 'Oil Boom and Crisis in Contemporary Nigeria',
    Review of African Political Economy, 13, May-August 1978,
    91-100.
Gona, Aaron T., 'Nigeria: Class Struggle and Foreign
    Policy', Africa Development, 5 (1), 1980, 75-94.

Joseph, Richard, 'Affluence and Underdevelopment: the
Nigerian Experience', Journal of Modern African Studies,
16 (2), June 1978, 221-39.

Madiebo, Alexander A., The Nigerian Revolution and the
Biafran War (Enugu: Fourth Dimension, 1980) passim.

Nnoli, Okwudiba (ed.), Path to Nigerian Development (London:
Zed, 1982).

Nzimiro, Ikenna, 'The Political and Social Implications of
International Corporations in Nigeria' in Carl Widstrand
(ed.), Multinational Firms in Africa (Stockholm: Almqvist
& Wiksell, 1975) 210-43.

Ojedokun, Olasupo, 'The Changing Pattern of Nigeria's
International Economic Relations: the Decline of the
Colonial Nexus, 1960-1966', Journal of Developing Areas,
6 (4), July 1972, 534-54.

Ojo, Olatunde J. B., 'Nigeria's Self-Reliant Strategy:
the Prospect for Self-Reliance in the Contemporary International Tributory System', African Studies Association,
Bloomington, October 1981.

Oni, Ola and Bade Onimode, Economic Development of Nigeria:
the Socialist Alternative (Ibadan: Nigerian Academy of
Arts, Sciences and Technology, 1975).

Onimode, Bade, 'Imperialism and Multinational Corporations:
a Case Study of Nigeria' in Aguibou Y. Yansane (ed.),
Decolonisation and Dependency: Problems of Development in
African Societies (Westport: Greenwood, 1980) 145-70.

Osagie, E. and K. Awosika, 'Foreign Capital and Firms in
Nigeria', Quarterly Journal of Administration 9 (1),
October 1974, 61-76.

Osoba, Segun, 'The Nigerian Power Elite, 1952-65' in Peter
W. Gutkind and Peter Waterman (eds.), African Social
Studies: a Radical Reader (London: Heinemann, 1977)
368-82.

Osoba, Segun, 'The Deepening Crisis of the Nigerian National
Bourgeoisie', Review of African Political Economy, 13,
May-August 1978, 63-77.

Osoba, Segun, 'The Economic Foundations of Nigeria's Foreign
Policy in the First Republic, 1960-1966' in I. A.
Akinjogbin and Segun O. Osoba (eds), Topics on Nigerian
Economic and Social History (Ife: University of Ife Press,
1980) 208-33.

Owosekun, Akinola and Moses Otigba, 'The Nigerian Enterprises Promotion Decree: Impact on Indigenous Ownership'
in J. F. Rweyemamu (ed.), Industrialization and Income
Distribution in Africa (London: Zed for CODESRIA, 1980)
168-90.

Oyebode, Akindele B., 'Towards a New Policy on Decolonisa-
tion' in Bolaji Akinyemi (ed.), Nigeria and the World
(Ibadan: OUP for NIIA, 1978) 96-115.
Rimmer, Douglas, 'Elements of the Political Economy' in
Keith Panter-Brick (ed.), Soldiers and Oil (London: Frank
Cass, 1978) 141-65.
Schatz, Sayre P., Nigerian Capitalism (Berkeley: University
of California Press, 1977).
Shaw, Timothy M., 'Nigeria's Political Economy: Constitu-
tions, Capitalism and Contradictions', ODI Review, 2,
1980, 76-85.
Soleye, O. O., 'The Politico-economic Position of Multina-
tional Corporations: a Nigerian Example' in Carl Widstrand
(ed.), Multinational Firms in Africa (Stockholm: Almqvist
& Wiksell, 1975) 196-209.
Turner, Terisa, 'Multinational Corporations and the
Instability of the Nigerian State', Review of African
Political Economy, 5, January-April 1976, 63-79.
Turner, Terisa, 'The Transfer of Oil Technology and the
Nigerian State', Development and Change, 7 (4), 1976,
353-90; revised version in Petter Nore and Terisa Turner
(eds), Oil and Class Struggle (London: Zed, 1980), 199-
223.
Turner, Terisa, 'Two Refineries: a Comparative Study of
Technology Transfer to the Nigerian Refining Industry',
World Development, 5, 1977, 235-56.
Tyoden, Sonni, The Political Economy of Nigeria's External
Relations (London: Zed, 1983).
Usman, Bala, For the Liberation of Nigeria (London: New
Beacon, 1979).
Usore, E. J., 'Foreign Oil Companies and Recent Nigerian
Petroleum Oil Policies', Nigerian Journal of Economic and
Social Studies, 14, 1972, 301-14.
White, P. V., 'Nigerian Politics: Class Alliances and
Foreign Alignment' in U. G. Damachi and H. P. Seibel
(eds), Social Change and Economic Development in Nigeria
(New York: Praeger, 1973) 209-29.
Williams, Gavin, 'Class Relations in a Neo-colony: the Case
of Nigeria' in Peter Gutkind and Peter Waterman (eds),
African Social Studies: a Radical Reader (London:
Heinemann, 1977) 284-94.
Williams, Gavin, 'Editorial: Nigeria', Review of African
Political Economy, 13, May-August 1978, 1-7.
Williams, Gavin, 'Introduction' and 'Nigeria: a Political
Economy' in Gavin Williams (ed.), Nigeria: Economy and
Society (London: Rex Collings, 1976) 1-54.
Williams, Gavin and Terisa Turner, 'Nigeria' in John Dunn
(ed.), West African States: Failure and Promise (Cambridge
University Press, 1978) 132-72.

Index

Index